PENGUIN PLAYS

# THE REAR COLUMN, DOG DAYS, AND OTHER PLAYS

Born in 1936, Simon Gray was educated at Portsmouth Grammar School and Westminster, at universities in Canada and France, and at Cambridge. He now lectures in English literature at Queen Mary College, London. He is the author of a number of television plays, including *Sleeping Dog*, *Death of a Teddy Bear*, *Pig in a Poke*, and *Man in a Sidecar*, and the novels *Colmain*, *Little Portia*, *Simple People*, and (under the pseudonym Hamish Reade) *A Comeback for Stark*. His first stage play, *Wise Child*, was produced in 1957. Since then he has written *Dutch Uncle* (1969); *The Idiot* (1970), an adaptation of Dostoyevsky's novel; *Spoiled* (1971); *Butley*, winner of the London Evening Standard Best Play award for 1971 (available from Penguin); and *Otherwise Engaged*, winner of the London Evening Standard Best Play award for 1975, the Play and Players Best Play award for 1975, and the New York Critics Circle and the New York Drama Desk awards for Best Play in 1977. *Otherwise Engaged and Other Plays*, published by Penguin, includes *Two Sundays* and *Plaintiffs and Defendants*. Productions of *Molly* and *The Rear Column* were given off Broadway in New York City during 1978.

ALSO BY SIMON GRAY

*Plays*

Sleeping Dog
Wise Child
Dutch Uncle
Spoiled
The Idiot
Butley
Otherwise Engaged,
Two Sundays *and*
Plaintiffs and Defendants

*Novels*

Colmain
Little Portia
Simple People
A Comeback for Stark
(under the pseudonym
Hamish Reade)

# THE REAR COLUMN,
# DOG DAYS, AND OTHER PLAYS

## SIMON GRAY

PENGUIN BOOKS

Penguin Books Ltd, Harmondsworth,
Middlesex, England
Penguin Books, 625 Madison Avenue,
New York, New York 10022, U.S.A.
Penguin Books Australia Ltd, Ringwood,
Victoria, Australia
Penguin Books Canada Limited, 2801 John Street,
Markham, Ontario, Canada L3R 1B4
Penguin Books (N.Z.) Ltd, 182–190 Wairau Road,
Auckland 10, New Zealand

First published in the United States of America in simultaneous hardcover
and paperback editions by The Viking Press (A Seaver Book)
and Penguin Books 1979

LIBRARY OF CONGRESS CATALOGING IN PUBLICATION DATA
Gray, Simon James Holliday.
The rear column, Dog days, and other plays.
I. Title.
[PR6057.R33R4   1979b]     822'.9'14     79-11244
ISBN 0 14 048.155 9

Printed in the United States of America by
Offset Paperback Mfrs., Inc., Dallas, Pennsylvania
Set in Caslon Old Face

All rights whatsoever in this play are strictly reserved, and application for
performance should be made before rehearsal to Judy Daish Assoc. Ltd,
Globe Theatre, Shaftesbury Avenue, London W1, England.

# Contents

THE REAR COLUMN  vii

MOLLY  75

MAN IN A SIDE-CAR  137

DOG DAYS  193

# THE REAR COLUMN

This book is dedicated to the memory of Clive Goodwin,
to whom I owe more than I can say.    S.G.

# Author's Note

I had a purple patch between March 1969 and February 1971 when I managed three flops in a row. *Dutch Uncle,* produced by the Royal Shakespeare Company, was a farce that depressed its audiences, appalled the reviewers (one of whom based on it his entire case for bringing booing back to the theatre) and shamed myself and my loved ones: a clear example I think of a flop total; then came an adaptation of *The Idiot,* which didn't do as badly by its audiences, but was so comprehensively done over by reviewers anxious to establish their Dostoievsky credentials that the National Theatre, which during rehearslas and previews had predicted great success, withdrew the play from its repertory more quickly than it decently could. This flop d'estime was followed by *Spoiled,* which though well enough received by the reviewers (apart from a fellow-failure of a dramatist who seized the opportunity to upgrade himself by saluting me as the worst playwright in England), ran for three weeks to a handful of agrophiles at the Haymarket, and was a flop merely.

I seem in retrospect to have spent most of this period with my head down, to conceal as I went about my daily business cheeks that flamed easily and eyes that watered over trifles. The only glimmer of compensation came from my old friend and sticker-by Tony Gould, who over a long lunch in a Chinese restaurant (probably) told me the story of Stanley's march to the relief of Emin Pasha, and more particularly the fate of his rear column, left behind in the encampment of Yambuya, by the banks of the Arruwimi River, in the Year of Grace 1887. There were times during the working years that followed when, stuck in some Yambuya of my own making, with five characters I could neither completely abandon nor conduct to their final destinies, I regretted the lunch more than the flops from which it had promised redemption. In the worst patches I turned away to write other stage plays — *Butley, Otherwise Engaged, Dog Days* and *Molly*; and two television plays — *Plaintiffs and Defendants* and *Two Sundays* — but in between I always, for shorter or longer periods, returned to Yambuya: and a few months ago, some seven years after I first heard the story, got Mr Stanley to come back at last, and bring a painful relief to us all.

*7th December, 1977*

At the time of going to press THE REAR COLUMN was scheduled to be presented by Michael Codron at the Globe Theatre, London, on 22 February 1978 with the following cast:

| | |
|---|---|
| BONNY | Donald Gee |
| JAMESON | Jeremy Irons |
| WARD | Simon Ward |
| TROUP | Clive Francis |
| BARTTELOT | Barry Foster |
| STANLEY | Michael Forrest |
| JOHN HENRY | Riba Ackabusi |
| NATIVE WOMAN | Dorrett Thompson |

Directed by Harold Pinter
Designed by Eileen Diss
Lighting by Nick Chelton

# Act One

## Scene One

*A large store room in the Yambuya Camp, on the banks of the Arruwimi River, the Congo. It is June, 1887. Late afternoon.*

*There are boxes back left and back right of stage. Between them, back stage centre, large double doors. A canvas flap, stage right. A large table, centre stage. Some travelling chests which also serve as chairs. Stage left, a travelling desk and a chair, a settee.*

*The double doors are partly open, to let in light. There are two turtles, attached by lengths of string to the table legs.*

*BONNY is studying the room, clearly having just entered it for the first time. He goes to the work desk, gives something on it a cursory, rather contemptuous glance, goes over to the table, lets out an exclamation, picks up a turtle, then the other one. Puts them on the table.*

JAMESON (*enters through flap*). Oh, Mr Bonny — you've met Herman and King, I see.

BONNY. Oh. I was hoping I'd met some soup.

JAMESON (*laughs*). One evening, no doubt. But one needs time to prepare.

BONNY. It doesn't take long to boil up a pair of turtles, does it?

JAMESON. I meant for the loss.

BONNY. What, they're pets, are they?

JAMESON. Well, they've kept the Major and myself company through some pretty lonely times. When he was ill, they were all I had to talk to, and when I was ill I used to imagine the three of them passing riotous evenings together. I got them from one of the village chiefs on my first trip out after Stanley's departure. He assumed I was a slaver, come to steal his wife and ransom her for food. He offered me these before I could put him straight — I couldn't speak much of the lingo then.

BONNY. What was the wife like?

JAMESON. I didn't see her, but I'm sure she wouldn't have made into soup.

BONNY. No, but she might have done for a pet. Then when you'd finished with her, you could have traded her in for the soup.

JAMESON (*laughs politely*). This one's Herman because he reminds me of a German Professor of Zoology under whom I once studied, and this is King because he reminded the Major of the horse on which he was taught to ride, as a child in Sussex. Two patient, comforting, slow-witted fellows from our past, whose own pasts go far further back than ours. If you look at Herman's markings, you'll see he must be nearly a hundred.

BONNY. Oh. (*He looks quickly, without interest.*)

JAMESON. While King is a mere stripling of some six decades. I'm sorry to ramble on. One's got out of the habit of succinctness these last two months. Where are your two companions, by the way?

BONNY. Troup's dealing with his Soudanese, and Ward with his Zanzibaris.

JAMESON. You've got your men down already have you, good.

BONNY. Oh, I didn't have charge of any men — as I'm the one with medical training Mr Stanley made me responsible for the mules.

JAMESON. Did they give you a bad time?

BONNY. Let's say we only understood each other when I was having them fed.

JAMESON. In that respect, they don't seem too unlike the men.

BONNY. A bit unlike your men, in that they were at least fed. I took a stroll around the compound after I'd done with the brutes. You're in a bad way here, aren't you? A very bad way. (*Pause.*) How many have you lost?

JAMESON. Nineteen Zanzibaris, twelve Soudanese.

BONNY. Well, you'll lose a few more tonight. Fever, ulcers on the back and legs — malnutrition, in other words. What have the poor devils been eating?

JAMESON. Much the same as the Major and myself. The odd
fish they buy from the natives, or a goat, sometimes a fowl.
But the staple diet is the manioc root. For the Soudanese,
that is. The Zanzibaris won't eat meat, so for them it's
manioc and more manioc. Of course they won't cook it
properly. The manioc has to be boiled slowly and then drained.
They toss it into the pot then swallow it straight down. It
frequently swells in their stomachs . . .

WARD *enters.*

The Major and I have given at least twenty cooking
demonstrations between us. But they pay no attention.

BONNY. Was it like this when Mr Stanley was here?

JAMESON. Perhaps the Soudanese had a little more meat, and
the Zanzibaris a little more fish, as Mr Stanley is famously
clever at trading with the natives. But some of the
Zanzibaris had begun to die before he left.

WARD. In other words, you've been having a rather grim time.

JAMESON. It's not particularly pleasant to watch men dying.
They seem, the Zanzibaris especially, to settle into death
before they become properly ill — as if death itself were the
disease. They lie in their own dung waiting — the flies come
up — well, you've seen and smelt for yourselves. At first we
tried to keep them on the move, our policy was work and
more work, but once we'd built the palisades and fenced
ourselves in there was no work, to speak of. We can't let
them out except in small details to gather wood, and even
then they try to quarrel with the natives or what's worse
trade them their guns for food. And as we'd rather be
surrounded by natives who are reasonably friendly and
unarmed . . . So we're left with the camp routine, and that's
not adequate. These men are porters by nature, used to
marching for long periods and to camping for short ones.

WARD. So the fact of it is, they're dying of hunger and
boredom.

JAMESON. In a sense, Mr Ward. Though it doesn't quite
catch the feeling of the two months they've spent doing it in.

WARD. And how many have died of a flogging?

JAMESON (*after a pause*). One.

WARD. But there's been more than one flogging, I take it? I
saw a creature out there whose back was in ribbons.

JAMESON. There have been several floggings, Mr Ward. Once they'd realized they could get a chicken or some fish or even a goat for their rifles, and once they'd started thieving — the Major began by issuing warnings, and when they didn't take was forced to back them up with floggings.

WARD. Which doubtless haven't taken either.

JAMESON. An old debate, Mr Ward. We have no way of knowing, have we? how many we've deterred. We only know how many haven't been. You blame us for it, then?

WARD. Good God, no. Once you start, you have to go on, and nobody's yet discovered an alternative to starting. I can't really see that there's anything here to surprise. Constant sickness punctuated by regular floggings — the inevitable conditions of a large, stationary camp in the Congo. The only solution is to get moving as quickly as possible.

JAMESON. Amen to that!

TROUP (enters). It appears I'm not to get one after all, can you believe it? It's not enough that we find Stanley gone in spite of his reassurances that he'd wait on us, it's not enough that we were misled on that, but it turns out that after weeks of hard travelling by day and the utmost misery and discomfort at night, I'm still to be deprived — what the devil am I to do?

WARD. Mr Troup is talking of a bed, Mr Jameson.

JAMESON. A bed? But weren't you issued with a bed in London?

TROUP. Oh yes, Mr Jameson, I was issued with one, and here's my chit to prove it — you see, it entitles me to one bed at the expedition's expense. When I met with Mr Stanley at the Falls, I presented him with this chit, signed by Mr MacKinnon of the Committee, and he said that as all the beds were packed in the steamer, I'd have to wait until we met up here. Well, here I am, and here's my chit, but as there's no Stanley, there's no bed. (He laughs bitterly.) Anyway, that'll teach me a little savvy. I saw a bed lying free on the wharf at the Falls, but I refrained from taking it. And what happened? Old Ward here too it instead. He was quite right, by God, if I'd known the plight my scruples were to land me in, I'd have fought him for it, I would you know, Ward!

WARD. Yes, old chap, I know, but look, there must be a spare bed somewhere in the Camp, there always is.

TROUP. Oh yes, three. Three spare beds. But according to the

Major, they belong to Mr Stanley, and are on no account to be touched. According to the Major. Though why the devil he thinks Stanley would object —

JAMESON. Mr Troup, I think I can help you. Mr Parke brought up an extra bed for Jephson, who fortunately brought his own. Parke asked me to add it to the loads for him, but he and I are good friends, I'm sure he wouldn't mind my letting you have the use of it.

TROUP. What? You mean there is a bed — I shall have a bed — tonight, you mean?

JAMESON. This very minute, if you like.

TROUP. No, no, it's just that — (*laughs*) after sleeping on wet grass between damp blankets — or propped against trees — I can hardly grasp — it's uncommonly kind of you, Mr Jameson, thank you.

BARTTELOT (*enters, through the flap, carrying a wooden stick with a metal tip*). Ah, Mr Troup, Mr Ward, here you are, I've been looking for you, and Mr Bonny. We must be careful that your Soudanese, Mr Troup, and your Zanzibaris, Mr Ward, are kept separate from those already in the camp. We've had a bout of sickness, as you've probably noticed, and there's no point the fresh men being contaminated. We'll have to put guards on them or they'll drift — they'll drift — and Mr Bonny, your mules, a guard on those too, if you please. Mule meat is something of a delicacy with the Soudanese — with Mr Jameson and myself, come to think of it, eh Jamie? (*He laughs.*) Well gentlemen, by this time you'll have some idea of our situation. I've no doubt you're as disappointed to find Mr Stanley gone as Mr Jameson and I were when we were left behind to wait for you. But he was anxious to make all possible speed to Emin Pasha, and pull him out before the Mahdi gets to him and with luck we'll either catch him up or not be too far behind him.

BONNY. As I understand it, we have to wait on for more porters.

BARTTELOT. Yes, Mr Bonny, another six hundred. We have nine hundred loads, each one of which Mr Stanley believes essential — food, quinine, rifles — and including the ones you've brought up just over three hundred porters. So we can't move until we have the other six hundred.

TROUP. Where are they going to come from? As Bonny, Ward and I were the only officers left behind —

BARTTELOT. They're being brought up by Tippu-Tib.

WARD. Tippu-Tib!

BARTTELOT. That's right, Mr Ward. Tippu-Tib. He and Mr Stanley came to an arrangement here before Stanley set out.

BONNY. Who is Tippu-Tib?

WARD. He's an Arab slave trader. Half Arab that is, and half Manyema. Which makes him wholly abominable.

BARTTELOT. But a particular friend of Mr Stanley's. You know him then?

WARD. By reputation, of course. No one who's spent any time in this part of the Congo could fail to. And I've come across his auxiliaries, who usually turn out to be his relatives as well. I've also come across his victims. I met poor Deane at Stanley Falls a year ago, just after the Arabs had burnt him out.

JAMESON. But on that occasion Tippu-Tib wasn't the Arab responsible.

WARD. Oh, Tippu is always the Arab responsible. This country is really his bazaar, you see, and the people in it his merchandise, and every Arab a relative, and every relative an agent.

BARTTELOT. Nevertheless, as I said, he and Mr Stanley are the greatest of friends.

WARD. They both choose their friends wisely.

JAMESON. And they have an agreement for the porters.

BONNY. When is he expected then, Major, with the porters?

BARTTELOT. Mr Stanley couldn't be precise. But he was hoping they'd arrive shortly after you.

BONNY. Any day now then.

WARD. Did you yourselves take part in these arrangements with Tippu-Tib?

BARTTELOT. No, Mr Stanley and Tippu-Tib kept themselves to themselves during the time the Arabs were in the Camp. None of the other officers had the pleasure of being introduced to him either, he has an aversion to any shows of white strength, apparently, we scarcely got a glimpse of him.

TROUP. And this is the man we're to wait for! An Arab slaver who distrusts white men —

JAMESON. He doesn't distrust Mr Stanley.

BONNY. Have you heard anything of him since he left?

JAMESON. Oh, just rumours. A few weeks ago the natives were full of talk of Arabs, I went over to explore but couldn't find any trace — the natives have a particular interest in Arabs, of course, they fear them as slavers but desire them as food.

TROUP. Food!

JAMESON. They believe they can take their cunning into their own systems, by eating them.

TROUP. But look here — do you mean to say — I thought cannibalism had been wiped out in these parts, by Stanley himself when he was here before. There was a long report in *The Times*, only last year —

WARD. The local chiefs probably haven't received their copies yet.

JAMESON (*laughs*). The problem is, Mr Troup, that it's hard to wipe out an appetite. Mr Stanley made the chiefs promise to stop gobbling each other up —

WARD. As he made the slavers promise to give up slaving. A promise in the jungle may become a fact in London, but you don't believe that Tippu-Tib is going to hire our six hundred men, do you? Or that Stanley believes he is.

TROUP. But good God — good God — Stanley told us nothing of this sort of thing in London. We signed on to march direct to the relief of Emin Pasha — and instead here we are hanging about waiting for some brigand of an Arab to enslave some porters —

BARTTELOT. While outside there are cannibals and inside three hundred hungry and contagious niggers. Exactly, Mr Troup. That is our situation, and will remain our situation until Tippu-Tib arrives to release us from it.

WARD. What is Mr Stanley's alternative proposal?

BARTTELOT. Alternative to what?

WARD. In the event of Tippu's not turning up shortly. He's notorious for a number of things, but not for his punctuality. At least I've never heard of it.

BARTTELOT. There is no alternative.

WARD. But in the event of his not turning up at all.

BARTTELOT. There is still no alternative. Mr Stanley will accept
no alternative to the safety of his loads. He is clear that he
expects them and must have them. There is no alternative, Mr
Ward. Tippu-Tib must turn up. And until he does we shall
have to make the best of it.

WARD. But surely — (*He stops.*)

JAMESON. You'll be wanting to settle into your quarters —
there's a shower behind my tent. The water comes up from the
Arruwimi, it's dirty, warm and it smells, I'm afraid, but it's wet.

BARTTELOT. We've been in the habit of eating at sun-down, if
that suits you. We've kept a goat specially for this occasion —
though we've been tempted by it often enough, haven't we,
Jamie? — so at least this first night you'll have meat rather
than manioc. By the way, an unnecessary warning, I'm sure,
but anything you have in the way of provisions should be
kept locked in your trunks — they're not above trying to slip
into the tents, we caught one just the other day — and your
rifles, goes without saying.

WARD. Actually, Major, I've no provisions whatsoever. So I'd
be very glad to have what's coming to me as soon as you can
manage it.

BONNY. Yes, I'm right out of tea.

BARTTELOT. I'm sorry, Mr Ward. There's nothing coming to you
that I know of.

TROUP. Six months provisions, guaranteed by the Committee.

WARD. To be provided when we got our men up here.

BARTTELOT. I know nothing about it.

TROUP. But they must surely have been left behind by Mr Stanley.

BARTTELOT. Very possibly. But as Mr Stanley left no instructions
on the matter, there's no way of knowing.

TROUP. But what about you and Jameson? Have you had yours?

BARTTELOT. Mr Stanley did give some out before he left, yes.
But he left me no authorisation to give you any.

TROUP. My authorisation comes from the Committee in London.

BARTTELOT. Then perhaps you should take it up with the
Committee in London.

WARD. Personally I shan't be needing jungle provisions in
London, at least as long as there are still shops and restaurants
there. Anyway, my chit is signed personally by Mr Stanley.

BARTTELOT. Then it's to Mr Stanley you must apply,
when we catch up with him.

TROUP. We need our provisions now, sir.

BARTTELOT. I can't help you, sir.

TROUP. But you can, sir. They must be here, among the loads
Mr Stanley left behind.

BARTTELOT. As Mr Stanley didn't say, how can you know
that?

WARD. Ratiocination, possibly. In that if Mr Stanley owes us
some provisions, which he does; and has left behind a large
number of loads, which he has; and arranged for us to wait
here with you, to help bring up those loads, which he did;
then he's scarcely likely to have taken our provisions on with
him; which one can therefore conclude he hasn't.

BARTTELOT. Are you making fun of me, sir!

WARD. No, Major. I was simply helping you to a conclusion.

BARTTELOT. Well, one may conclude anything with Mr
Stanley, as a sure way of ending up in the wrong for it. But
one thing one can be sure about, in the matter of Mr
Stanley's intentions, is that his instructions are to be
carried out to the very letter, and only to the very letter,
however inconvenient that may be to the rest of the world.
Mr Jameson will confirm that as Commanding Officer of
this Rear Column, I must do as Mr Stanley said, but I may
on no account do what I think he might have said, had he
been here to say it. Isn't that so, Mr Jameson? I sympathise
with you, of course, and if my Commanding Officer weren't
Mr Stanley, you'd find your Commanding Officer a very
much more obliging fellow, believe me.

TROUP. Do you mean to say that we're not to have our provisions
simply because Stanley forgot to include them in his
instructions.

BARTTELOT. But we cannot say that he forgot. He may well
have remembered not to include them.

TROUP. And why should he do that?

BARTTELOT. Because — because — I don't know, how should I?

TROUP. This is nonsense, nonsense! You tell us we're not to
have provisions which we were guaranteed as members of this
expedition, provisions that do not belong personally to Mr
Stanley, because in your view Mr Stanley is some sort of —
some sort of — punctilious lunatic. Well sir, let me remind
you that I have had dealings with Mr Stanley, and a saner and
more practical man I've never met. Sir, I believe you're making
us the victims of some private misunderstanding between Mr
Stanley and yourself.

BARTTELOT. Have no fear of that, sir, there's no misunderstanding
at all between Mr Stanley, and myself. I understand him only
too well. Certainly too well to allow myself to be the victim of
your misfortune. He wouldn't hesitate to use this opportunity
to ruin my career, my reputation at home —

WARD (after a pause). Stanley will ruin your career and your
reputation if you furnish us with provisions that are rightly
ours?

BARTTELOT. Ask Mr Jameson if I'm over-stating the case?

JAMESON. The Major has reason to be careful, where Mr
Stanley's orders are in question. Mr Stanley on an
expedition is a very different man from Mr Stanley on the Falls
or sitting with Mr MacKinnon on the Committee in London.
Jephson, Parke, Stairs — all the officers who've gone on with
him would concur.

BARTTELOT. And it is through his orders, some of them
impossible to perform, that he gets at us. He's as savage with
initiative as he is with inefficiency. Well, he'll not get at me,
sir, not any more. And I'm sorry if others must suffer for it.

TROUP. Can we see these orders, Major? As we're to be so
strictly governed by them?

BARTTELOT (after a pause, during which he stares at
TROUP). You would have seen them in due course, Mr
Troup, whether you'd requested to or not.

TROUP (reads them through quickly). There's very little to them,
and what there is can scarcely be said to have been written in a
spirit of animosity. (Passing them to WARD.) Rather the
reverse.

BARTTELOT. He knew that I would not be the only one to read
them.

TROUP. I see he expressly requests you to take Mr Ward's, Mr Bonny's and my advice — along with Mr Jameson's.

BARTTELOT. No, Mr Troup, he tells me to ask you for your advice, not take it. The responsibility remains entirely mine. It's in the same sentence — heed their advice while being solely answerable for the decisions. At a first reading you will fail to detect, as Mr Jameson and I failed to detect, the real subtlety of what he's written. Or notice a major anomaly.

WARD. I certainly can't find an anomaly — or even much in the way of subtlety. It's all most emphatic, down to the number of brass-rods we're to pay to the porters per day.

BARTTELOT. The brass-rods — oh yes — he'd be emphatic about the brass-rods. He knows the value of a brass-rod in the Congo as a Jew knows a sovereign in Kensington.

JAMESON. But apart from the brass-rods he is emphatic. But without being precise.

BARTTELOT. Exactly. Exactly. And look — see what he says about the palisade.

WARD (looks). Merely that you're to build one. Which you have — an admirable one. What could be more sensible?

BARTTELOT. Ah, but what follows the order — (He recites.) For remember, it is not the natives alone who may wish to assail you, but the Arabs and their followers may, through some cause or other, quarrel with you and assail the camp.

WARD. Well?

BARTTELOT. Well, Mr Ward, you yourself have confirmed our worst suspicions. By Arabs whom can he mean but Tippu-Tib. So Stanley has gone out of his way to warn us against a man he claims as his friend, on whom he has made us depend, without whose arrival we cannot move!

WARD. But good God, of course he'd warn you! He knows better than anyone — friend or not, Tippu-Tib is a very dangerous man. But he also knows that Tippu is the only man in the Congo who could raise six hundred porters, by whatever means. Tippu is both totally indispensable and completely untrustworthy. That is the nature of the beast!

JAMESON. But as you've pointed out, he leaves us with no alternative.

WARD. And as Major Barttelot pointed out — with considerable force — there is no alternative. If the loads are essential, then the porters are essential. If the porters are essential —

TROUP. So is this Tippu-Tib. Exactly! I must say (*laughs*) if this is all!

BARTTELOT. It isn't all! Or rather it is all — and that's the damned subtlety of it. Not what he's put in, but what he's left out!

TROUP. Oh this is the sheerest — the sheerest — how could he cover every contingency — look, you tell us that Stanley always gets at you through his orders — well, surely you examined him on every sentence when he took you through them.

BARTTELOT. I did not.

TROUP. Why not?

BARTTELOT. Perhaps, Mr Troup, because he didn't take me through them.

TROUP. That's irregular, I admit — but then he's not a military man — but you could have gone to him yourself, I suppose you read them before he left?

BARTTELOT. You suppose incorrectly. Mr Stanley made it impossible — quite impossible — for me to read them until he'd marched out of the Camp.

TROUP. But the fact remains there is nothing there to prevent you giving us our provisions. Good God, man, can you not see — I have two ounces of sugar, an ounce of tea — Mr Ward tells you he has nothing — Mr Bonny is out of —

BONNY. Tea.

TROUP. And the only reason you offer for denying us is that Stanley hasn't actually written it down that you should give us them. As if he didn't have enough on his mind —

BARTTELOT. Mr Stanley's last verbal orders to me. delivered before Jephson and Stairs as witnesses, was that I was on no account to exceed his written orders. On no account!

TROUP. You were on no account to exceed written orders that he prevented you from reading until he'd gone?

BARTTELOT. This is a trivial subject, trivial! There are more important matters — look outside, sir, at the state of the niggers Stanley's left us with — he made sure to take only the healthy with him — don't doubt that — there's sickness, pilfering — and you fret at me with your tea and sugar — by God, I've said my last word on the subject. The subject is closed! (*He exits through the flap.*)

TROUP. Well, it's not closed as far as I'm concerned — I've no intention —

JAMESON. Mr Troup, your bed. Shall we go and find it?

TROUP. What? Yes, yes, the bed! At least I have a bed! (*He laughs bitterly.*) I'm much obliged to you, Mr Jameson. (*He follows* JAMESON *through the flap.*)

WARD. I remember a governess rather similar to the Major. Her most infuriating prohibitions always depended upon some illogically spiteful but unuttered edict of my father's. It's no good blaming me, it's your papa says no. But he hasn't said no. But he would if you asked him. In fact our papa hadn't the slightest interest in us, and would have said yes to anything. Did you have a governess like that, Bonny?

BONNY. No. But this governess'll say yes, don't you worry.

WARD. What makes you think that?

BONNY. Mr Jameson's face.

WARD. Ah, I see. That's why you kept the peace, was it? Because you'd read Mr Jameson's face?

BONNY. Well, there was no good going on at him, was there, it just made him more determined.

WARD. And did you like him for that?

BONNY. I didn't like him or dislike him. I recognised him for what he is.

WARD. And what's that?

BONNY. Our Commanding Officer. (*He exits.*)

WARD *stares after him, then walks around the store-room, stops to look at the turtles, then walks casually on to Jameson's desk, picks up a sketch, studies it.*

JAMESON *enters, as if expecting to find the room empty. Stops on seeing* WARD.

WARD. You've bedded old Troup, then?

JAMESON. He couldn't get off with it fast enough. He was probably afraid I'd change my mind and wrestle it back from him.

WARD. I was just admiring your work — it is yours, I take it?

JAMESON. Yes. A plover, he rested ten minutes on a branch right outside my tent this morning. I shall have to wait until I get home to do full justice to his colouring — the forehead's light brown — reddish brown, really — and the crest here (*coming over, pointing*) is blacker than I've managed with charcoal — so is the top of the head. And the cheeks are a delicate grey, as is the lower half of the throat. The whiteness of the paper is about right for the whiteness of the rest of the throat, but the wing crests are a wonderful ash-green — and no paper would serve for the white bar across the centre of the wing — and the eye — imagine an ochre iris around the black pupil.

WARD. That collection in one of the small huts — it's entirely yours then?

JAMESON. Why yes. Yes it is.

WARD. Good God, I thought it had been done by four men at least. A lepidopterist, an ornithologist, an entymologist and an ethnologist. What unified them must be the artist.

JAMESON. Or perhaps a dilettante, who separates them. Do you sketch, Mr Ward?

WARD. A little. Which is how I do most things. So I'm the dillettante, Mr Jameson, and now you've come face to face with the real article, you'll have to drop your pose. Unless, of course, it's assumed for the Major's sake.

JAMESON. Major Barttelot and I have been together in rather difficult circumstances recently. We've had to depend on each other too much, in sickness, and in health, to assume poses with each other.

WARD. Good Heavens, that sounds rather like a marriage!

JAMESON. I already have a marriage.

WARD. Really? And children?

JAMESON (*after a pause*). Two. At least I trust and pray two. The second was due last month.

WARD. May I congratulate you. Not least on your wife, who must be very understanding.

JAMESON. She is, Mr Ward. Thank you.

WARD. Did Mr Stanley choose you to stay behind with the Major, or did the Major choose you, or did you choose yourself?

JAMESON. It was understood that Stairs was to be left behind, but at the last moment Mr Stanley changed his mind, and appointed me. Mr Stanley being Mr Stanley, he offered no explanation. Have you any further questions?

WARD. I'm sorry, I've been impertinent. It's just that — look — I know from my own experience of this continent how quickly one can come to brood on a subject when cut off — isn't it possible that you and the Major —

JAMESON. Went a trifle mad together? Yes, quite possible. Nevertheless Stanley did threaten to destroy the Major's reputation.

WARD. Why?

JAMESON. Perhaps the Major wasn't used to being spoken to as Mr Stanley is used to speaking to gentlemen who accompany him on his expeditions. And Mr Stanley was even less used to being answered as the Major answered him.

WARD. And because of this — this clash of temperaments, Stanley would go to the length of ruining a man —

JAMESON. At the moment, Stanley is almost as powerful in London as he is in Africa. He'd only have to speak a few words — and Stanley is too jealous of his own fame to care much about another man's honour. The Major is a military man from a military family. His honour means a great deal to him.

WARD. Yet Stanley did make him Commanding Officer of his Rear Column. That could be construed as an honour.

JAMESON. It could also be construed as one of his insults. The Major was appointed Senior Officer to the Relief of Emin Pasha, and has been left behind to guard the supplies. He is a brave and active man, rendered temporarily inactive.

WARD. A sort of Samson, blinded and chained. And yet you were left with him — so Stanley showed some compassion to the Major. And to the rest of us, I suspect. Bonny has already singled you out as the peacemaker.

JAMESON. We had all of us better keep the peace, Mr Ward.

WARD. Oh, I shan't give you any more trouble, my word on it. And old Troup is really a decent enough fellow who's never been to the Congo before and has been out of bed too long — one good night'll probably settle him.

JAMESON (laughs). Well, you've only to settle Mr Bonny, and we shall be all right.

WARD. Mr Bonny has already informed me that he's quite settled. It seems that he likes his Commanding Officers to be commanding, which the Major evidently is. Did you know, by the way, that he's the only white man on the whole expedition who's being paid for his services. Can that be because he's the only one among us whose services are worth hiring? Whatever you say about Stanley, his recruitment drive in London was a spectacular success — why, they said at the Falls he'd actually got some rich nincompoop to pay for the privilege of marching with him, God knows how much! (*He laughs.*)

JAMESON. One thousand pounds, Mr Ward, and in view of what I've learnt so far, I count it a bargain as well as a privilege. So the Major is for honour, and Troup, I presume, is for honour, and Bonny for money, and I for study — what about you, Mr Ward, what are you here for?

WARD. I'm a patriotic Englishman, Mr Jameson.

JAMESON. I see.

WARD. And as Emin Pasha is an eccentric German employed by the Egyptians to maintain their interest in South Equatorial Africa, it is surely the duty of all patriotic Englishmen to sign up with a Welsh adoptive American to rescue him from a rampaging Muslim. While at the same time helping the Welsh adoptive American to extend a little more Belgian influence along the Arruwimi River. Isn't it?

JAMESON. You believe the rumours then? That Stanley is really doing all this for Leopold of Brussels?

WARD. Certainly not. He's using Leopold of Brussels so that he can do it all for Stanley.

JAMESON. But if you don't believe the cause is noble —

WARD. Noble! (*He laughs.*) There are no noble causes in the Congo, and never have been. In the Congo there are only cannibals and other natives, Arab slavers, European interests and magnificent opportunists. Along with birds, butterflies and snakes, of course, for artists and naturalists like yourself.

JAMESON. Then what are you doing here?

WARD. I haven't the slightest idea. All I know is that after three years travelling around the continent, I was suddenly desperate for the sight of England. Nothing could have persuaded me to stay on another month except, it seems, the very first opportunity to do so. Stanley's expedition was the first opportunity. Perhaps it's simply the fickleness of the dilettante who decides to put up with something he's tired of, for a change, eh?

JAMESON. Or the impulse of a serious man who's not yet discovered what it is he came here to find out.

WARD. Unless, finally, I'm an unwitting agent of one of history's more grandiose schemes.

JAMESON. What would that be?

WARD. Why, to ruin the reputation of a certain Major — from Norfolk, is it?

JAMESON. Sussex, it is.

WARD. In his Sussex family, with his Sussex hunt, and in his London clubs. Think, if only Gordon hadn't fallen at Khartoum the Mahdi wouldn't be driving on to destroy Emin Pasha, Stanley wouldn't be in the Congo, and ergo: I wouldn't be quarrelling with the Sussex Major for my flour, coffee, sugar, tea and gentleman's relish, at Yambuya, on the banks of the Arruwimi River, in June, this year of Grace, 1887.

JAMESON (*laughs*). Well, whatever the whirligigs of history or fate, Mr Ward, I believe I'm glad they've brought you to us.

BARTTELOT (*enters through the flap*). Ah, you're still here then. (*To* JAMESON.) I was looking for Bonny, as a matter of fact. Thought I'd better find out whether he brought up any quinine. He's not in his tent.

JAMESON. Well, he hasn't come in. He went off some time ago.

BARTTELOT. Oh.

JAMESON. He may be having a shower.

BARTTELOT. Looked there. No one in the shower.

*Pause.*

WARD. In that case, I'll be able to have one. (*He goes towards the flap.*)

BARTTELOT. Don't forget, Mr Ward. Roast goat. Roast goat and palm wine at sun-down, eh?

WARD *exits.*

BARTTELOT. You've been having a chat with him, then?

JAMESON. Yes.

BARTTELOT. Ah. And what's he like — when he's not drawling out his sarcasms.

JAMESON. Oh, rather sympathetic. Certainly intelligent.

BARTTELOT. You like him, then?

JAMESON. I found him rather a relief. (*Hurriedly.*) I mean, from what I'd feared earlier.

BARTTELOT. God Jamie, I wish I had your knack — but by God, what a business, eh! Hardly arrived and they're set against me. Even Stanley couldn't have hoped for such a swift success — grown men at each other's throats — over what! Fortnum and Mason's! That's the joke of it! And that Troup — (*pacing about*) dead set, dead set against me —

JAMESON. Ward assures me that now he's got a bed he'll calm down.

BARTTELOT. What, a bed, how?

JAMESON. I remembered Parke's — the one for Jephson —

BARTTELOT. There you are, you see! And I didn't think of it — not at all, all I could think was that he was after me for one of Stanley's beds — and now the bad feeling's there!

JAMESON. We'll find a way to win them around.

BARTTELOT. Hah! You'd find a way all right, Jamie. (*Pause.*) If I weren't here.

JAMESON. Oh now come, old man, you mustn't give in —

BONNY *enters through the flap.*

BARTTELOT. Ah, Bonny! Here you are — I've been looking for you.

BONNY. One of the nigger boys only just told me, sir. I was talking to Troup in his tent.

BARTTELOT. What? Talking to Troup?

BONNY. Yes, sir.

BARTTELOT. Well Bonny, we'd better have a think about our medical supplies, eh?

JAMESON. I'll see you at mess. (*He exits.*)

BARTTELOT. Right, Jamie, at mess. Yes, first thing is to make sure we keep our supplies separate from Stanley's — Oh, that reminds me — here's a (*takes a little package from his pocket*)

as you're desperate, not much I'm afraid, almost at the end
myself, but enough to make you a pot at least.

BONNY. That's — that's very kind of you, sir.

BARTTELOT. Not at all. Not at all. (*Pause.*) Now there's one
other matter. I need your advice on. I've been ill.

BONNY. Yes. Mr Jameson mentioned that you and he —

BARTTELOT. This is something different. Something a medic
can't detect — (*Pause.*) I don't sleep at nights, not for months,
not since Stanley left, get the shakes, the fever, nightmares,
that sort of thing and I can't — I find my temper, well,
scarcely seems to be mine any more as if — how to explain it
— as if I were being — being poisoned, do you see?

BONNY. Well, you probably are, Major, from what Mr
Jameson was telling me of your diet here.

BARTTELOT. No it's not the diet, Jameson sleeps like a top
most nights. He has the same diet. These nightmares, I tell
you — and headaches — I can't go on with them. (*Pause.*)
Well? What do you — ?

BONNY. Morphine, sir.

BARTTELOT. Morphine! Certainly not. Morphine's not the
answer. (*He looks at him.*)

BONNY. No, Major, it isn't. The answer is obvious enough. A
return to a different life, different food, a different country. In
other words, the answer for you is England.

BARTTELOT *looks at him, waits.*

But as the answer's out of the question —

BARTTELOT. Why?

BONNY. I beg your pardon, sir?

BARTTELOT Why is it out of the question?

BONNY. Well — because you're in command here, sir.

BARTTELOT. It might be better for everybody if I weren't.
(*Pause.*) Jameson — is more — more fit.

BONNY. Mr Jameson isn't an army man, though, is he, sir?
He's a gentleman of leisure, from what I can make out.

BARTTELOT. Mr Jameson happens to be the finest man I've
ever met.

BONNY. But Mr Stanley appointed you the Commanding Officer.

BARTTELOT. But between you, you and Troup and Ward and Mr Jameson — you could — (*pause*) do you understand what I'm asking?

BONNY. Yes, I do.

BARTTELOT. Well then, man!

BONNY. I'm not sure my recommendation would carry much weight.

BARTTELOT. But you would write one for me?

BONNY. Naturally, sir. If you ordered me to.

BARTTELOT. Ordered you to?

BONNY. I could hardly write a letter recommending that you be invalided home, without your asking me to, first. Which you have done. And I agree.

BARTTELOT. With the recommendation?

BONNY. To write the letter. It is an order, isn't it?

BARTTELOT. Of course it isn't an order! What value would a letter have that I'd ordered you to write — good God man, you have qualifications, you can judge a situation and act accordingly. Nobody would challenge a doctor's findings.

BONNY. That's true, sir, yes. But then I'm not a doctor.

BARTTELOT. Not a doctor?

BONNY. I'm a medical orderly. And that's less than third class in the medical profession. Did you take me for a doctor?

BARTTELOT. I didn't think about it one way or another. I assumed you had medical experience, I assumed — as they signed you up — you'd be, yes, properly qualified —

BONNY. I'm properly qualified as a medical orderly. And a medical orderly's services come considerably cheaper than a properly qualified doctor's. I expect Mr Stanley took that into account when he appointed me.

BARTTELOT. In that case, we've been at cross-purposes, haven't we?

BONNY. No, sir. (*Little pause.*) Well, at least I understood.

BARTTELOT. What? What did you understand? (*He moves towards him threateningly.*)

BONNY. Well, that you wanted my assurance, in as much as I could give it, that you're fit to carry on.

BARTTELOT. You want me to stay, do you?

BONNY. Yes, I do.

BARTTELOT. Why?

BONNY. Because you're the Commanding Officer. And if we're to be here a while yet, then Mr Stanley will be getting further and further away from us. The country is dangerous, there are cannibals around, there could be fighting. And this Tippu-Tib, who sounds as likely to attack us as give us our nigger porters. We'd need you then, very badly, however nicely Mr Jameson were to run things in the meanwhile.

BARTTELOT. You'll do for me, Bonny. You'll do for me very well.

BONNY. Thank you, Major. (*Little pause.*) You'll do for me too, if I may say so. (*He turns, makes to go out, stops.*) Oh sir, I shan't —

BARTTELOT. What?

BONNY. Needless to say, it shall never be mentioned by me that this conversation took place. The others might misconstrue —

BARTTELOT *stares at him.*

BONNY. And thank you again for the tea, sir. Much appreciated. (*He goes out.*)

BARTTELOT (*stands, for a moment, then lets out an exclamation, loud, of despair. He begins to stride up and down*). Damn — damn — damned insolence!

*He drives the point of his stick into the ground, plucks it out, strides up and down.*

(*Bellowing.*) John Henry! John Henry! (*He continues to stride, and as lights fade to black, still striding and jabbing his stick into the ground, at the very top of his lungs.*) John Henry!

**Scene Two**

*About an hour later. The stage is in darkness.* JAMESON *enters.*
*through the flap. He strikes a match, puts it to the lamp.*
    BARTTELOT *is sitting at the table, his hands to his face.*
    JOHN HENRY *is sitting at the end of the table staring*
*straight ahead.*
    JAMESON *takes in the scene, quickly lights the other two*
*lamps, goes over to* BARTTELOT, *puts a hand on his shoulder.*

BARTTELOT (*jumps, removes his hands*). Oh — oh Jamie — there
    you are! Well, supper, eh? Manioc soup, prime cuts of manioc,
    pudding of manioc —

JAMESON. Not tonight, old man. Can't you smell the goat?

BARTTELOT. What, by God, yes — goat, eh, how did you —
    oh, oh yes, those others, they've arrived, it's for them. (*He*
    *looks, sees* JOHN HENRY.) What? (*Stares at him.*) Ah, that's
    right, there's a good boy, John Henry, told him to sit down,
    not on the floor like a monkey, but at the table, like a human
    being, eh John Henry — and then when I — I — you just sat on,
    eh? Yes, that's a good lad, now go and get the palm wine,
    John Henry. Palm wine. Fancy that. (*He gets up.*) Falling
    asleep — and a nice sleep, a dream not a nightmare, I've got a
    feeling the old pater was in it, we were walking across the
    paddocks, a spring morning — smelt something good — perhaps
    it was the goat, eh? Well, now I'm back, they'll be here in a
    minute —

JAMESON. Look, something's occurred to me that may help —
    What do you say to giving them half their six months'
    provision now, and leave it to Stanley to give them their other
    half when we get up with him. That way, you'll be recognizing
    their claim, while still respecting Stanley's ultimate authority.
    Do you see?

BARTTELOT. But it would still be a breach.

JAMESON. Yes, but if you don't give them anything then they
    could complain to Stanley and it might suit him to take their
    side. There was nothing in my orders, he could say, and no
    reason that you shouldn't have obliged these men.

BARTTELOT. And so he gets me either way! For being in breach
    of his orders if I do, or failing to exercise my command if I
    don't!

JAMESON. Ah, but if he says you shouldn't have given them even half their provisions, then Ward, Troup and Bonny would have to come to your defence, you see. And Stanley wouldn't like that.

BARTTELOT. I don't know, Jamie. I don't know. All I know is that I'm well and truly in Stanley's web and whatever I do — I'll have to think — make a decision — but you believe that would be all right, do you?

*There is a pause.*

Look, old man, I must tell you. I — the fact is, I've just done something rather shameful. I asked Bonny if he could have me invalided home. (*He looks at* JAMESON, *distressed.*) It suddenly seemed a solution, you see, that as a medical man he could get me out of all this — a letter would do it, that was my thought. Then you and the others could do as you like, wouldn't have me to contend with. I'd be out of his trap honourably and the rest of you'd be out of his trap too, d'you see? But it's not to be. He's not a doctor, it turns out. Just a medical orderly. I'd have to order him to recommend me to leave — you can imagine what Stanley would have made of that — how he could get at me as far worse than a coward — a cunning coward. Eh? (*He laughs.*)

JAMESON. Poor old boy. I don't blame you, not at all, I'm only sorry —

BARTTELOT. No, don't be soft on me. I did wrong. I shouldn't have tried. But you know, there's something I want you to understand. I couldn't have done it. Couldn't have left, I'm sure of that. All I wanted was the letter in my pocket, that meant I could if I wanted to, you see? Something I could — could touch as — to confirm I'd made a choice — a choice not to go back even though I'd been let off. I'd never desert. Not desert you, old man, after the two months we've been through. I count you my closest — my closest —

TROUP *comes through the flap.*

Ah, Mr Troup — well, I hear you have a bed, thank God for that, eh?

JOHN HENRY *enters with a jug.*

And here's the palm wine — on the table — there's a boy — now the glasses —

WARD *enters.*

BARTTELOT. Ah, here you are then, Ward — showered and — and
— and one for Mr Ward too, John Henry — now the jug — be
careful not to spill, we've only about a quart of the stuff left,
old Jameson bought it from the cannibals, so you see they have
their uses, Troup, eh? (*He laughs*.) Not brandy, I know, but not
as fierce as you'd expect from a cannibal brew —

*As* JOHN HENRY, *having filled* WARD's *and* TROUP's
*and* JAMESON's *glass comes to fill his,* BONNY *enters.*

Ah, Bonny — Mr Bonny first, John Henry — that's right, there's
a boy, and now mine — John Henry's quite a little find of
mine, used to be one of Mr Stanley's boys, eh, John Henry? He
was in the tent the morning Stanley was leaving — Stanley's
tent — all the hullabaloo and John Henry crying, weren't
you, John Henry, because Stanley had chosen to take one of
his other boys instead, heartbroken because of it, eh, John
Henry? And when Stanley marched out — by God, what a
business he makes of it, struts yards ahead of his officers —
poor old Jephson in a terrible state of indecision, whether to
keep him company or maintain a respectful ten yards behind,
Parke and Stairs trying to look unconcerned, at the back, but
getting caught up in the Zanzibaris who wouldn't move fast
enough for all the damned fuss, drums rolling, pipes blowing,
and all the time Stanley not seeing the farce of it all, strutting
along eyes focussed on posterity by way of the London *Times*
and his publishers, old Jameson did a marvellous sketch, one of
the Soudanese he left for us to bury managed to die just as
Stanley passed him, old Jameson got him in the sketch, eyes
rolling, what was it you called it, A Faithful Zanzibari says his
Farewell to H. M. Stanley, Esq. H. M. standing for His
Majesty, hah, hah, not Henry Morton by God, and above it
Jameson's put, what was it, homage to a great man. (*He
laughs*.) And there was little John Henry trailing behind,
blubbering away, right out of the Camp, hoping right to the
end His Majesty would pardon him and take him along after all,
but I knew he wouldn't, knew he'd send him back and next
morning — next morning I kept a look out for him, found him
skulking with the Soudanese, and took him on. After a
shower, of course. Now John Henry showers once a day, don't
you, John Henry, and is my personal boy, sleeps outside my
tent — tell them how Mr Stanley came by you, John Henry.

JOHN HENRY. Tippu-Tib, he give me Mr Stanley.

BARTTELOT. That's right, our old friend Tippu-Tib. He

captured John Henry from one of the villages, and made a
present of him to Stanley the last time Stanley was in these
parts. Stanley made him his chief boy, then when he went
back to England, stuck him in a missionary school at the Pool.
Collected him when he got back three months ago. And leaves
him behind all over again. Jameson and I've spent hours grilling
him about Tippu-Tib, haven't we, Jamie, but he only knows three
things about him, Tell us, John Henry, is Tippu-Tib a good man,
good man?

JOHN HENRY. Tippu-Tib good man.

BARTTELOT. And is Tippu-Tib a bad man.

JOHN HENRY. Bad man, bad man.

BARTTELOT. Now tell us why he's called Tippu-Tib? Why name
Tippu-Tib?

JOHN HENRY (*lifts his arm, points it about*). Tippu-tippu-tippu,
tib, tib, tippu tib, tippu tib.

JAMESON. Onomatopoeic, you see.

BONNY. What?

JAMESON. The noise of the rifle, when Tippu and his men come
firing on the villages. Far more exact than bang, really.

WARD. Tippu's real name is Hamed bin Mahamed el Marjebi. But
I never thought to ask why he was known as Tippu-Tib —

BARTTELOT. No, but Jameson did, eh Jamie? Anyway, those
are the three things that John Henry knows about Tippu-Tib,
that he's good, that he's bad, and how he got his name.

WARD. Which is one thing more than we know about most
people.

BARTTELOT (*laughs with false enthusiasm*). Very neat, Mr
Ward. Very neat.

JAMESON. Gentlemen, before you finish your glasses, may I
propose a toast. To the Rear Column.

BARTTELOT. To the Rear Column.

TROUP. )
WARD.  ) To the Rear Column!
BONNY. )

BARTTELOT (*catches Jameson's eye*). I've been thinking —
rather Jameson and I've been putting our heads together —
and what do you say to this? Three months provision now,

three months when we catch up with Stanley. Eh? What do you say? Troup?

TROUP. Well, sir, given your — your uneasiness with Mr Stanley's orders, that seems fair enough.

WARD. I think it's a marvellously sensible compromise. (*Glancing at* JAMESON.)

BONNY. Certainly do for me.

BARTTELOT. Very well, gentlemen. Now I've something to show you.

*He looks to* JAMESON, *winks, goes to a crate, brings it over, swings it up, jabs the point of his stick in, prises up the lid, and begins to plonk down items.*

One and a half pounds of coffee. One pound of tea. One and a half tins of salt. One and a half tins of jam and of chocolate milk. One tin of cocoa and milk. One tin of sardines. One of sausages. One pound of fancy biscuits. One third of a tin of red herring. Half a pound of flour. One pot of Liebig. One quarter of a pound of tapioca. Times three, of course.

*During this drums have begun to pound.*

TROUP. Oh, I see, This is a *month's* rations.

BARTTELOT. No, this is three months.

WARD. Three months' — that!

BARTTELOT. It is.

TROUP. But good God, who made up these provisions?

JAMESON. Fortnum and Mason's. They'd have done us quite nicely for an afternoon at Lord's Cricket Ground, don't you think?

TROUP. Good God, good God!

BARTTELOT. So there you, gentlemen! One half of what we were quarrelling about. And now perhaps you'll understand something about Mr Stanley, the greatest African explorer of our age! He has his expedition provisions made up by Fortnum and Mason's. (*He laughs.*)

*The drums increase in volume.*

Now if you excuse me while I put a stop to the accompaniment — (*He goes to the doors, unlatches them, throws them open.*)

*From outside, fires flaming; low keening sounds; the drums louder; dim shapes everywhere.* BARTTELOT *strides into their midst, with his stick.*

JAMESON. The Zanzibaris — the Major has a running battle with them every night —

BARTTELOT (*off*). That's enough of the drums — damn you, enough I say —

*The drums diminish, without stopping.*

JAMESON. There's a particular couple I call the Minchips because it's a Dickens-sounding name, and they're both out of Dickens — he'd have set them in the Mile End Road. The husband's as lazy a vagabond as you could expect to meet — lies on his side all day while the wife collects wood, bargains for food, gathers manioc — then at night after he's eaten he retires to his tent and cleans his rifle while the wife plays for him on the drums, I think she starts all the others off, and she's always the last to stop —

BARTTELOT (*still shouting, off*). Quiet I say — quiet —

WARD *goes towards the door, watches.*

TROUP *joins him.*

BONNY *pours himself some more palm-wine.*

*There is now only one drum beating.*

JAMESON *goes over to his desk, picks up the picture, looks at it.*

*Drum plays a few seconds longer, then stops.*

*On this tableau:*

*Lights.*

*Curtain.*

# Act Two

**Scene One**

*The Same. Six months later. Morning.*
*The doors are open. Outside, blazing sun-light and intense heat. Off, the sound of a voice, faint and unidentifiable, although it is Ward's. A thudding sound, also faint, follows each count.*

WARD. Forty-five, forty-six, forty-seven, forty-eight, forty-nine, fifty, fifty-one, fifty-two, fifty-three, fifty-four, fifty-five, fifty — (*Stops, pause.*) Take him down, will you? Down! Take him down!

*Movements, voices off. There is a pause.*

*TROUP enters through the main doors, goes to the water bucket, pours himself a mug of water, sits down, wipes his forehead, drinks.*

*BONNY enters. He is carrying salt and bandages. He puts them in a box. Goes to the water bucket, pours himself a mug of water.*

BONNY. Jameson's due back this morning, isn't he?

TROUP. Is he? (*Pause, sips. Laughs.*)

BONNY (*looks at him*). What?

TROUP. Well, you're not setting any store by that, are you?

BONNY. Not setting store by it, no. Just wanting to find out.

TROUP. Well, you don't have to wait for him — I can tell you. There're rumours. As he knew before he left.

BONNY. There're rumours in the villages here. They may turn out to be facts further down.

TROUP. They're always rumours, never facts.

BONNY. But he thought these were worth following up.

TROUP. Of course he did. As they coincided with a distasteful duty.

BONNY. Oh well, can't say I blame him. He's a gentleman, after all.

TROUP. And the rest of us aren't?

BONNY. Oh, I only meant he's not an officer.

TROUP. Some of us try to be both. Not that I blame him either, if he can get away with it. But I wonder that Barttelot lets him, he wouldn't let me, or Ward, it's a collective responsibility, we take votes on it, we should all stand by the decision.

BONNY. But Jameson voted against, didn't he? This time.

TROUP. This time, last time and the time before.

BONNY. Still, what would be the point of a vote, if we all had to vote one way.

TROUP. That's not my complaint.

BONNY. But what is your complaint?

TROUP. Only that Jameson doesn't take any of the —

BARTTELOT (*off*). Here you nigger — move that nigger out of the way —

BONNY. What?

TROUP. It doesn't matter.

BARTTELOT (*enters, followed by* JOHN HENRY). Water.

JOHN HENRY *goes to the cask, pours a mug of water.*

BARTTELOT. Ward went over. Over by five. We entered fifty on the log, damn nuisance!

JOHN HENRY *brings the mug over to* BARTTELOT, *who swills it down, hands the mug to* JOHN HENRY, *who goes over, pours more.*

BARTTELOT. Jameson should be back by now, he likes to get in before the heat — God what a business, Ward going on, thought he'd never stop. (*He takes the mug from* JOHN HENRY *again, drinks.*)

BONNY. No, but I don't understand what your complaint is.

TROUP. It doesn't matter.

BARTTELOT. What complaint?

*There is a pause.*

BONNY. About Mr Jameson's absence, wasn't it?

BARTTELOT. What about his absence?

TROUP. I was just saying that it was unfortunate that Jameson missed the flogging.

BARTTELOT. Why? Do you think he would have enjoyed it?

TROUP. They're meant to be a joint responsibility. We're all supposed to stand by the majority decision.

BARTTELOT. And when has Jameson rejected the majority decision?

TROUP. My point is simply that he should see it through with the rest of us.

BARTTELOT. He's seen enough of them to know how they go.

TROUP. But he voted against, and then stayed away.

BARTTELOT. And so?

TROUP. It's a way of keeping in the clear, isn't it?

BARTTELOT. Clear of what?

TROUP. The responsibility, of course.

BARTTELOT. Oh, what are you talking about, Troup? Somebody had to go up river to check the rumours —

TROUP. And does that someone always have to be Jameson? And always when there's a flogging?

BARTTELOT. Jameson goes because he's learned the lingo and is good with the natives. All right. (*Pause.*) All right?

TROUP (*grunts*). He'll bring back some sketches.

BARTTELOT. What?

TROUP. I said he'll bring back some nice sketches, of birds and leaves and toads and butterflies, and whatnot, I expect.

BARTTELOT. Let's hope he brings back some news of Tippu-Tib, eh?

TROUP. Whether he does or not, he'll bring back some sketches.

BARTTELOT (*after a pause*). Well?

TROUP. Well, he's down in the log as dissenting, *and* down in the log as absent from proceedings. In the six months I've been here he's not supervised the floggings once.

BARTTELOT. And in the six months you've been here you haven't stopped complaining, to one of us about the rest of us, to the rest of us about one of us, if it's not the flogging it's wood patrol, if it's not wood patrol it's — it's something else.

BONNY. I'm sorry if I've given you cause for complaint.

TROUP. You still haven't answered the facts, have you?

BARTTELOT. What facts?

TROUP. I've done my turn on the floggings, Bonny's done his, you've done yours and so's Ward.

WARD (entering wearily). Done what?

TROUP. Your turn on the floggings.

WARD. Over-done it, I think, didn't I? This time.

BARTTELOT. By five strokes, what came over you, anyway?

WARD. Sorry. I didn't keep count of my counting. Let's just hope he didn't, either.

BONNY. He couldn't. Anyway not after the first twenty. He wasn't conscious.

WARD. How very fortunate. After all, what would one do if he asked for the last five strokes to be taken back. (He laughs weakly.) Anyway, I gave orders for two days remission in chains, hope that's all right?

BARTTELOT. What! No, it's not all right! You should have spoken to me first.

WARD. Yes, well, sorry again. I felt as it was my mistake I must make up in some way —

BARTTELOT. You made the mistake, it wasn't for you to make it up.

WARD. Well, what do you suggest we do? Eh? Eh? (Fiercely.) Anway, what difference does it make whether it's three or five, he won't last the night, will he Bonny?

BONNY. I shouldn't think so.

WARD. There! You see! (Puts his face in his arms.)

TROUP. You all right, old man?

WARD. Yes, yes, thank you.

TROUP (to BONNY). You'd better give him some quinine.

BONNY. Is that all right, Major?

BARTTELOT. How are the stocks?

BONNY. Beginning to run low.

TROUP. Still, if a man's ill, he must have medicine.

BARTTELOT. He can only have medicine if there's medicine to give him.

TROUP. But it's no good making sure there's medicine to give him by not giving him any.

WARD (*laughs*). Very neat, Troup, very neat.

TROUP. It wasn't meant to be. Because it's not funny when you think about it. If Barttelot starts refusing us medicine —

BARTTELOT. I've never refused when Bonny's said it's absolutely necessary. Nevertheless the fact remains there soon won't be any medicine.

WARD. Oh, don't squabble over my health, I'm all right, I tell you, short on sleep, that's all, my tent isn't conducive to it, the glow from their fires throws up peculiar images and their voices go on very shrill and the whole effect — you know it occurs to me, at least it did occur to me, when I'd counted to twenty-three strokes or twenty-four, somewhere in that passage anyway, the twenties it did occur to me that old Jameson was quite right, he usually is, you know, when he put forward the argument that we should abandon flogging for a while, we really are losing them fast enough at what's the current rate, one and an eighth a day Bonny worked it out at, from starvation, sickness etc, for us not to need to flog them to death too.

BARTTELOT. It's the one matter on which Jameson is not right. We have no choice. If a nigger thieves or deserts or trades his rifle for food or sleeps on sentry duty, he is to be flogged.

TROUP. But we do have a choice, that's what I was saying. If Jameson votes against, and now Ward votes against, it only needs one more vote — then what would you do?

BARTTELOT. I see. You intend to vote against, do you, in future.

TROUP. Or Bonny might.

BARTTELOT *turns, looks at* BONNY.

BONNY. What, me? Of course I wouldn't.

BARTTELOT (*to* TROUP). Well?

WARD. If Troup votes against, I shall have to vote for. I agree
with the Major. But I'll tell you what, Troup, shall we make a
deal, take it in turns, that way we honour the law and
satisfy conscience, how many judges manage that? With the
Major's permission of course.

BARTTELOT. I don't give a damn what you do between you as
long as discipline is maintained. If you all voted against I'd
enter it in the log and still have them flogged. And by God!
order whichever of you I wanted to supervise it. And now
that we've cleared that up, I've work to do — (*He exits.*)

WARD. Work, what work?

BONNY. He's counting the brass-rods. He started last night, in
here. I was just going to bed, he came bursting in, didn't even
notice me, started pulling the cases out — then at dawn he was
into the tents —

WARD. Well, it put him in a good humour for the flogging, didn't
it? I saw him joking with a couple of Zanzibaris just before I
began the count, you were at his side Bonny, as you usually are,
was it a good joke?

BONNY. It wasn't a joke. He was grinning at them.

WARD. Grinning at them?

BONNY. He's discovered that they're more frightened of him
when he grins at them.

WARD. Really? Well he's got an excellent set of teeth. Why,
that might solve our problem, instead of lashing a man to the
post and having him flogged, we can lash him to a post and
have Barttelot grin at him. Fifty, fifty-five times, it wouldn't
make any difference . . .

BONNY. Yes, it would. They'd go off from fright even quicker.

TROUP. They hate him.

WARD. They hate us all.

TROUP. But they hate him most. He goes out amongst them
looking for trouble, poking at them with his damned stick, as if
trying to stir them up.

BONNY. Perhaps that's what he's trying to do. Stir them up to
life. Hate might sustain them a day or two longer —

TROUP. That's not why he does it. He does it because he hates them back.

WARD. So do I.

TROUP. What?

WARD. When I see them lying about in the compound, in their sickness, as if they were the image of sickness itself. Or while they stand there, heads lolling, while I supervise one of them flogging another of them to death. That makes me hate them.

TROUP. We can't go on week after week — something must be done, and soon.

BONNY. But what do you propose, Troup?

TROUP. Simply that we do something, anything, to get on the move. Look here, Bonny, this is confidential.

WARD (*laughs*). Yes, do be discreet old man. By the way, that woman I saw you with last night —

BONNY. What? What woman?

WARD. I saw you in silhouette, tip-toeing past my tent —

BONNY. Then you were seeing things.

WARD. Yes, lots of things, you and the woman among them. But you've got a way with the ladies, haven't you? Old Troup here was telling me the other day how you managed coming out on the boat, you had to travel tourist as you were on the expedition's expense, isn't that right, old man, but before you were three days out — you did say three days, didn't you, Troup? You'd insinuated yourself among the ladies in First Class, by making free with little remedies for *mal de mer*, and ended up dining between two absolute beauties, Troup called them, didn't you, Troup, at the Captain's table. Two absolute beauties?

TROUP. Look here, Ward, I didn't mean — I didn't intend any slight —

WARD. Of course you didn't, he was most complimentary about your gifts, Bonny, he didn't end up at the Captain's table between two absolute beauties, did you, Troup, even though you went first at your own expense, he was envious, you see, so there's nothing to be ashamed of in taking a Zanzibari or Soudanese or native lady by the neck, eh, as long as there's no outraged husband —

BONNY (*gets up, comes over*). Lift your arms.

WARD. What?

BONNY. Lift your arms.

WARD *does so*.

BONNY (*feels in Ward's arm-pits*). Swollen. (*He puts his hand to Ward's brow*). You'd do better lying down.

WARD. No, I wouldn't.

BONNY. Well, if you don't lie down soon, you'll fall down later.

WARD. Right. I'll wait until then.

BONNY. Then you're a fool. And that wasn't me or a woman you saw last night, it was your delirium.

TROUP. Look here, let's get back to what's important. Can I speak plainly?

WARD (*laughs*). Plainly, Troup. Good God! You certainly can.

TROUP. What, look, I'm not advocating going behind Barttelot's back, but simply that we all have a reasoned and proper discussion —

WARD (*gets to his feet, as sudden noises off*). He's here!

TROUP. What?

JAMESON *enters through the flap. He is carrying a shoulder-bag.*

WARD. Welcome back, old man. (*He shakes his hand.*)

JAMESON. Thank you. Troup — Bonny — how are you —

TROUP. Any news?

JAMESON. Oh, nothing very definite, I'm afraid, although —

BARTTELOT (*comes striding in*). Ah, here you are then, Jamie, thank God, I was getting worried, well, what news, what news?

JAMESON. None really, I'm afraid. Lots of rumours, but I didn't actually find a native who'd seen an Arab. Mark you, there was a great deal of excitement, more than usual, but the only significant thing was that in the village by the second river bend — where the Chief wears those boots Stanley gave him — a more preposterous figure — (*He laughs.*)

BARTTELOT. Well, what about him?

JAMESON. I know it doesn't sound much, but you see, he claimed he hadn't heard anything at all, not even a rumour.

TROUP. It certainly doesn't sound much, other than that there might be one honest nigger in the Congo after all.

JAMESON. No, my impression was the opposite. I couldn't be sure the other chiefs were telling the truth, but I was quite sure he wasn't. He knew something —

BARTTELOT. By God, you mean you believe he's seen Tippu-Tib?

JAMESON. Not quite that. But perhaps an Arab or two.

BARTTELOT. But by God, that's something. That's something more than we've had this last six months!

TROUP. But you're only guessing. It doesn't seem much to me, to go on.

JAMESON. There was one small piece of evidence. Just outside his village I came across the remains of a feast, a few bones —

BARTTELOT. An Arab feast?

JAMESON. Oh no, quite distinctly a native feast. But an exceptional one. An Arab might have furnished it.

TROUP. Furnished what? A goat?

JAMESON. No, no. Himself. He might have been caught and eaten. But really there was no way of knowing, because if it was an Arab, he was presumably in the belly of the Chief who said there wasn't.

WARD. That's what's called digesting the evidence.

JAMESON. There were only a few digitals sucked clean and a couple of shin bones to go on. It could equally well have been a nigger from one of the other villages who'd come up too far, and the chief might well have been emphatic about there being no Arabs because he didn't want a fuss over his meal. I can't say.

BARTTELOT. And nothing else?

JAMESON. No.

BARTTELOT (*after a pause*). So we're no further ahead?

JAMESON. Not really. I'm sorry.

BARTTELOT. Not your fault, old man.

JAMESON. Still, the bearer of no news — I say, (*to* WARD) you don't look at all well, your fever still running?

WARD (*gestures*). Oh, I'm much better. Much.

JAMESON. That's good. By the way, I caught the most beautiful parakeet, I shall have to stuff him this evening — and look — (*He takes a sketch out, shows it to* WARD.)

BARTTELOT (*to* BONNY). You'd better come and have a look at a Soudanese lying on the bank, some sort of green bile coming out of his mouth —

WARD. Ah, and here's our Stanley-booted Chief. Yes, I see what you mean, embarrassed but replete — certainly a large, illicit meal not far from his memory —

TROUP. No! no! (*Suddenly loud.*) What are we going to do? Are we going to look at Jameson's sketches, or study sick Soudanese we can't do anything for anyway, or are we going to talk, to talk for once about what we're going to do? This situation can't go on, don't you see, Barttelot, you Jameson, surely you see — all we have to show for six months' waiting, for some sixty dead men, is a loathsome story of shin bones and cannibalism. It's the last straw. (*Pause.*) Don't you see! We must act! We must act!

BARTTELOT. And what action do you suggest we take?

TROUP. Stanley can't possibly want us to linger on here —

BARTTELOT. I assure you he does.

TROUP. Well, for how long? Another month? Another two months? What use will we be to him then? He might already have reached Emin Pasha, for all we know. He might even be dead, they might all of them have been massacred by the Mahdi —

BARTTELOT. Yes.

TROUP. And meanwhile we're to go on waiting?

BARTTELOT. Yes.

TROUP. Rot among rotting niggers for no reason? Or wait for them to turn on us when we're in the middle of one of our floggings and tear us to pieces, do you really think that's what Stanley would want? Tippu-Tib's not coming. We all know it. There will be no six hundred porters. There's nothing to wait here for —

BARTTELOT. Except one's honour.

TROUP. Your honour, you mean, with Stanley. Oh, come man, your silly feud with Stanley is eight months past, he's long forgotten it, if he's even alive. Don't you see —

BARTTELOT. I see what you're proposing. It's desertion.

TROUP. I'm proposing that we act with common sense. I tell you, Barttelot, whatever you may claim, Stanley is not a murdering maniac.

BARTTELOT. I never said he was.

TROUP The other night you accused him of attempting to poison —

WARD. A figure of speech, old chap. A figure of —

TROUP. Well, his attitude to Stanley is poisoning us, that's the point. Good God man, those orders of his you're so frightened of contravening, they were written on the supposition that Tippu would be here months ago — Stanley didn't even deal with the contingency that's arisen, he never expected it.

BARTTELOT. You've forgotten the brass-rods.

TROUP. What? You mean we're running out of those, too? Then we'll certainly have a rebellion to deal with, the only thing the niggers look forward to is their brass-rods —

BARTTELOT. We're not running out. Stanley's left us enough to pay the men for another six months. Another six months, Troup.

*There is a pause.*

JAMESON (*suddenly laughs*). No, just a minute old man, you've forgotten that we also have to pay Tippu's men on the march. He'd take that into account.

BARTTELOT. I did. If Tippu's men had been paid from the day Stanley left, we'd still have enough for another six months. As Tippu's men haven't arrived we've enough for another year and a half. This from Mr Stanley, who knows the value of a brass-rod in the Congo as a — a Jew does of a sovereign in Kensington. So there you are, Troup, there's your evidence, Stanley acknowledges through the brass-rods that we might have to wait, and wait, and wait.

*There is silence.*

TROUP. Then what about the quinine, how do you explain that?

WARD. Perhaps he got Fortnum and Mason's to package the quinine.

BONNY. In my experience of medical supplies, there are never enough of them. Specially quinine.

TROUP (*goes to sit down*). Oh this is all — all speculation. The fact of the matter is, we don't know what Stanley intended — if only you'd found some way of getting him to take you through those damned orders. I still don't understand how it is you didn't get the chance, did he refuse to let you read them before he left, what?

JAMESON. I really don't see the value of going back —

BARTTELOT. No, I'll tell you what happened, Troup. I wasn't going to give him the satisfaction. That's what happened.

TROUP. What satisfaction?

BARTTELOT. Of watching me read them. When I went to his tent to get them he wasn't even dressed, that's how much — how much — he was just getting into those damned ridiculous togs he puts on specially for his marches, I had to stand there, to stand there while he crammed himself into those knicker-bockers he wears for showing off his calves and then his Norfolk jacket, which he thinks turns him into an English gentleman, and his German officer's cap, which he thinks turns him into a — a — German officer, and all the time strutting about gobble-de-gooking John Henry here who was blubbering away, and gobble-de-gooking the Soudanese in Soudanese and Zanzibaris in Zanzibari or the other way around for all I knew, to let me see the niggers were more important than his own senior officer, and sending messages to Jephson and Parke and Stairs — and in the middle of it all he shoved the orders into my hands and went on gobble-de-gooking, and when he saw I'd just shoved them into my pocket, that I was just going to go on standing there watching him with a smile he was forced to come back to me, and by God how he hates that, standing eye to eye with another white man. Well, Major (*He does a poor imitation of a high voice with a nasal twang.*) not interested in your orders? I take it, I said, I take it they don't apply until you've left the camp, Mr Stanley. Besides there's really no need, sir, as they shall be carried out to the letter, whatever they are. But not beyond the letter . . . or to your own letter . . . something like that, because I turned on my heel, and walked over here, leaving him to get on with his circus — so Troup, now you know why it was impossible, and why I wasn't going to give him the satisfaction, I hope it's given you some, eh?

TROUP. I can't believe it! You mean he actually invited you, — I can't believe it!

WARD. If you'll excuse the observation, old chap, one of your small weaknesses is that you can't believe what you clearly know to be true, it's far too human to be anything else, surely. You can believe it, can't you? If you try?

TROUP. Do you really find all this *amusing*, Ward?

WARD. Well yes, it's odd, I admit, but I put it down to my temperature or temperament —

TROUP. Well, because you didn't want Stanley to have the satisfaction, what it comes to is this. We have no idea what to do next —

BARTTELOT. We wait.

TROUP. For death?

JAMESON. Oh, I don't really think it'll come to that —

BARTTELOT. In view of the brass-rods anything else would be desertion. And that's what Stanley hopes for.

WARD. Well, actually Major, the brass-rods have nothing to do with anything at all. The perfectly simple and reasonable explanation for them came to me while you were describing — with great vivacity may I say — your last meeting with Stanley and then I became so engrossed with the — sorry — sorry — the delightful interchanges between yourself and our good Troup that I forgot to mention — and then you've such an assertive manner, do you see?

BARTTELOT. What are you talking about?

WARD. What?

JAMESON. It's his fever — (*goes to him*) old man, do lie down.

BONNY. I warned him.

WARD. Nonsense, no old boy, I'm quite — if you don't mind — the brass-rods, yes, the reason Stanley left them behind, yes, well it's because they're damned heavy, you see. Took as many as he calculated he'd need, and left us to bring up the rest with the porters, which porters and what porters being an entirely different question, but what would be the use of them if they weren't to bring up the brass-rods among the other things, eh?

*There is a pause.*

JAMESON. He's perfectly right, of course.

TROUP. Of course! My dear old Ward — well — so there we are, the rods mean nothing. Surely you agree?

BARTTELOT. It's a — possible — explanation.

TROUP. Well now can we — can we discuss it in a different atmosphere, I've been partly to blame, I admit, we bring out the worst in each other at times, eh, Major?

BARTTELOT. We wait. That's what we must do. For Tippu-Tib, or for a message from Stanley, or for news that Stanley is dead. We wait.

TROUP. No. No, I'm not going to wait. I'm going home. Who's coming with me? Ward, Jameson — you must see this is madness — come with me —

JAMESON. Excuse me, may I? (*Gently, takes* BARTTELOT's *stick.*) Stanley appointed me to stay with the Major, my place has been with him from the beginning — (*Moving gently towards* TROUP.)

WARD. There's no doubt honour's involved somewhere, you know, Troup, even if one can't — can't quite —

BONNY. I'm staying too. If you're interested, that is.

TROUP. Honour, there's no honour —

> JAMESON *springs forward, with stick upraised, as if to strike* TROUP, *knocks him out of the way, and brings it down again and again, violently.*
> TROUP *has lurched back with a cry of terror.*

JAMESON (*fishes up a dead snake with the tip of the stick*). Probably the mate of that one I got a few days ago — or were you simply after a spot of shade and a drop of water, can't blame you for that. (*He loops it over the rafters.*) You all right?

TROUP. What? All right? Yes, yes — what does another snake or two matter in all this madness.

BARTTELOT. When will you be leaving, Mr Troup?

TROUP. I can't go on my own, you know that.

BARTTELOT. One of us would accompany you, with the soundest of the Soudanese. We won't let you end up in the belly of an Arruwimi, don't worry.

TROUP. That's not what I meant. I stand by the majority decision.

BARTTELOT. We've each decided for ourselves, what our duty is. If you think yours is to leave —

TROUP. I'm staying.

BARTTELOT. In that case, Mr Troup, perhaps you will allow me to get on with my duties. Mr Bonny, shall we go and look at the Soudanese — (*He goes towards the flap.*)

BARTTELOT (*turns, looks at* TROUP). But by God, Troup, by God I shall put it in the log! (*He goes out.*)

TROUP. The log? What does he mean? We had a discussion, I stand by the majority decision — does he mean I was proposing to desert, to abandon you and Stanley — he can't put that in the log! I shall — I shall write a letter to the Committee in London, to Mr William MacKinnon himself, stating my position. I shall get it on record that there was never any question — never — (*He goes out.*)

WARD. I wonder who he thinks is going to deliver his letter, or perhaps he'll ask for a majority decision to pop over with it himself to, what's the address, somewhere in Cutter's Lane, Holborn, isn't it? I say Jameson, that's a fine specimen you slaughtered there, much better than its wife or husband, was it? Are you going to add it to your collection or have you got one already, how you sense these things! The way you moved I thought — I thought you were going to strike down old Troup or even the rest of us, all of us, a single blow, while you were away I've taken up sculpting again, but fretfully, fretfully, tried to model Herman and King, but they would keep their heads in, because of Bonny's remarks about cooking them, you know, I was looking forward to showing you, but it's rotten work, rotten work I'm afraid, I (*swaying as he speaks, and collapses just as*):

JAMESON (*gets to him quickly, to support him*). My poor old fellow — here — let me — better get you to bed —

WARD. No, not to my tent. Not to my tent, if you please.

JAMESON. Well then, come — (*He helps* WARD *over to settee.*) There, lie down.

WARD. Sorry, sorry, Jameson — did you know I went on to fifty (*very brightly*) five and a fraction, didn't matter though, Bonny says he'll die anyway, it became a bit hypnotic, you see, telling off the strokes, and he got into a rhythm you know, his arm sweeping back and then forward, and then the scream, and then my voice, and his arm sweeping back and the screams stopped, and my voice, and his arm, and my voice —

JAMESON. It must have been quite horrible for you.

WARD. No, no, it was quite pleasant, (*fretfully*) quite pleasant, don't you see, could really have gone on and on, why don't you do it, Jameson, don't you enjoy it, Troup says Barttelot lets you off, is that true?

JAMESON. I supervised it once or twice, before you other chaps came up.

WARD. And didn't you find it pleasant?

JAMESON. No. But I didn't have a fever when I did it, perhaps that helps.

WARD (*sitting up, very brightly*). What about your wife and child, children you pray and trust, it must be awful for them having you away, when people count on you so much, if we need you here she must need you there, do you ever think about them, do you, Jameson, do you worry if they're all right?

JAMESON. Yes.

WARD. And I worry about you, you know, when you're away, so does Barttelot tramping about at top speed ordering floggings and kicking niggers and grinning, have you heard about his grinning? And worrying about you, he misses you, doesn't he?

JAMESON. You're really rather ill, you know. You must try and sleep.

WARD. No, but Jameson —

JAMESON. You must sleep. You must.

WARD. But you'll look in on me later, won't you?

JAMESON. Of course. (*He goes to the doors, makes to shut them.*)

WARD. Oh, don't shut them, if you please.

JAMESON. Oh, I think so. They'll light their fires, and the din —

WARD. Oh, I don't mind, truly I want the light please.

JAMESON (*hesitates*). All right, I'll leave them half and half — (*He half closes the doors, then turns, looks at WARD, goes out through the flap.*)

*The stage dims slowly to night. WARD is tossing and turning on his bed, in a troubled and feverish sleep.*
*Suddenly a blaze off, and cries. The light of a large bonfire getting brighter and brighter. Voices chattering.*
*The drums begin, as at the end of Act One.*
*WARD lets out a cry. Sits upright. The drums continue.*
*WARD stares wildly about, then fixes his gaze on the snake which appears, in the changing light from the blaze, to be writhing.*
*WARD stares transfixed, then begins to babble, shaking his head and clasping himself tightly. He is shivering. He moans, lets out shrill cries.*
*TROUP enters, through the flap, carrying a lamp. He goes to WARD's bed.*

WARD. The worm, the worm — (*Pointing.*)

TROUP. What worm? (*He turns.*) Good God! (*Laughs.*) It's only Jameson's snake — (*He goes to the rafter, pulls it down.*)

WARD. Be careful — be careful — Jameson will want it.

*TROUP puts the snake on the table, then goes to the doors.*

BARTTELOT (*off*). Stop it, damn you! Stop it, I say!

TROUP. There's old Barttelot on his rounds again, eh? Having a go at Mrs What-d'you call her, Minchip —

BARTTELOT (*off*). Damn you, will you stop it!

*The drums begin to quiet, as at the end of the previous scene.*

TROUP (*closes the doors, comes over*). I say, old boy, you've got it badly, eh?

WARD (*is sitting up, shaking hideously*). You mustn't go away again, you mustn't leave me again.

TROUP. No, no, of course not, old man, I'll sit by you. (*He gently pushes WARD back.*) There now, old man, that's better, isn't it? I'll be here, you'll be all right, eh?

*JAMESON enters through the flap, also carrying a lamp and some blankets, comes over, looks down at WARD.*

Not too good, eh?

JAMESON. No. (*He begins to put blankets over WARD, assisted by TROUP.*)

WARD. Jameson, Jameson — you there? (*Teeth chattering.*)

JAMESON. Yes. Right here.

WARD. You will stay, won't you?

JAMESON. Yes. Yes, I'll stay.

BONNY (*enters through flap*). Here we are, some quinine, compliments of the Major.

TROUP. Thank God for that.

BONNY (*goes to* WARD, *lifts his head*). Now get this down you — (*He administers it.*) There we are.

WARD. Thank you, Jameson.

BONNY. He's very bad. Very bad. If he'd lain down at the beginning — somebody'd better stay with him.

JAMESON. Yes, I'm going to.

BONNY. Then the rest of us better leave him in peace.

TROUP. Right. If you're sure —

JAMESON. Quite sure.

TROUP. Well then — (*He puts his hand on* WARD's *shoulder.*) Good night, old man.

BONNY. Good night.

JAMESON. Good night.

TROUP *and* BONNY *go towards the flap.*

BARTTELOT. Ah, you're all here are you, how is he?

BONNY. At the crisis. Jameson's going to sit with him.

BARTTELOT. Ah. (*He comes over to the bed.*)

TROUP *and* BONNY *exit.*

BONNY. Good night, Major. (*As he goes.*)

*There is a pause.*

BARTTELOT. He's had the quinine then?

JAMESON. Yes.

BARTTELOT. Ah. Well, be careful, Jamie, don't want you going out on us, we can take turns.

JAMESON. No, I'll be all right.

BARTTELOT. Ah. (*Pause.*) Well — (*He puts his hand on* JAMESON's *shoulder.*) Good night, old Jamie.

JAMESON. Good night.

> BARTTELOT *hesitates, turns, goes out through the flap.*
>
> *There is a silence.*

WARD. Jameson!

JAMESON. Yes.

WARD. Jameson, are you there?

JAMESON. Yes, I'm here.

> *There is a silence.* JAMESON *sees the snake, goes over, picks it up, then draws a chair to the bed, arranges the lamp so that the light falls on him. He takes a knife from his pocket, and begins to skin the snake.*
>
> *On this, lights.*

## Scene Two

*Some days later. Night.*
*A brazier is the first glow, followed by the other lights.*
WARD's *make-shift bed has been disestablished.* JOHN HENRY
*is moving around the table, clearing away the remnants of a meal.* BARTTELOT, BONNY *and* TROUP *are seated around the brazier.* BARTTELOT *is smoking a pipe. After a pause,* JAMESON *gets up, goes to the brazier, stokes it up.*
*Off, a single drum starts, very low, almost a murmur.*

BARTTELOT. There she goes.

TROUP. I can't hear her. Oh yes. Still, they're very quiet tonight. Do you think they know? I mean, they might have felt something today. From us. The way we've behaved.

BONNY (*laughs*).

TROUP. Well, she's beating very soft, and the others haven't joined in. How do you explain that?

BONNY. Not by sentiment, anyway. The wonder is she can play at all, after what the Major did to her last night, eh Major?

BARTTELOT (*as if not listening*). Mmmmm?

TROUP. Why does she do it anyway, what do you think, Jameson?

JAMESON. What? Oh — (*coming from the brazier to sit down*) for the magic, I should think. As long as Mrs Minchip plays, the sickness will stay off Mr Minchip.

BONNY. Seems to work. They die around him, but every morning he's as fresh as black paint, except for a few patches of red and blue from the Major's stick or boot, eh Major?

JAMESON. Yes, well it's really very reasonable. Mr and Mrs Minchip are evidently genuinely attached to each other. Her continuing to play the drums for him in spite of the Major's attempts to stop her, only proves it to both of them. And so provides them both with a reason for living.

BONNY. There you are, Major, you're part of her magic too.

BARTTELOT. Mmmm? What do you mean?

BONNY. Well, you're helping to keep their marriage together and that always takes magic. Are you going to go out to them?

BARTTELOT. No, no. Not tonight. It would be wrong tonight.

TROUP. And they *are* very low. I tell you they feel something of what we're feeling. (*Pause.*) There! She's stopped altogether!

WARD *enters through the flap. He is carrying a large tray, on which is an object covered with a handkerchief. Under his arm, a bottle of brandy.*

BARTTELOT. Ah, there you are at last. What have you been up to?

WARD. Gentlemen, my apologies for the delay. There's a little something I gave myself to, in an idle kind of way, during my convalescence that I hesitate to present to public view (*putting the tray on the table*) but I hope that my main contribution (*holds up the brandy bottle*)

*Laughs and cheers.*

will help to render the other more tolerable. And his own to the evening has been so extreme that, however inadequately, he must be honoured. So gentlemen, Troup old man, if you would — (*hands him the brandy bottle*)

TROUP *pours into glasses.*

While I propose, thank you old man, a toast —

OTHERS (*standing*). A toast!

WARD. To our tender and succulent benefactor! (*He removes*

*the hankerchief, to reveal the head of a goat, modelled in clay.)*

*Exclamations and applause.*

WARD. To dear old Nanny!

OTHERS (*laughing*). Dear old Nanny!

JAMESON (*studying it*). But look here, old man, it's a real piece of work, something really done — the mouth is wonderful, quite wonderful — the sardonic grin, the twist there of the lips, the very essence of goatiness —

TROUP (*belches*). The substance being somewhere else.

WARD (*to* JAMESON). I'm not thoroughly shamed by it, I admit.

BONNY. The funny thing is, I shall miss him.

TROUP. That's charitable, Bonny, considering the devil never stopped trying to kick you.

BONNY. The devil's always trying to kick me, in some manifestation or another.

JAMESON. Now the brandy's arrived — (*taking a newspaper packet out of his pocket*) may I present my little — (*Holding it out. They take from it a cigar each, with little exclamations.*)

BARTTELOT (*pocketing his cigar*). I'll hang on to this a little longer, by God, it's good, Troup, damned good! Thank you for it.

BONNY. We all owe Troup thanks for it. He's sweetened the atmosphere around you.

BARTTELOT. What? (*He looks at* BONNY.) Oh. (*He laughs.*) Neat Bonny, very neat.

JAMESON (*who has been about to thrust the cigar newspaper into the brazier, checks himself*). Good Heavens, here's something — the personal column. If the gentleman who waited outside the Savoy on Friday of last week at the appointed hour should care to do so again this week, he will receive a full explanation, and an assurance of —

TROUP. Assurance of what?

JAMESON. It stops there.

BONNY. An assurance of nothing, then.

TROUP. Or of everything.

JAMESON (*looks at date*). Fourteen months ago. Well, let's trust the matter's been settled between them, whatever it was.

TROUP. Oh, it's obvious what it was. The writer is a lady and her message is addressed to a — well, gentleman.

JAMESON. Well, go on, old man. Give us the whole scene.

TROUP. Well, well it's a sacred tryst, what? They meet, let's see, they meet every Friday, for a few precious moments. They don't touch, scarcely speak, look into each other's eyes —

JAMESON. And what happened on that last Friday?

BARTTELOT. I'll tell you what, she has a fierce pater who locked her in, and the gentleman in question's an officer — penniless but true, they're planning something dashing — an elopement — eh?

BONNY. Mark my words, it's either money or — the other thing. If it's the other thing he didn't turn up because he's tired of waiting for it, if it's money she's not giving the other thing until she's got her hands on it.

JAMESON. How does that end?

BONNY. Oh, in the usual way. With an arrangement. The question is how *that* ends?

WARD. How does it usually end?

BONNY. Why, if it's bad, in the law courts. And if it's worse — in church.

BARTTELOT. Careful, Bonny, careful.

TROUP. Oh, I say, why is that worse?

BONNY. Because then it never ends.

JAMESON. Ah, but that song, Bonny — the one you were humming in the shower — I believe you're a sentimentalist at heart, like all cynics.

BARTTELOT. What song?

BONNY. Oh, just a song —

BARTTELOT. Sing it for us.

BONNY. What?

BARTTELOT. Sing it for us. (*Little pause.*) Come on, Bonny!

BONNY, *after a moment, stands, sings a Victorian love song, delicately and with feeling.*

TROUP (*rises, emotionally*). Gentlemen, to a young lady — a young lady in Highgate!

REST. A young lady in Highgate!

BARTTELOT. And a young lady in Sussex!

BONNY. To a young lady in Pimlico. Another in Maidenhead. A third in Greenwich!

BARTTELOT. No no, only allowed one, Bonny.

BONNY. Ah, then I choose — a young lady in Clapham!

REST (*laughing*). A young lady in Clapham!

WARD. To them, all plain and pretty, amiable and otherwise the true, the false, the young, the old — so long as they be ladies!

TROUP. You're worse than old Bonny — you've taken them all!

BONNY. No, he hasn't. Just one. Pretty, amiable, young and true on the way to the altar! Plain, false, old and otherwise from there to the grave!

BARTTELOT. You go too far, Bonny! Too far! Remember Mrs Jameson!

BONNY. Oh, I'm sorry, I didn't mean to give —

JAMESON. Oh good Heavens, I can easily refute our Bonny — by inviting you all to take dinner in my home this day a year hence. Mrs Jameson and I and our (*hesitates*) children will be grateful for the chance to prove that what begins in church can continue ever more happily, please God! Will you come, all of you? Mrs Jameson would be so pleased.

BARTTELOT (*solemnly*). Mrs Jameson!

REST. Mrs Jameson.

*A respectful silence.*

JAMESON. Or of course, *two* years hence, depending on circumstances known to us all —

*Laughter.*

WARD. And that's the real interpretation to put on the message in the Personal Column — it's not written by a lady at all, but by some desperate fellow trying to do business with Mr Tippu-Tib. Who is now outside the Savoy —

JAMESON. Or indeed inside it, with his six hundred porters turned waiters.

*Laughter.*

BARTTELOT. You know what my pater says, he says 'It's a funny old world.' And he's right. Here we all are, we've had our quarrels and our worries, God knows — old Troup and I are a pretty peppery couple of fellows from time to time, eh? But here we are — and somewhere out there, Stanley, please God, as Jamie said — and tonight — well tonight, my spirit's at peace with him. I'll never like him, I can't promise to like him but by God I can't help wishing him safety, and an evening of fellowship like this one. Eh?

REST. Hear, hear!

TROUP. And I'll wager he's wished us the same, eh? And look, I want to endorse everything the Major's said — whatever — whatever the hazards — we are — we remain

BONNY *is quietly pouring himself more brandy.*

united, I mean we've forged a bond — between us — that — that — speaking for myself I know will last to the end of my life. I shall look back on this Christmas together to the — to the end of my life.

*There is a pause.*

JAMESON. Amen to that.

BARTTELOT. Bonny, give us a carol, there's a chap. My heart yearns for one.

BONNY *begins to sing 'The Twelve Days of Christmas'.*

OTHERS *join in. Half-way through the drums begin, very low, scarcely noticeable.*

BARTTELOT *has put his hand on* JOHN HENRY's *shoulder.*

*As they sing, lights and:*

*Curtain.*

# Act Three

## Scene One

*The same. Six months later. It is morning.*

*The doors are open. Around the room are various pieces of sculpture, in clay, heads of natives, animals, etc; and some sketches, stuffed birds, stuffed snakes.*

*A NATIVE WOMAN, naked, her arms tied behind her, a halter around her neck and attached to a rafter, is squatting on the floor, right.*

*WARD is seated on a packing case, modelling her head in clay.*

*BONNY enters, drifts over, watches WARD, then sits down at the table, close to the woman. There is a silence. He stares at the woman, suddenly smiles at her.*

*The WOMAN smiles back.*

*BONNY laughs.*

*The WOMAN laughs back.*

*BONNY laughs again.*

*The WOMAN laughs again.*

BONNY. Funny, they squat for hours without an expression until you laugh at them. And they always laugh back.

WARD. Yes, they have very pleasant dispositions. Unless of course she was laughing at you for laughing at her — who can say whether the man is playing with the cat or the cat with the man . . .

BONNY. More like cattle than cats. Although she might have a game or two in her . . . eh, my darling? (*He laughs.*)

*The WOMAN laughs.*

WARD. Could you, do you think, hold back on your wooing a while — I'd prefer her to keep her head still. Besides, the days when you were the Lothario of Yambuya are over by some months, aren't they — ever since our Commanding Officer delivered his *en passant* homily on what he'd do, by God, to any white man he caught, by God! etc, etc.

BONNY *yawns, puts his feet on the table, his head back. Begins to hum.*

WARD (*glances at him with irritation*). Why don't you join our Commanding Officer, he'd be glad of your company, I'm sure.

BONNY. Where is he?

WARD. Having a word.

BONNY. Who with?

WARD. A couple of Soudanese who fell asleep on watch last night. The second provisions tent, I believe it was. Some of Stanley's medical supplies are in there, so he should be lathering up nicely, you'll catch him at his climax if you run.

BONNY (*after a slight pause*). Anything missing?

WARD. Mmmm?

BONNY. Anything missing?

WARD. Why don't you scamper over and see for yourself, there's a good man.

BONNY *gets up, goes over to the water bucket, tries to pour himself some. It is empty.*

BONNY. John Henry! John Henry!

WARD. Oh for — do stop shouting, Bonny! He won't come. At least, not for you.

BONNY. Well, he'd better, for his sake. If the Major finds out he's forgotten the water — John Henry!

WARD (*throws down the clay in disgust*). He's probably unconscious, you fool.

BONNY. What? (*Little pause.*) Oh.

WARD. Didn't you hear his screams?

BONNY. No.

WARD. Really not? About midnight, from his master's tent?

BONNY. No.

WARD. Nor his master's bellow, stick and boot?

BONNY. No.

WARD. How do you manage those slumbers of yours? You seem

to have found the secret that eludes everyone but the niggers on watch and the dying, of course.

BONNY. Perhaps I've given up worrying.

WARD. But what have you taken up to give up worrying? (*He looks at him.*) Eh, Bonny?

BONNY. The thing about you, Ward, is you can't let up, can you? You set out to make him worse, the way you went on at him in mess, counting off the niggers who'd died or escaped this last month —

WARD. I was merely trying to engage his attention, with a little mental arithmetic.

BONNY. Yes, well you left him in a proper state, then banging your hand up and down to the drums — that's probably why he went off and battered John Henry.

WARD. Ah, I see. And that's why you needn't concern yourself with his health. Don't types of your rank have to take the Hippocratic oath, Bonny?

BONNY (*after a pause*). Oh, shut up, Ward.

WARD. You feel no professional obligation, to minister to him, eh?

BONNY. What am I meant to do? He hasn't consulted me, has he?

WARD. And he won't. He's far too frightened.

BONNY. What of?

WARD. You.

BONNY. Oh very funny, Ward.

WARD. You can have my next year's ration of goat if he isn't.

BONNY. You honestly mean to tell me that Barttelot's frightened of *me* —

WARD. Barttelot? Good God, Bonny, you'd better not go about confusing our Commanding Major Barttelot with his battered little nigger of a serving boy. No, no, get it clear in your head, they're fearfully distinct, you know. The battered little nigger of a serving boy is the one who's frightened of you, even though he needs your skill and bandages. The Commanding Major Barttelot is the one you're frightened of, and with good reason, as he's quite clearly mad. And now you've got something to report to the Major, you'll hurry along, won't you, please, and report it?.

BONNY. You want me to tell him that you say he's mad, do you?

WARD. Yes please.

BONNY. Why?

WARD. So that I can tell him what it is you've started taking to give up worrying. Then he'll have you flogged, I should think, and I'd quite enjoy that. Wouldn't you?

BONNY. I warn you, Ward, if you make any trouble for me with Barttelot, I'll make a damned sight more back.

TROUP *enters. He looks very ill, thin and yellow complexioned.*

BONNY. Oh hello, old man, how are you?

TROUP *pays no attention, goes on to the water bucket.*

BONNY. You really shouldn't be up you know.

WARD. There you are, old man, Bonny's just made out his favourite prescription. That should make you feel better.

TROUP *drops the cup, comes back to the table, sits down.*

BONNY. I'll get you some water — (*He rises.*)

TROUP. No, you won't.

TONNY. You're thirsty, aren't you?

TROUP. Yes, but you won't get any water. You'll go out for it, but you won't come back with it.

BONNY. What do you mean?

WARD. You know what he means. He means that you'll go out for it but you won't come back with it.

TROUP. Because you haven't asked him, have you?

BONNY. I haven't even seen him to speak to this morning.

TROUP. But you're not going to ask him, are you?

BONNY. Of course I am. I said I would. But I also said I didn't see the point because we all know what the answer's going to be.

TROUP. What about you, Ward, will you speak up for me?

WARD. Of course. But I won't do any good, old chap. Quite the reverse, I'm afraid.

TROUP. I see. So I'm to die then? Is that it? To die without making a fuss.

BONNY. Look, I don't think it's quite that bad —

TROUP. Oh yes it is. Oh yes it is. I'm weaker every time I come
out of it. I shall die all right, I've known it for days now. I
shall die. Die here in this place because a lunatic, a lunatic —
(*He stops, trembling.*)

WARD. I say, old man, be careful. The faithful Bonny, you know,
is at your side.

TROUP. I don't care. I'm past caring. You tell him I saw him,
Bonny. He didn't know I was watching, but I saw him, from
my tent flap. I saw the lunatic go out and —

BARTTELOT (*enters, carrying his stick and a basket*). Two
rotting fish! Two rotting fish!

WARD. Three dying niggers, four flogging gentlemen —

BARTTELOT. What?

WARD. Oh nothing, just what promised to be an amusing
anecdote of old Troup's you've interrupted, what were you
saying about two rotting fish —

BARTTELOT. That's all her husband thinks she's worth, smirking
outside as if he were redeeming from a pawn shop — (*going
over to the woman, untying the rope from the rafter*) come on,
get up, get up, he's bought you back with two rotting fish —
go on, get along with you — and take these with you — (*He
hooks basket around her neck*) tell him to choke on them
himself — (*He grins at her, she cowers away from him*) go, get
along with you — (*He propels her out through the door*) swears
there isn't a goat to be had, stinks like a goat himself, a
morning wasted catching her for two rotting fish — well, I got
them to admit it at last, they'd been asleep all right, thank God
they hadn't got into the boxes, none of them opened and they're
not cunning enough to put the lids back on — by God if any of
the medicine had been touched Stanley'd never have believed
it was the niggers — not with a chance like that — Troup,
you're closest to the tent, did you hear anything last night?

TROUP. I'm still ill, thank you for asking. Worse, as a matter of
fact.

BARTTELOT. What?

WARD. Still ill, thank you for asking. Worse as a matter of fact.

BARTTELOT. I'm talking to Troup, Ward.

TROUP. I said I'm worse.

BARTTELOT. But you're up, aren't you?

TROUP. Oh yes. Yes, I'm up, Barttelot.

BARTTELOT. Slept through the night, did you?

TROUP. No, Barttelot. No sleep. None at all.

WARD. Loyal Bonny did, though, didn't you, Bonny? Slept like
a top.

BARTTELOT. Well then, did you hear anything, see anything?

TROUP. Oh yes. I saw and heard quite a lot.

BARTTELOT. What?

WARD. He saw and heard —

BARTTELOT. From the provisions tent?

TROUP. No. Not from there.

BARTTELOT. Well, Ward, what about you?

WARD. Screams, oaths and blows from your tent. From the
provisions tent, nothing. So I'm afraid I can't help you either,
sir.

BARTTELOT (*goes over to the water*). Well, we've got to find
out who's responsible, there's a clutch of Soudanese scum
who're up to some mischief — (*Tries to pour water.*)

WARD. How remarkable.

BARTTELOT. What?

WARD (*after a little pause*). Why, that anyone in the compound,
apart from your energetic self, of course, could be up to
anything as taxing as mischief.

BARTTELOT. Well, you're damned well not are you, been idling
in here all day — John Henry, John Henry! Where is the little —

BONNY. Haven't seen hide nor hair of him, Major.

WARD. From which we can conclude, sir, that he must still be out.

BARTTELOT. Out where?

WARD. Of his senses. And after the kind of night you had together,
it's not to be wondered at, is it?

BARTTELOT. You drank the last drop of water, I suppose,
Ward, but damn if you were going to get some more for the
rest of us, eh?

WARD. Damn me, sir, if I was.

BONNY. I'll go, Major, I was just about to fetch some for Troup anyway — (*Getting up.*)

BARTTELOT. Thank you Bonny.

WARD. Before you go, Bonny, would you kindly ask the Major what you promised old Troup here you'd ask him.

BONNY. What?

WARD. Before you go, Bonny, would you kindly ask etc.

BONNY. It's only what I've already mentioned, Major. I explained that the situation being what it is —

BARTTELOT. You know the situation, Troup. You've known it for months. There isn't any.

TROUP. Yes, there is. There is!

BARTTELOT. But it's not ours, Troup. It's Stanley's. We've used up ours.

TROUP. So. So I'm to die —

BARTTELOT. You're not going to die.

TROUP. — because the rest of you used up our stock before I could get ill, is that what it comes to?

WARD. Yes, even you must find that a trifle bizarre, sir. That poor old Troup's superior robustness has had such an unhappy effect on his health. (*He laughs.*)

BARTTELOT. What?

WARD. Yes, even you must find that a trifle —

BARTTELOT. By God, Ward, how sick I am of your jokes.

WARD. Ah, but fortunately — for you — you don't need quinine to recover from them.

BARTTELOT. But I know how to stop you making them.

WARD. So do I, sir. Some humanity, or failing that, a dash of intelligence, in the running of this camp. Or did you mean bellow, boot and stick, as usual.

TROUP. You're just going to stand by, then, and see me die, are you, Barttelot? My death shall be on your head. I've written to MacKinnon, my letter to be conveyed to him with the rest of my effects, Ward, if you'll be so good.

WARD. Of course, my dear chap. Though I should point out that having over a hundred dead blacks on his head already —

BARTTELOT. That's right, Troup. You can die if you want to. I've long wanted you gone, you've never had anything to give to the Rear Column but bluster when you're well and snivelling now you're sick. It's not medicine you lack, Troup, but fortitude.

TROUP (*after a pause*). You refuse me, then.

BARTTELOT. Of course I refuse you.

TROUP. And that's your last word?

BARTTELOT. I hope so. Though knowing you —

TROUP. Very well. I give you warning, Barttelot. I shall help myself from Stanley's supplies.

BARTTELOT. What? (*Pause.*) What did you say?

TROUP. I shall help myself —

BARTTELOT. By God — by God, you already have, haven't you? It was you, wasn't it, in the provisions' tent last night! It was you! I'm going to open every load, every one, and if there's a drop of quinine missing, I'll — by God, Troup, I'll have you flogged for the thieving nigger you are.

TROUP (*runs over to him*). You're mad, Barttelot, a lunatic, a lunatic! I saw you last night, I watched you, I wrote it down, It's in my letter to MacKinnon, don't forget the letter, Ward —

WARD. Certainly not, old man.

TROUP. Everybody'll know you for what you are — do you know what he did last night?

BARTTELOT (*advances on* TROUP, *grinning*). Hah, hah, hah, hah! Hah hah hah hah!

JAMESON *appears at the door. He is carrying equipment, as in Act Two, Scene One. He is not, at first, noticed.*

Hah hah hah hah!

TROUP. You, you —

WARD. Ah, welcome home, old man — oh, the Major and Troup are just sharing a joke on the subject of the Major's sanity.

BARTTELOT. Hah hah hah hah!

TROUP *draws back a fist, to strike* BARTTELOT. BARTTELOT *thrusts his face closer to* TROUP.

Hah hah hah hah!

JAMESON *moves very swiftly, catches* TROUP's *arm, pulls him away. He stands between* BARTTELOT *and* TROUP, *facing* BARTTELOT.

Ah — ah, there you are, Jamie, you're back then are you?

TROUP. He's trying to murder me, murder me, Jameson — well — (*trying to pull* JAMESON *away*) let him do it so everybody can see — go on, Barttelot, kill me, kill me now, in front of everybody —

BARTTELOT. By God I will, Troup, if you don't get out of the Camp and back to England. I'm sending you home, now, this minute.

TROUP. See, see, he's frightened of me because I saw him — Oh, I saw him —

JAMESON. Please. Please, listen to me. (*Little pause.*) I've news. I've seen Tippu-Tib.

BARTTELOT. What? (*As if dazed.*) Seen him?

JAMESON. Yes. He sends his greetings and his apologies for the delay.

BARTTELOT. The delay! For the delay — after a year!

JAMESON. But he solemnly undertakes to be with us shortly, with the porters. He swore it to Allah, and in friendship to Stanley. Apparently he lost his first catch through a series of monstrous misfortunes — escape, sickness, capsizing boats, but he sent messengers to let us know — presumably they were the cannibal victims. But his second lot, with a large guard of his Arabs, are on their way. He's just had word. He's going back to the Falls to bring them up himself.

BARTTELOT. About — about three weeks then! A month at the most!

JAMESON. His own calculation was a month.

BARTTELOT. By God — by God — of all the wonderful — but what was he doing in these parts, if his slaves are at the Falls?

JAMESON. Coming to see you. But I told him that as he'd seen me, you'd prefer him to get back to the porters —

BARTTELOT. By God yes — and Stanley — any news of Stanley?

JAMESON. He must be alive as he'd have heard if he were dead.

He's a rather extraordinary chap, our Tippu, by the way, you'll enjoy —

BARTTELOT (*is pacing about, talking almost as if to himself*). So Stanley's still alive, the porters coming up — can't be more than a month away — we'll meet him on the march, by God — with the loads — with the loads — how d'you do, Mr Stanley, here are your supplies, sir — by God we've beaten you, Stanley — beaten you, sir — (*He goes on out through the doors, and his voice, off.*) Up on your feet, scum, up on your feet, you're going to learn how to walk again — up I say — up with you — by God I've beaten him — march — march along I say — I've beaten the devil — (*His voice fading, but sounding now and then.*)

TROUP. So we'll be moving from this place after all, is that what you mean, Jameson? Is that it?

JAMESON. Yes, old man. That's it.

TROUP. But what about me, what's he going to do about me? I told him, you see, I let him know that I'd seen him — oh why did I, why did I? Now he'll send me home to die in the jungle, or leave me here to perish by myself while you march on —

JAMESON. My dear old chap, there's no question of your being left, or of your being sent home, and certainly not of your dying. I do assure you.

TROUP. Oh, I shall die, Jameson, one way or the other. He'll see to that. Anyway I won't live without quinine, and he won't let me have any of Stanley's, that's how he'll do it —

JAMESON. But there's no need of Stanley's. I've got some. Here. (*He takes a phial out of his equipment.*) I've always kept some of my personal stock in reserve for my expeditions, in case I'm taken with a fever away from base — but I shan't need it now, shall I? Besides, I've never felt so well in my life.

TROUP. Oh, thank you, Jameson. Thank you. God bless you. God bless you. (*He bursts into tears.*) I'm sorry, I'm sorry — (*He sinks to his knees.*) Oh Jameson —

JAMESON *lifts* TROUP *up, holds him.*

BONNY. He should be in bed.

WARD. Well, why don't you put him there.

JAMESON. Yes, I'm sure you're the chap he needs —

BONNY. Yes, come along, old man, let's get you down. (*He puts his arm around* TROUP, *who is in a state of semi-collapse, and leads him off.*)

*There is a pause.*

WARD. Well. (*Smiling.*) You got back in the nick of time.

JAMESON. I've never moved so fast in my life. (*Little pause.*) How are you?

WARD. I'm anxious to hear about your adventures, what sort of chap is Tippu after all?

JAMESON. Oh very amusing. I kept storing away all sorts of things to tell you, (*going to the water bucket*) he goes in for a grand, not to say flamboyant style of hospitality, I've done one or two sketches of him in characteristic postures, I must show you later, by the way, oh, and I picked up a spectacular lizard and a butterfly I've never seen before, he fluttered over Tippu's head on my second morning and settled in a branch — (*Makes to pour himself water.*)

WARD. I'm afraid it's empty. John Henry being hors de combat, let me get you some.

JAMESON. No, no, I'm not really thirsty, I stopped for a drink when I came in. I wasn't thirsty then either, but one gets into the habit of taking a drink where one can as if it'll make up for the times one can't, which of course it doesn't. (*He laughs.*) But you haven't told me how you are?

WARD. All I can really say is that I'm no worse.

JAMESON. No worse?

WARD. Than the rest of us. I haven't been beating children senseless, for instance. But then that's the Major's way, not mine. Nor have I been stealing morphine from Stanley's supplies. But then that's Bonny's way, as it turns out.

JAMESON. Ah, I did wonder, before I left —

WARD. Troup's way you know about, as you caught the climax of his performance.

JAMESON. Yes, poor old Troup.

WARD. For my part, I've mainly lolled.

JAMESON. Lolled?

WARD. Yes, about and about, you know. Inflaming the

inflammable, goading the goadable and despising the despicable. That's been my way.

JAMESON. But I see you've made an attempt — (*Indicating the head of the woman.*)

WARD. Yesterday afternoon I dragged myself over to the river-bank, where I lolled in the hope of catching you in an early return. But all I saw were the corpses of two drowned niggers, rolled along by the sluggish current, and a few minutes later one nigger drowning. He sank some yards from me but bobbed up half an hour later, his head tangled in weeds, to be rolled off in his turn. I took him to be a deserting Zanzibari.

JAMESON. I'm sure there was nothing you could have done.

WARD. No, there wasn't, really.

JAMESON. Thank God you didn't go in after him. That current — you wouldn't have had a chance.

WARD. Not much of one, certainly.

JAMESON. So you mustn't reproach yourself.

WARD. Oh, I haven't been. Nor have I reproached myself for not reproaching myself, if you see.

JAMESON. Well I don't quite —

WARD. What I'm trying to say is, well, that given our different forms of degeneration, you were quite right to lie about seeing Tippu-Tib. False hope is probably our only hope now.

JAMESON. I didn't lie about seeing Tippu-Tib. I spent three days in his camp.

WARD. I see. Then you lied about what he said.

JAMESON. I reported him absolutely faithfully.

WARD. But you can't have believed him!

JAMESON (*after a pause*). Of course not. It was understood between us at once that his lies were a courtesy. Kindness, even, so that I shouldn't feel obliged to accuse him of treachery when hopelessly outnumbered. As I said, he's an excellent host, he really went to extravagant lengths to make me comfortable. (*Pause.*) I hoped you wouldn't be taken in. I shall need your support more than ever when the month is up and the doubts return.

WARD. And the whole process starts again. Although we shan't survive a whole year this time.

JAMESON. But if we can stretch the month into two and then three — until Stanley comes back, or we have news of his death. We have a chance. (*He smiles.*) At least we'll survive until tomorrow.

WARD. Of course if we were all like you, we could survive here for ever. And you could certainly survive without us, couldn't you?

JAMESON. Not quite. (*Pause.*) I say, would you like to have a look (*going to equipment*) at my rendering of Tippu, I think I've caught something of his —

WARD. No! No I wouldn't! (*Little pause.*) I'm sorry, I know it's infernally weak of me, I admire you more than any man I've ever met, and I'm flattered, flattered of course, that you should have counted on me for your support, even though I know you could manage without it, but it's just that — at the moment I wish — I wish you hadn't — no, that's not fair — I hadn't insisted on the truth. I'm sorry. Infernally weak. But then I am. I've learnt that much — (*He turns, goes towards the flap, stops, looks at* JAMESON.)

JAMESON. I'm sorry. If I'd realised —

WARD. Don't worry. You *can* count on me. For what I'm worth. (*He exits.*)

JAMESON *stands for a moment.*

*From off,* BARTTELOT's *voice, roaring out orders, and the sound of the Soudanese, and the Zanzibaris, calling to each other excitedly, coming near, then turning, going further off.*

JAMESON *goes to the doors, draws them almost closed, but allowing light to enter, comes back, stares at his equipment, then after a moment takes out a dead parakeet, gutted; then a small object, presumably the butterfly; looks at it; takes out several more objects, a bowl and a wooden spoon; finally his sketch pad and note-book. Opens the note-book, sits looking at it.*

JOHN HENRY *enters through the flap, limping bruised, carrying a water-bucket. He looks furtively over at* JAMESON, *who watches him go to replace the empty water-bucket with the full one, and then turn to go out.*

JAMESON. John Henry. John Henry — come here.

JOHN HENRY *comes over.*

Are you all right?

JOHN HENRY *nods.*

Well, you will be from now on. I promise you. No more bruises. No more. All right? (*He pats his head.*) Now you go and find your master, eh?

JOHN HENRY *nods, goes out through the flap.*

JAMESON *sits for a moment, looks at the sketches, then puts his face in his hands, as if tired. The voices off become less and less distinct. The lights fade slowly down to darkness.*

## Scene Two

*A couple of hours later.*
   *The set is in darkness. There comes from the darkness a low murmur, an exclamation, silence. Then another exclamation. BARTTELOT enters, left, carrying a lamp. JOHN HENRY is at his side. There is another exclamation. BARTTELOT goes over to the work desk, holds the lamp up. JAMESON is slumped over the desk, asleep. On the desk his note-book. His sketch-pad has fallen to the floor. BARTTELOT lights the lamp near the table, gives his own lamp to JOHN HENRY, who lights the other lamps.*
   *JAMESON groans heavily.*

BARTTELOT (*stands looking down at him. Then puts a hand on* JAMESON's *shoulder.*) All right, Jamie. All right, old boy. It's only me.

   JAMESON *lifts his head, sees* BARTTELOT, *lets out a cry of terror.*

   Only me, Jamie. Only me.

JAMESON. Oh, I'm — I'm sorry.

BARTTELOT. A bad dream, eh?

JAMESON. Yes.

BARTTELOT. And are you properly awake now?

JAMESON. I'm not sure.

BARTTELOT. Well, I'm no dream, I can tell you. (*He laughs.*) I've had them on the march, up and down and around the

compound, then out into the jungle, making them walk, making
them feel their legs again, you see, the halt, the maim,
tomorrow I'll have the strongest moving with loads, some will
have to carry double when Tippu's lot arrive, we've lost so
many, but by God we won't lose another one, not another one
— John Henry — go and get some manioc — manioc, John
Henry — tell you the truth couldn't keep still myself, thinking
of his face — the expression on the devil's face.

JOHN HENRY *has gone out for the manioc.*

— when he finds every one of them intact, eh? Well, Mr
Stanley, what sort of year have you had? Let me tell you about
ours — oh, and here's our Mr Jameson, Mr Bonny, Mr Ward
and even Mr Troup, you do remember us, I take it, or had you
thought us dead, sir. Or deserted even? By God — by God —

JOHN HENRY *returns, pours the manioc.*

That's the boy, John Henry, keep off that bad leg, eh? (*He
drinks.*) Well, Jamie — and what about Emin Pasha, I thought
of him when I was marching them, first time for nearly a year
I remembered him. Make nonsense of the whole business if
Stanley hasn't got him out, if the Mahdi got to him first, eh?
All that we've been through because of Emin Pasha, and none
of it to do with him, just a battle between Stanley and
ourselves, and ourselves and the damned niggers, and ourselves
and ourselves, eh? (*He drinks, looks at* JAMESON.) But I'll tell
you something. He nearly won, old man. He did. If you hadn't
come back God knows what — Troup called me a lunatic and —
by God he was right. Because last night I committed the act of
a lunatic and Troup saw me at it. It was your Mrs Minchip who
drove me to it, on her drums, I sent John Henry out, and they
went silent, then started again, and — I couldn't endure it,
couldn't endure it, but I did, you see, instead of going out and
giving her a cuff myself I endured it, until the others had gone
to bed, and then I went out, walked over them, trampled on
them where they lay, or put my stick into their sides and stirred
them out of the way with the point, walking in a straight line
to their tent, and when I got there I went up to the woman
squatting there, beating away, and I grinned at her, you know
how my grin works, a grin and then a cuff, how they fold before
it, but this time not a bit of it, she kept on pounding away, not
even seeing me, and then I looked up, and there was his face
in the slit of their tent, peering out and grinning back at me,
and beneath that another slit, freshly cut, the barrel of his

rifle sticking out of it straight at me, right at my chest, you see, and the woman pounding on, so I looked back at him, grinning at his grin to wipe it off, and I could see him losing his nerve, the barrel wavered, so I bent over the woman, you see, didn't know what I was doing until my teeth were in her neck. Sank them deep into her neck, to stop her on the drums at last. I looked back at the slit and I thought now — now you nigger, if you dare — with her blood still around my mouth, and I laughed into his face. Laughed into his face with his woman's blood around my mouth and his gun against my chest. It was a good laugh, a good long laugh, all the time I was waiting for the rifle to go off, thinking now, nigger, do it now — until I turned and walked away, stepping on them again, on their arms and legs and bellies and faces and when I got back to my tent I remembered the blood was still around my mouth. I licked at it with my tongue. Licked it off with my tongue. Drank some manioc to get rid of the taste, and more manioc to keep the dear old pater, you see, from watching his son lick up nigger blood from around his mouth — or Stanley seeing — what I had come to. And there was John Henry — and so he got the brunt of it, poor little mite. Poor little mite. You see. Had to tell you myself. Before you hear it from Troup. (*Pause.*) Well, Jamie — what do you think of me now?

JAMESON. Why, exactly as I've always thought of you, old man.

BARTTELOT. You don't despise me for it.

JAMESON. No.

BARTTELOT. That's a relief. I care what you think of me, you know. Always have. You, with your strength — well, you know that. (*Pause.*) By God, you know, I may be the wrong man for the Rear Column, that's why he chose me, but I did one good thing, right at the beginning, I had the beating of Stanley right at the beginning, when I made him give you over to me.

JAMESON. Give me over to you?

BARTTELOT. One of Parke, Jephson or Stair will remain behind with you, Barttelot, he said. You may choose. And I said, None of them, thank you, Mr Stanley, the man I want is Jameson. Jameson, Jameson, he said, but Jameson isn't an officer, he's a paying gentleman. And I said, It's Jameson I want, Mr Stanley. And he gave me a Stanley look, and I readied myself for a row, instead he whinnied out some laughter, Very well, he said. Very well. But I advise you,

Major Barttelot, for the sake of harmony between you, not to tell him he's staying behind at your request. Even Jameson, gentleman though he is, might come to hate you for it. Stanley, the great judge of men! Didn't know you as I knew you, even then — and that's where I had the beating of him. And beaten him all over again by telling you. Although I've waited until today to do it, I admit, and probably wouldn't have today if — if —

JAMESON. Fate hadn't worked things otherwise.

BARTTELOT. That's it, old man! That's it!

JAMESON. But then fate, being fate, never does. At least in as much as you've been mine, and didn't.

BARTTELOT. All I can say is, in spite of everything, I wouldn't have had it different.

JAMESON. Amen to that!

BONNY *enters through the flap.*

Ah, Bonny, here you are then — Jameson and I were just having a glass — John Henry, a glass for Mr Bonny —

JOHN HENRY *pours* BONNY *a glass.*

*Off, the drums start, with a flourish.*

BARTTELOT. There they go, eh Jamie? So that's all right then — well, they've something to celebrate tonight, John Henry, go tell them with the Major's compliments that tonight they may play their drums — but low, tell them — low.

BONNY (*meanwhile, spotting* JAMESON's *fallen sketch-pad, picks it up*). Brought back some drawings too, eh?

JAMESON. Yes.

BONNY. So quite a successful trip, what with one thing and the other.

JOHN HENRY *goes out.*

BONNY (*looking through the pad*). Any of Tippu-Tib?

BARTTELOT. What, Tippu, I must have a look at those, get to know the devil on different terms, eh? By God, it'll be hard to keep a check on my tongue when he comes in here — How d'you do, Mr Tib, glad to make your acquaintance at last, sir —

WARD *enters through the flap.*

Ah, here you are, Ward — here's a glass of Yambuya

champagne for you — and *I've* got good news — fish stew
tonight.

BONNY. What?

BARTTELOT (*laughs*). No, it's all right, Bonny, three I picked
up down-river when I was marching the men, not the rotting
pair this morning — Jamie, you haven't heard about that yet,
Bonny and I caught ourselves a woman yesterday, hobbled her,
brought her back, her man came in this morning with two
stinking fish —

*The drums have quietened.*

TROUP *enters through the flap.*

Troup, by God, you've come — here — a glass for Troup — but
should you be up, even for Yambuya champagne, old man —
here — (*pouring him a glass*) should you be?

TROUP. Thank you. Jameson's quinine, you know — (*He clears
his throat.*) Um Major, I want to say — say before everybody
— that — I said some things this morning I — I deeply regret,
accused you of all sorts of nonsense, which Bonny tells me — I
realise was just — just delirium —

BARTTELOT (*pause*). Well — you and I have had our — our —
what's passed is passed, eh? That's the thing — let's drink
instead — drink to, to —

WARD. Tippu-Tib. (*He glances at* JAMESON.)

BARTTELOT. Why, yes — Tippu-Tib, damn his soul!

REST. Tippu-Tib, damn his soul!

BONNY. I saw him a minute ago, yes, here he is — (*Flicking
open the sketch pad.*)

BARTTELOT. What, let's see, why that's as good as your famous
A Faithful Zanzibari says his Farewell, Jamie — what slyness,
what pomp, eh, and his rifle — the one Stanley gave him —
over his chest — hah, hah, hah!

JAMESON *puts his hand to his forehead.*

BARTTELOT *goes to get the manioc jug.*

WARD (*to* JAMESON). Are you all right?

JAMESON. Yes, yes — just a touch tired —

BONNY *is casually turning over pages of the pad.*

TROUP (*to* JAMESON). I'm very conscious of my debt to you,
Jameson. For the quinine — and everything else.

JAMESON. Oh.

JOHN HENRY *enters.*

BARTTELOT. Ah, there's a good boy — well done John Henry,
well done — (*Coming back with the jug.*)

BONNY (*lets out an exclamation*). What's this?

JAMESON (*looking up*). Mmmm?

WARD *saunters over to look.*

BARTTELOT *comes over with the jug, offers to pour for*
TROUP.

TROUP. No thank you, Major, feeling a bit — a bit — (*Goes, sits
down.*)

BONNY. A little girl tied to a tree.

JAMESON. Oh. (*Little pause.*) Yes.

BARTTELOT *comes over, looks over* BONNY's *other shoulder.*

BARTTELOT. What, what is it, Jamie?

BONNY *turns another page, stares at it.* WARD, BARTTELOT
*also stare.*

WARD. But she's — they're —

BARTTELOT. Can't make it out, what's going on?

*There is a pause.*

JAMESON. It's a cannibal feast. (*Pause.*) I happened to mention to
Tippu that once or twice I'd come across the remains of one,
but never the beginnings or middle of one. So the next
morning he invited me to accompany him and some of his
chaps to a village where a couple of Tippu's men had been
doing a bit of slaving. Among their merchandise was a girl of
about thirteen, I suppose — that girl. I bought her from them,
at Tippu's suggestion, for five brass-rods, and then we took her
off to a cannibal chief Tippu knew of, who was told he could
have her for lunch on the understanding that I did drawings of
him while he was at it, and Tippu got a goat for our supper.
(*Pause.*) To my knowledge it's the first time the whole process
has been recorded. (*Pause.*) He was my host.

WARD. You bought the girl, then watched her being killed and

prepared for the pot and cooked and eaten. And made sketches
of it?

BONNY. And here, asleep under a tree, that's him is it, afterwards?

JAMESON. Yes.

BARTTELOT (*quietly*). What have you done?

JAMESON. What? (*He looks around at their faces.*) Nothing very
terrible, surely. The girl had already been caught by slavers,
she was bound to end up in the pot — they have no other use
for them at that age. Good Heavens, we've flogged them to
death, we've watched them die by the score, what does it
matter, one nigger girl — (*He stops, looks at* WARD.)
Yes. I see. I suppose I've slightly lost my — my — My curiosity
and the uniqueness of it evidently blinded me to the — the —
(*stops*) I'm sorry.

BONNY. Tippu-Tib doesn't have any of these, by any chance, does
he?

JAMESON. Some rough versions, yes.

BONNY. Did you sign them for him?

JAMESON. Yes.

BARTTELOT. Do you know — do you know — what he'll do
with them? Why, he'll head straight back to the Falls and
show them — show them around to everyone, everyone. The
story will be all over the Congo, in England, in London, on the
first steamer — that we participated — participated in a
cannibal — a cannibal —

BONNY. They'll say you ate your share of her, too.

BARTTELOT. All these months — this year — of waiting and
hoping — and then just as the end is in sight you — you — with
your damned — your damned — collection — you bring us
down!

*The drums increase, and increase, through* BARTTELOT's *next
speech, almost drowning it towards its end.*

Why, it's all been for nothing, nothing! Worse than nothing,
to dishonour, to disgrace — by God man, after all this you've
destroyed us, worse than death, worse than desertion, in
England, with Stanley, here, destroyed — destroyed — is
that why Stanley gave you to me, because he knew, he knew
you'd — you'd — (*he is shaking, as if in a fit*) do his work for
him, you and Stanley, is that what it was, — (*he holds his*

stick towards JAMESON, *makes as if to thrust it into him,
then wheels around, sees* JOHN HENRY) I told you — I told
you to stop them, told you, (*gouges the stick into* JOHN
HENRY) little black — scum — scum — (*as the pounding of the
drum is at its fullest pitch*)

WARD *runs over to stop* BARTTELOT.

BARTTELOT *shakes him off savagely, then rounds on him
raises his stick, makes to thrust it into* WARD, *then turns,
flings open the doors, on the darkness, with fires burning,
drums pounding, strides off.*

BONNY *goes over to the door, stares out.*

WARD *goes to* JOHN HENRY, *bends over him, then
straightens.*

TROUP *is sitting, motionless.*

JAMESON *is sitting, motionless.*

*The drums stop, There is silence.*

BARTTELOT (*off*). Hah, hah, hah, hah! Hah, hah, hah —

*There is a shot.*

*Silence.*

WARD *moves towards the doors.*

*There are sudden cries, shouts, off.*

BONNY *pushes the doors closed before* WARD *reaches them,
locks them. Turns his back to them.*

BONNY. If you go out there they'll do the same to you. And
then come on in and do the same to us. (*Pause.*) We'll get him
in the morning.

WARD *hesitates, then turns away. Looks at* JAMESON. *He
goes over to him, looks at him.*

JAMESON *looks slowly up at* WARD.

*There is a pause.*

TROUP (*in a dull voice*). Now perhaps you'll listen to me. Now
perhaps we can go home.

BONNY *goes over, helps himself to manioc from the jug.*

WARD *puts his hand on* JAMESON's *shoulder.*

Go home at last, eh?

BONNY *drinks.*

*Lights fade slowly on this tableau, to darkness, as the drums
start up again excitable, unrhythmic.*
*The same. Some days later.*
  *The doors are slightly open. From off, the sound of voices,
Zanzibari, Soudanese. BONNY is moving about, doing an
inventory of the boxes, but slowly. The sound of STANLEY's
voice, off, commanding. BONNY straightens, listens.*
  STANLEY *enters through the doors, pulling them wide.*

STANLEY. Well Bonny, Parke is back from the Falls, with
  some news. He spoke to Mr Troup, who is in excellent health,
  and has booked his passage back to Southampton. He is also
  in excellent voice. His self-justifications and denials have fuelled
  the scandal, God knows what form the story will finally take
  when it appears in *The Times*, but it will certainly have
  precedence with the public over my own poor efforts, who
  will want to read of the successful relief of Emin Pasha when
  there are tales of Barttelot's lash and Jameson's experiments
  in slaughtering, cooking and consuming infant girls to wallow
  in, eh? Mr Jameson, by the way, is dead.

BONNY. Oh.

STANLEY. He died at a Mission House between here and the
  Falls. He went too fast, in no state to travel, though if he'd
  had quinine with him he would probably have survived, why
  he didn't have quinine is another of the incomprehensible — as
  there is quinine here — is there not? But let us be charitable
  and assume that his neglect of himself had something
  Roman in it. If not Roman, then at least English. He was
  buried by Mr Ward, some nonsense about a Union Jack
  draped over a coffin rough-hewn from a tree — no doubt a
  bugle carved on the spot to sound a lament, eh? Pshaw! The
  good people at the Mission were much moved, being
  ignorant at the time that they were officiating over the
  remains of a celebrated cannibal, with his good friend, the
  opium fiend.

BONNY. I can't be sure it was Mr Ward who took the laudanum —
  all I know is that some is missing —

STANLEY (*looks at him*). Mr Ward left the Mission House, and
  has completely vanished. You, on the other hand, Bonny, are
  here, the only survivor, in the moral sense, of the Yambuya

fiasco. So let us make sure that your reputation is unsullied, eh?

BONNY. Thank you, sir. I felt somebody had to stay behind until you —

STANLEY. I'm not interested in your motives, Bonny. One can't plan motives only results. But there's no way of planning for gentlemen like Jameson, or a maniac like Barttelot. I did my best. I knew him to be a danger to us all, that's why I left him behind, in this place, where he could do no harm. (*Laughs.*) With an English gentleman to keep a check on him. And a set of orders that couldn't have been simpler, clearer or more flexible. All he had to do was to follow my orders. Easy enough, easy enough, even for a maniac, eh?

BONNY. At least you rescued Emin Pasha.

STANLEY. Who resents it bitterly, being comfortable and probably safe where he was. By the way, Bonny, where did you bury my John Henry?

BONNY. Outside the compound, with all the other — um —

STANLEY *looks at him, then bends, begins to pull off one of his boots.*

BONNY *waits.*

STANLEY. Be so kind as to take those damned turtles to the kitchen, would you?

BONNY *releases the turtles, takes them out through the flap.*

STANLEY *straightens for a moment, then begins to take off the other boot.*

*Curtain.*

# MOLLY

# Author's Note

*Molly* is an adaptation for the stage of the earliest of my television plays — *Death of a Teddy Bear* — which was written for BBC's Wednesday Play about ten years ago. Brenda Bruce, Hywel Bennet, Rachel Kempson and the late Kenneth J. Warren played the original Molly, Oliver, Eve and Teddy; Warris Hussein was our director; Kenith Trodd the producer; and Gerald Savory wiped the tape.

The source of *Death of a Teddy Bear* was the Alma Rattenbury case, an account of which I came across in a paperback called (I think) *Ten Famous Trials*, left discarded in a railway compartment. I was on my way from London to Cambridge to supervise Trinity undergraduates in (probably) Hobbes, or Hume, or Aeschylus or some such, and had a briefcase full of essays to mark. I flicked through the pages of the paperback — it was stained and swollen as if a dog had urinated over it — in the cursory manner of one who has something of more consequence on his mind, plucked out a handful of essays, and settled down to the book. When I arrived at Cambridge I left the book where I'd found it, but for the rest of that day, and for many subsequent days and (especially) nights, I was haunted by Mrs Rattenbury's story — or what of it I could perceive behind the dozen pages or so in which her trial had been described. So when Kenith Trodd asked me if I'd like to try my hand at a full-length television play, the subject was already fully there, and at least partially shaped, even though unwritten. Which is perhaps why I didn't go back to Mrs Rattenbury herself, neither to her trial nor to reconstructions of the crime. I based my play on the effect that the dozen pages had had on me (the specifics being pretty well forgotten), changed the names, and hoped that my sense of the drama would find its own form. *Death of a Teddy Bear* was not, therefore, *about* Mrs Rattenbury and the murder in which she was involved, although of course without her it would never have been written.

I felt strongly enough about *Death of a Teddy Bear* not to

want to lose it to television — not realising then that the BBC, after showing it twice, was simply going to chuck it away (see *The New Review* Vol. 3 No. 27) — and about five years ago I wrote the first stage draft. I followed as closely as I could the emotional line and the basic structure of the original, extending some scenes and subtracting those that depended on the mobility of the camera, and so inevitably, and against my intentions, altered the tone of the whole. Further drafts altered further, and I might have left the final draft in a drawer if it hadn't been for the discovery that the television version no longer exists. So in a sense its recent production (at the New Spoleto Festival, in Charleston, last Spring) and its present slightly different (slightly re-written) production (at the Watford Palace Theatre) and its publication in *The New Review* must be attributed to 'Wiper' Savory, who left me with no alternative but to preserve the play in the only form now left.

N.B. Terence Rattigan's play, *Cause Célèbre*, is also based on the Rattenbury case. I haven't seen it, but gather that it started life as a radio play a couple of years back, and unlike *Molly*, concentrates on the trial. I believe there have been other Rattenbury plays, but have no details of them.

MOLLY was first presented in Britain in November 1977 at the Watford Palace Theatre, with the following cast:

| | |
|---|---|
| MOLLY | Mary Miller |
| TEDDY | Raymond Francis |
| OLIVER | Anthony Allen |
| EVE | Barbara Atkinson |
| GREAVES | Arthur Cox |
| POLICE CONSTABLE | Stephen Enns |

Directed by Stephen Hollis
Set design by Christopher Morley
Costume design by Ann Curtis
Lighting by Brian Harris

# Act One

**Scene One**

*The play is set in the 1930s.*

*Living-room of a house. It has three doors: one stage right, which leads into the conservatory, part of which is visible on the stage; one back, that leads into the kitchen, dining-room etc; and one left, that leads to the hall, front door, and other offices and stairs. In the room is a cocktail cabinet, new and of the Thirties, amply stocked; an arm-chair; a large sofa; tables, chairs, all in the style of the Twenties and Thirties.*

*The curtain rises on the room, empty. Light beginning to fade. There is a pause, and then MOLLY, wearing a light coat, a silk scarf, enters slowly through the conservatory. She takes off her scarf, drops it onto the sofa. She stands listless, then takes from her coat pocket her cigarettes and a lighter. She lights a cigarette, draws on it deeply, then stares around her with an air of desperation, goes to radio, turns it on, listens for a moment to music, makes an irritated expression, turns the radio off, goes to drinks table, pours herself a drink, takes a sip as, above, sound of door opening.*

TEDDY (*off, up*). Moll! (*Calling.*) Molly!

MOLLY (*hesitates*). In here darling.

*There is another call of MOLL, then a door slams. The sound of footsteps, coming down. MOLLY puts down glass, walks swiftly out through the conservatory, vanishing exactly as the door, left, opens and TEDDY enters, saying irritably MOLL as he does so. Sees the room empty, makes an irritable exclamation, goes over to the conservatory, shouts MOLL! He is in his mid-sixties, has a deaf aid, elaborate and visible and of the Thirties, and an air of slightly bogus physicality. Shouts again. MOLL-LY*

EVE *enters from the back. Looks toward the conservatory.
She is a woman in her mid-fifties, severely dressed and severe of
expression; spectacles; and an air of brisk efficiency.*

TEDDY (*off*). Damn it! (*He comes back from the conservatory,
sees* EVE.) Oh, hello Evie, where's Moll?

EVE (*speaking loudly*). She's gone for a walk.

TEDDY. When?

EVE. About an hour ago.

TEDDY. Then why didn't she ask me. (*Goes to cocktail cabinet.*)
I could have just done with a walk.

EVE. You were taking a nap.

TEDDY. But I didn't want to. I wanted to go for a walk. I
spend the whole afternoon waiting for her to make up her
mind whether she wants to go or not —

*Pours himself a large Scotch.*
EVE *sees* MOLLY'*s scarf, goes over to it and deftly and
surreptitiously picks it up, and puts it on one of the tables,
where it is unlikely to be noticed.*

and then I go upstairs to get a book and sit down on the bed
with it for a moment and — (*Adds soda water to his Scotch,
splashes it.*) Damn, damn! (*Looks at* EVE.)

EVE. I'll get a cloth —

TEDDY. Oh sit down Evie, sit down. I can manage — (*Mops up
the soda with a handkerchief.*) Sorry Eve, I'm always a
grump if I doze through the afternoon — like a bear with a
headache — what'll you have, one of your dry-as-dust sherrys?

EVE. Oh, no thank you, Teddy, I really ought to get back to the
kitchen —

TEDDY (*pours* EVE *a sherry*). Tell me, Evie, do you think Moll
wants to stay. We've been here a month now but she makes me
feel as if we only just moved in yesterday, or we're going to
be moved out tomorrow, but we're never going to have the
part in between, has she said anything to you? (*Brings her the
sherry.*)

EVE. Thank you. Well, she's said she likes it here.

TEDDY. What about you?

EVE. Oh yes. Very much.

TEDDY. That's good, because we need you, Evie. Your hitching on to us was real luck, you keep us orderly. Don't you think of abandoning us.

EVE. That's very kind of you, Teddy.

TEDDY. Well, it's her England, that's what she said she wanted. And it'd do for me if she settles for it. Wish I didn't sleep so much, that's the only thing. Never slept like this in Canada. Never had time to. But then I had a business to run, bills of lading to get out, had to meet the ships at sometimes two in the morning, did you know that, Evie? (*Pause.*) Funny thing is I miss the smell of fish. The whole town smelt of it, the uptown streets, it got into the stores. I didn't notice it until I'd left. Hey, it's getting dark. That's something else I'm not used to, your English springs. We don't have springs in Canada, just a sort of wink between winter and summer. But then we have our falls, you don't have falls, do you?

EVE. No, we only have autumns, I'm afraid.

TEDDY. What? Well, I don't like her out in the dark. Wandering about. She used to tell me England's got the best climate in the world, you know what I think now I've seen it, it may be the best climate, but the weather's terrible. (*Laughs.*) Not my idea of friendly either. (*Goes back to cocktail cabinet.*) Now in Nova Scotia, move into a village they'd be right round asking what they could do to help, inviting us over, but we've been here two whole weeks, and who do we know, Dr Gracey, when I need him to look after my ears.

EVE. More people know Tom Fool than Tom Fool knows people.

TEDDY. Who?

EVE. Tom Fool.

TEDDY. Tom who?

EVE. Fool.

TEDDY. Well I don't know him, somebody in the village?

EVE. It's a saying.

TEDDY (*not having understood*). Oh. Ready for another? (*Coming across with the bottle.*)

EVE. No I won't, thanks —

TEDDY *pours sherry.* EVE *just manages to catch it.*

TEDDY. You know what woke me up? I thought I heard her

singing, that one about the seals of Nanaimo, and playing the piano — I heard it quite clear, every note, so it must have been a dream — she was going to try and write more songs once she got back here, that's why she wanted a place with a piano in it, but she hasn't played it yet — I'm going to get on to her about that, this evening. Did you know I got that seal song played over Station RCVX — knew the owner — he put it out across the whole of Nova Scotia. Bob Hoskins. He was a good friend of mine. In hardware. You ever been married, Evie?

EVE. No.

TEDDY. Why not?

EVE. I'm afraid no one ever asked me.

TEDDY. That's the girl. (*Laughs.*) Hey, Evie, mind if I ask you a delicate question?

EVE. No.

TEDDY. You sure?

EVE. Well, as I'm living in your house, you have a perfect right to know anything about me you want. Within reason, of course.

TEDDY. Am I paying you enough?

EVE. Yes, quite enough, thank you, Teddy. No thank you. You're more than generous. Now if you'll excuse me I really must go and have a look at the dinner. (*Gets up and goes out.*)

TEDDY. Oh.

*Sits for a moment, then gets up, goes to the cocktail cabinet, adds a dash of Scotch, squirts soda water, splashes it slightly, makes as if to mop it, gestures irritably, goes over to the conservatory, stands looking through.*

What the hell's she playing at?

*There is a ring at the door-bell, left.* TEDDY *makes no move.*

EVE (*appears from back*). Somebody at the door.

TEDDY *still makes no move.* EVE *makes to speak again, instead goes off, left.*

TEDDY (*turns, walks to the door, back, stands at it*). Hey Evie, I'm getting really worried —

EVE *re-enters from left, accompanied by* OLIVER. OLIVER *is a boy of about seventeen, awkward and not particularly attractive. Dressed in his Sunday clothes, as for an interview.*

TEDDY *turns away from the door, sees* OLIVER *and* EVE.

EVE (*coming over to* TEDDY). It's a boy from the village.

TEDDY. What? Is Moll all right?

EVE. He says something about a job.

TEDDY. What job?

EVE. I've no idea.

TEDDY (*goes over to* OLIVER). Well hello boy, what can we do for you?

OLIVER. Sir. They said at Sprinkley's there was a job.

EVE. That's the garage in the village.

TEDDY. What's your name, boy?

OLIVER. Oliver, sir.

TEDDY. What?

OLIVER. Oliver, sir. Oliver Treefe.

TEDDY. Oliver?

OLIVER. Yes sir.

TEDDY. Oliver what, Oliver?

OLIVER. Oliver Treefe, sir.

EVE. You'll have to speak up please, Oliver.

TEDDY. Sorry Oliver, I'm not picking you up.

OLIVER (*realising*). OLIVER TREEFE, SIR. (*In a bellow.*)

TEDDY. Oliver Treefsir, well Oliver Treefsir, what can we do for you?

OLIVER. They said (*in a bellow*) at Sprinkley's Garage a lady had been in to inquire about a boy, sir.

EVE (*to* TEDDY). It must have been Molly. (*To* OLIVER.) When did she come in?

OLIVER. This afternoon (*bellowing at* EVE) they said. They said she said there was a car needed looking after. Mr Goldberg's Alvis.

TEDDY. What?

EVE. Mr Goldberg's Alvis, Teddy.

TEDDY. Mr Goldberg hasn't got an Alvis. I've got it. Part of the

deal for the house. He left it for me for what he called a
consideration, he's probably bought himself a new car out of
the consideration, eh boy? Quite a business man, your Mr
Goldberg. (*Laughs.*)

OLIVER *laughs.*

TEDDY. Quite a businessman. It doesn't go, boy. Needs a lot of
tinkering. Can you tinker?

OLIVER. Yes sir.

TEDDY. Can, eh? That's right, don't undersell yourself, what
about a drink, we got some of that stuff you English call beer
somewhere and you look to be at the beer-guzzling age, eh
Evie? Like one? (*Goes to cocktail cabinet.*)

OLIVER. Well, no thank you very much sir.

TEDDY *begins to wrestle with a bottle of beer.*

EVE. Did the lady mention any special time to call, Oliver?

OLIVER. They said she said the evening would be best, Missus.

EVE. I see. And was it only about the car?

OLIVER. Well, they said she said it would be a bit of driving and
helping about the garden and odd-jobs. They said it was a
proper job, Missus.

EVE. Well, I'm afraid Mrs Treadley isn't here at the moment, but
I'll take down your details and let her have them. Who can give
you references, Oliver?

OLIVER. Well, there's Sprinkley's.

EVE. And anyone else?

TEDDY (*pours beer, which foams up over cabinet*). Damn! (*Mops
at it with handkerchief.*) First thing you've got to do is make her
go, second thing is to break me into her ways. I'm not used to
cars like your Mr Goldberg's Alvises, especially now my
balance's gone, so you'll have to show me how to handle her,
whether she needs coaxing or bullying, a car's like any machine,
a man's made her so she's going to have something wrong with
her. I used to do a lot of driving — ever heard of the Breton
Trail, that's in Nova Scotia. (*Bringing OLIVER his beer.*) Here,
get yourself outside of that —

OLIVER. Thank you sir.

TEDDY. That's in Nova Scotia, where the roads go straight ten yards before they turn around and go back five. In a Manson. By God I loved that car. Always knew where to tinker when she gave me trouble. Think I could get to love a car that used to belong to your Mr Goldberg, eh, that he left to rot and rust for a consideration? Eh?

EVE. I was just getting down some references, Teddy.

TEDDY. Oh.

EVE. Now who else besides Sprinkley's, Oliver?

OLIVER. I done some gardening with my Dad —

TEDDY. Who?

OLIVER. My dad, sir.

TEDDY. Your Dad — a reference from your Dad? We could all get references from our Dads' boy. (*Laughs*.)

OLIVER. No, I only meant —

EVE. Where else have you worked, Oliver?

MOLLY *enters the conservatory, stands watching for a moment, unseen by the others.*

EVE. Where else have you worked, Oliver?

OLIVER. Well — (*Pauses*.) — well I did some for Mrs Shepherd, Missus, but I stopped after a bit.

EVE. Indeed, why?

MOLLY (*enters*). Of course, you're the boy, aren't you, that Sprinkley's promised to send. I'm so sorry I wasn't here when you arrived, please forgive me.

OLIVER. That's all right, Miss.

MOLLY (*to* TEDDY *and* EVE). I popped in as I was passing the garage, when the thought struck, and then it slipped my mind, sorry darlings.

TEDDY. Where you been, Moll, old Evie was getting worried about you, out there in the dark.

MOLLY (*to* EVE). Were you, darling? There was no need, it was all quite friendly and above board. Well, what have you fixed up, between the three of you?

EVE. We're just sorting out the question of references.

TEDDY. Drink, Moll? (*Going to cocktail cabinet*.)

MOLLY. Thank you, darling, I'd love one.

TEDDY. We've just been trying to make out from your Oliver Treefsir here whether he's the sort that kills us.

MOLLY (*smiling at* OLIVER). Are you the sort to kill us, Oliver?

OLIVER. No Miss.

MOLLY. There we are, what more could we ask. You see, my husband's the sort that likes to drive very fast himself, but when he's being driven he likes it to be by the sort that drives very slow, don't you darling? But I can't drive at all, so I like everybody to drive fast, even the people in other cars.

TEDDY *comes over, hands* MOLLY *a drink.*

MOLLY. Thank you, darling. Now what about the gardening, are you going to do that for us too?

OLIVER. Well, yes Miss, I mean if you want —

MOLLY. Because we need a gardener to garden for us as well as a driver who won't kill us, Oliver, it's all in the most terrible tangle out there, some of the spring whatsits look quite alarming. What are your fingers like, can we see them?

OLIVER. Miss?

MOLLY. Can we see your fingers? (OLIVER *shows his fingers.*) Mmmm — yes, they look as if they could be green, you see we met a lady on the boat coming over from Canada who talked every lunch time and dinner time about gardening, and she said — do you remember, darling? —

TEDDY. What?

MOLLY. The herbaceous border lady, darling, she said that for gardens green fingers were quite essential, of course, and that the best way to make flowers grow was to talk to them and sing to them and even to recite poems to them, now would you be willing to talk and sing and recite poems to our flowers, Oliver? (*Looks at him seriously.*)

OLIVER. Um, well — (*Gives a little laugh.*)

MOLLY. Oh well (*smiling*). What about pulling up weeds and mowing the lawn instead?

OLIVER. Oh yes, Miss. I could do that. I mean, my Dad does the gardening for some of them in the village in the evenings, and I've helped him.

MOLLY. There you are then. You meet our requirements exactly, doesn't he darling?

TEDDY. What?

EVE. Excuse me, Moll, but I haven't quite found out how you can get hold of Mrs Shepherd.

MOLLY. Why do I want to get hold of Mrs Shepherd?

TEDDY. Hey, that boy's been standing there with a mitt full of beer and you ladies haven't let him take a sip of it — you have your drink, boy. Go on.

OLIVER *hesitates, then raises his glass, drinks.*

EVE (*to* MOLLY). Oliver used to work for Mrs Shepherd until she let him go.

OLIVER *finishes his drink.*

TEDDY. That's the boy!

MOLLY. Why did Mrs Shepherd let you go, Oliver?

OLIVER. She — well, she just said she didn't need me any more, that's all.

MOLLY. Oh. And if she had needed you any more we wouldn't be able to have you now, would we, so you see, Evie, Mrs Shepherd was only acting for the best, wasn't she Oliver, if we *can* have you now, that is? But omigod, how much are we to pay you?

OLIVER. Well, Miss, whatever — I don't know.

MOLLY. How much did Mrs Shepherd pay you?

OLIVER. Two pound a week, Miss.

MOLLY. Two pounds a week!

EVE. That would be the normal rate.

MOLLY. But it seems a mere trifle for chauffeuring us about and not killing us and keeping out weeds down and our flowers up and general handymanning, you would do a little handymanning wouldn't you, Oliver? I really think a minimum of four pounds a week, wouldn't you, darling?

EVE. Four pounds!

TEDDY. What?

MOLLY. Four pounds a week for Oliver, darling, includes handymanning.

TEDDY. Give him four and a half.

MOLLY. Four pounds ten, Oliver, there we are. Will you come to us for that?

OLIVER. Yes Miss! I mean, I'll have to talk it over with my Dad —

MOLLY. Of course you will. But even so, I think we've got you, haven't we?

OLIVER. Yes Miss.

MOLLY. Well then, Dad willing, when can you start, tomorrow?

EVE. Tomorrow's Sunday.

MOLLY. Monday then.

OLIVER. Yes Miss.

MOLLY. All settled darling, I had to use my wiles but I've brought him to it.

TEDDY. Another beer, boy?

OLIVER. Um, no thanks —

MOLLY. Oh, we mustn't keep him any longer (*taking the glass from* OLIVER, *winks at him*) he's got important matters to discuss with his Dad. Haven't you?

OLIVER. Yes Miss.

EVE. I'll see you out, Oliver. (*Leads him to the door.*)

MOLLY. See you Monday, Oliver.

TEDDY. 'Bye there, boy.

OLIVER. Sir. (*Shouting.*)

TEDDY. I like the look of him.

MOLLY. Did you really, darling? Can't say I did, pale, spotty and slightly furtive, I thought. But just the sort to know all about engines and lawn-mowers and things — (*taking off her coat*) and one never does know how to turn people down — (*Drops coat in chair.*)

TEDDY. Where did you go?

MOLLY. Further than I meant.

TEDDY (*sits down, looks at her*). Why didn't you take me with you?

MOLLY (*goes over to him, rumples his hair*). You were snoozing, my sweet, I hadn't the heart to wake you — (*kisses the top of his head, goes over to the cocktail cabinet with his glass, pours them both a drink*) — and it really wasn't very nice anyway, you'd have found me a terrible bore. I kept thinking I heard a tune I could write down and make into one of my silly songs, it was as if I were following it, through one field, then another, right to the river where the bridge is, I was sure it was there somewhere, like a person I was going to meet, but nobody came (*brings him his drink back*) nobody at all.

TEDDY. What? I missed all that.

MOLLY. I was just chattering.

EVE *enters, from left.*

MOLLY. Well darling, you got it all out of him, I take it.

EVE. What?

MOLLY. Mrs What'sit's address and the rest of it.

EVE. Mrs Shepherd's. Yes, I did. I hope you don't mind. I think she might be that lady we saw in the Post Office the other day, having a parcel weighed.

MOLLY. With a ridiculous hat and false teeth?

EVE. I didn't really notice her teeth.

MOLLY. What about her ankles, did you notice those?

EVE. Notice what?

MOLLY. Weren't they very thick?

EVE. I'm afraid I didn't notice her ankles, either.

MOLLY. Then it can't have been Mrs What'sit, darling, in the Post Office.

EVE. You've met her then?

MOLLY. Who?

EVE. Mrs Shepherd.

TEDDY. Who are you two nattering about?

MOLLY. Mrs Shepherd, darling.

TEDDY. Who's she?

MOLLY. We haven't the slightest idea, but Eve's got her address and she's determined to find out, aren't you, darling?

EVE. I'm sorry, Molly, I know it wasn't my place to interfere —

MOLLY. Oh Eve!

EVE. It's just that I don't think you should take people on without knowing anything about them, except what they tell you themselves.

MOLLY. Really, darling? I don't agree, we took you on without knowing anything about you except what you told us yourself, and that's worked out quite well.

EVE. I gave you three references!

MOLLY. Yes, darling but you don't think I read them. They were far too long, and bound to be flattering, which wouldn't have been fun, so I hired you in lieu.

EVE *picks up* MOLLY's *coat and scarf, takes them out to hall, left.*

MOLLY. Omigod! (*Sinks into a chair.*)

TEDDY. What?

MOLLY. I've offended Eve again.

TEDDY. What?

MOLLY. She really is the most humourless —

EVE *enters, from left.*

TEDDY (*not seeing her*). When's she going to feed us, that's what I want to know.

EVE. I'm on my way to the kitchen now.

MOLLY. Oh darling — (*to* EVE) I was only teasing, of course I read your references, they were divine, one from the two ladies in Richmond, one from the Doctor in Kingston and one from — from — wherever, but I remember it quite well, said you were scrupulous in violet ink and couldn't manage without you and no more could we, and you were right to insist on Mr What'sit's address, and I did rush us into the youth quite fecklessly, it was just that I felt funny about having forgotten him entirely, but I know he won't get away with anything, darling, with you to keep an eye on him, and if you ever bump into Mrs Shepherd again you can quiz her to your heart's content, all right, darling, all forgiven? Please. Pretty please with sugar on it?

EVE (*smiles*). Oh Moll. Now you're teasing me again.

MOLLY. No I'm not, darling. I mean it. Every word almost.

EVE (*still smiling*). It'll just be a few minutes, Teddy.

TEDDY. No rush, Evie, have another drink!

EVE. Then you'll never eat. (*Goes out back.*)

MOLLY. Omigod! (*Wearily. Lights a cigarette.*)

    TEDDY *watches her. There is a pause.*

TEDDY. Hey you, come here! (*Pause.*) Come on, come here, I said.

MOLLY (*concealing irritation, clearly knows what is to happen, gets up, goes over to* TEDDY). Sir?

TEDDY. Now my girl, how many's that since lunch?

MOLLY. Only one, sir.

TEDDY. Come on, Moll, the truth now. All the time you were gadding about out there.

MOLLY. Well, three. (*Pause.*) Four. (*Pause. Holds up five fingers.*) Ten. Twenty.

TEDDY (*not hearing*). Five, eh? Well, add on another four and one on top of that makes — one — two — three — four — five — six — seven — eight — nine — (*Slapping* MOLLY *on the bottom, laughing.*)

    MOLLY *giggles, cries ouch.*

TEDDY. Now get us another drink, girl.

MOLLY. My Lord.

    *Makes a little curtsey, takes his glass, pours him a drink and one for herself.*

TEDDY. And another thing, girl, what about getting to the piano, all your talk about your songs and you haven't touched a key since we moved in, that was another of Mr Goldberg's considerations — he can hire himself a whole band out of that one — I was telling Eve all about your seal-song and Bob Hoskins transmitting it over RCVX — (*takes her hand as she brings him the drink*) play it now, eh, Moll.

MOLLY. But darling, she's getting the dinner on the table.

TEDDY. What? Don't want to?

MOLLY. Not very much, darling. For one thing the piano's out of tune. And so am I. (*Looks at him from above, sadly.*) You come and sit here then.

*Takes him by the hand, leads him to the chair nearest the piano, then goes to the piano, begins to play uncertainly. The piano is out of tune.*
*MOLLY makes a face. After a moment she begins to sing, very loudly, but nicely, 'And did those feet'.*
*EVE enters from the back, stands listening.*
*TEDDY is evidently straining to hear, his foot beating out of time to the music.*

TEDDY (*as MOLLY is fading out*). There. There Evie. She wrote it herself. What do you think of it?

EVE. I think it's lovely.

MOLLY. Why Evie, you're tone deaf!

EVE. Perhaps I am. But I know a nice voice when I hear one. Dinner's ready.

*MOLLY comes over, takes TEDDY's hand; they go through back, and as EVE closes the door behind them; Lights.*

## Scene Two

*A week or so later. Mid-afternoon. The room is full of sunlight, the conservatory door is open.*
*OLIVER enters through the conservatory, furtively. He is wearing an open-necked shirt, baggy gardening trousers. He looks towards the kitchen, back, then towards the door, left, then goes to the sofa, on which is MOLLY's handbag. Opens the handbag, takes out a package of cigarettes and the lighter. Quickly extracts a cigarette, puts it in his pocket, then another, which he lights. Puts the lighter back in the handbag, closes it. Stands smoking, looking around.*
*EVE enters from the back. Stands watching OLIVER.*
*OLIVER, suddenly conscious of another presence, turns. They stare at each other.*

OLIVER. I've finished digging up them weeds around the garage, Missus.

EVE. And have you done the hedge?

OLIVER. No Missus, I — I don't know where the shears is.

EVE. We don't keep them in the sitting-room, Oliver. Perhaps they're under the potato sacking on the second shelf in the conservatory where I told you to put them the last time you used them, have you looked?

OLIVER. No Missus.

EVE. Have you put the weeds in the compost?

OLIVER. No Miss.

EVE. Then do that first. Then the hedge. And oh, Oliver — (EVE *gets an ashtray, comes towards* OLIVER, *holds it out.*) In here, please.

OLIVER *stubs out the cigarette.*

EVE. Now here are two things for you to understand, Oliver. Firstly, we don't like you wandering into the house whenever you feel like it, and secondly we don't like you smoking in the house, you left a saucer full of stubs in my kitchen after your lunch today. All right?

OLIVER. Yes Missus. (*Sulkily.*)

EVE. And by the way, I'm not Missus, I'm Miss. Miss Mace. (*Attempts a more friendly tone. Little pause.*) Is anything the matter?

OLIVER. Well, Missus — Miss. The only thing — well, I mean, I was told it was going to be fixing the Alvis and driving it mainly, that was my work, and there was a bit of gardening on the side, but I mean I've got the Alvis fixed, but I've only got to drive it twice in two weeks, it's been gardening all the time, and even painting the inside of the garage.

EVE. I see. Well, Oliver, if you're not satisfied with the conditions of your employment, you're quite at liberty to leave. Is that what you want to do?

OLIVER. No Missus.

EVE. Miss.

OLIVER. No Miss.

EVE. I'm sure you don't. So you'd better get on with it, hadn't you?

OLIVER (*after a pause*). Yes Miss. (*Turns to go.*)

EVE (*looks into the ashtray*). Oliver. What cigarettes do you smoke?

OLIVER. Any sort, Missus. Miss.

EVE. Including the sort that Mrs Treadley smokes?

OLIVER (*shrugs*). I don't know what sort she smokes.

EVE. She smokes this sort. (*Holding up stub.*) Did you take one of hers?

OLIVER. No Miss!

EVE. I think you did, Oliver. That's what you were doing in here, wasn't it?

OLIVER. No Miss, I never!

EVE. Please don't lie, Oliver.

OLIVER (*as MOLLY enters*). I'm not lying, Miss!

MOLLY (*looking from one to the other*). What's going on, it sounds thrilling!

EVE. I'm just trying to find out whether Oliver's been helping himself to your cigarettes.

OLIVER. I didn't, Miss.

MOLLY. Oh, I do hope you didn't, Oliver, I'm terribly low and I do hate to be caught without one. Shall I check and see how I'm off? (*Goes over to handbag, opens it, looks into the cigarette package.*) About a dozen, I suppose that'll do, could you remember some, Evie, if you're going shopping. (*Little pause.*) Are you doing something in the garden, Oliver?

OLIVER. I've got to put weeds in the compost and then clip the hedge, Miss.

MOLLY. Such a nice day for being outside.

OLIVER. Yes Miss. (*Smirks at EVE, goes out.*)

EVE. Molly, I know he helped himself.

MOLLY (*lighting a cigarette*). Yes, darling, I expect you're right.

EVE. Well, if there's one thing I hate it's a pilferer. And a liar.

MOLLY. Well we all have our pet aversions, I detest ghastly scenes and boys getting shrill all over something extremely trivial, darling.

EVE. I see. (*Turns, goes out, back.*)

MOLLY. I see. I see. Pretty please with sugar on it. (*Imitating first EVE, then herself.*) Oh God — (*She gets up.*) Evie! (*Makes to go back.*)

TEDDY (*enters, left*). Hey Moll, you nearly let me fall asleep again, you ready?

MOLLY. What? What for darling?

TEDDY. Our walk.

MOLLY. What walk?

TEDDY. Aren't you coming for a walk?

MOLLY. But darling, we worked it all out at lunch, now we've got the piano tuned at last I was going to try and settle to some song writing, and you were going to go for a walk.

TEDDY. We're going to Gwyllup, it's five miles.

MOLLY. No darling, we were going to *drive* to Gwyllup another day —

TEDDY. No, no, walk.

MOLLY. Anyway, not this afternoon —

TEDDY. You're smoking again.

MOLLY. So I am, I am.

TEDDY. If you don't want to, you'd better not.

MOLLY. But I do. I do.

TEDDY. Then we'd better get started.

MOLLY. No, I mean smoke — (*Stubs the cigarette out irritably.*)

REDDY. Do you or don't you, I can't make it out.

EVE (*enters back*). I'm just going to do the shopping.

TEDDY. What?

EVE. I've got down tomatoes, oranges, cauliflower, the beef to be collected, four skewers —

MOLLY. Oh darling, do come in properly, it can't be any good for your throat — baying at me from over there.

TEDDY. I'm going to walk to Gwyllup. The question is whether you are.

EVE. I'm sorry. I didn't mean to bay at you. (*Frostily.*)

TEDDY. I can perfectly well go by myself.

EVE. I just wanted to know if you wanted to add anything.

MOLLY. Add anything? To the skewers and the four cauliflowers?

EVE. To the shopping list.

TEDDY. When you two have sorted it out, whatever it is that's so important to you, I'll be upstairs in my room. I don't want to keep interrupting you ladies when you're nattering about something important — (*Going out, slams the door, left.*)

*There is a pause.*

MOLLY. Omigod! We go to all the trouble of getting that little man over from Guildford so that I can play the piano properly at last, and perhaps even, who knows? compose a song, and when I actually at last arrange to spend an afternoon at the piano, I find myself harassed with tales about youths stealing cigarettes, and grown men demanding to be taken for walks — it's too much, it's too, too much! (*Takes out a cigarette, lights it.*)

EVE *turns away, her face working.*

MOLLY (*looks at* EVE, *looks away angrily, draws on her cigarette*). Sorry darling. Didn't mean to be ratty. Forgive please. (*Little pause.*) Pretty please, with sugar on it.

EVE. I expect it *is* all my fault. *I'm* sorry, Molly. The truth is, I've got a bit of a headache, this weather's a little close for me. (*Attempts a little laugh.*) That always means it's going to rain. Sorry Moll.

MOLLY. Oh poor darling, can I get you an aspirin?

EVE. No — nothing does any good until it rains.

MOLLY. Anyway, you mustn't think of going to the shops — why don't you have a nice lie-down?

EVE. Oh, I'll be all right. Really. I shouldn't have made such a fuss over Oliver.

MOLLY. Someone's got to make fusses for us, darling, and as you're the only grown-up in the house, it'd better be you. We are childish, aren't we, Teddy and I?

EVE. Of course you're not.

MOLLY. Yes we are.

EVE. Well — I've always liked children.

MOLLY. Really, darling? I wouldn't have thought you'd much to do with them before.

EVE. Oh yes. I helped to look after some once. A long time ago.

MOLLY. Did you? (*Abruptly.*) I'd like a child. Do you think it's too late for me?

*Little pause.* EVE *looks embarrassed.*

MOLLY. I mean adopt one of course. Now that I'm back in England — home again. One could easily adopt one, couldn't one? What do you think?

EVE. I think it's the most marvellous idea!

MOLLY. After all, if we keep this place on, we've lots of room. He could have the small room as a bedroom, and the room opposite as a play-room and I could move across the hall to be next to him — and even if we don't stay here we could find somewhere else just as big — you see how I've been working it out?

EVE. Oh Moll!

MOLLY. And you wouldn't run away if we did?

EVE. I'd love it! And what does Teddy think?

MOLLY. Oh, I haven't mentioned it to him yet. One thing at a time for the poor darling — first England, then a child, then if we get on with that one perhaps another to go with it and so on, we may end up with a flock of them — (*laughing*) — we'd have to keep some out in the fields!

EVE.(*laughs*). Oh Moll!

TEDDY (*enters left*). I'm not going to doze through the afternoon, have you two fixed it all up between yourselves, yet?

MOLLY. Oh yes, darling, completely. Haven't we, Evie?

EVE (*smiling*). Yes.

TEDDY. Then you're ready to hike to Gwyllup? Or do I go on my own?

MOLLY. Oh darling, do you mind if I try out the lovely piano you've had fixed up for me? Do you?

TEDDY. You're saying no?

MOLLY. Darling, I will, if you like.

TEDDY. I'm going anyway, as that's what we arranged.

MOLLY. Besides, Evie says it's going to rain, and you know how bad that can be for your ears — why don't you take a little local stroll.

TEDDY. I'm going to Gwyllup. (*Pause.*) I'm going to Gwyllup.

MOLLY (*hesitates*). Then at least take your raincoat and your mackintosh hat.

TEDDY. What?

MOLLY. Your raincoat and mackintosh hat.

TEDDY. What for? It's not going to rain. 'Bye. (*Stamps out through the conservatory.*)

MOLLY. Oh damn, damn, what shall I do, if it rains into his ears — and he *will* go to Gwyllup too, he's so stubborn — and if I go after him now he'll just stump angrily along —

EVE (*getting up*). I'll take them to him. (*Runs to door, left, returns at once with hat and coat.*)

MOLLY. Oh thank you darling. But really somebody ought to go with him, I know it's a lot to ask — will you?

EVE (*hesitates, then smiles*). Of course Moll.

MOLLY. You are a darling — and they say Gwyllup's very beautiful.

EVE (*runs through the conservatory, with hat and coat. As she does so, she calls*). Oliver — Oliver — run after Mr Treadley, tell him to wait a minute, hurry, hurry!

MOLLY *stands listening for a moment, then goes into the conservatory, stands watching, still visible to the audience, then returns. Goes to the cigarettes, picks one out, lights it, puffs on it. Sits down to smoke. After a moment gets up, stands uncertainly, kicks off her shoes, then wanders over to the piano, picks out a tune, tries to play, then crashes a discord, sits puffing on her cigarette. Gets up, paces about restlessly, then goes to the cocktail cabinet, pours herself a gin, walks determinedly back to the piano, sits down, gets up, goes over, lights another cigarette, sits down with the drink.*

MOLLY. Alone at last. (*Pause, then in a desolate voice.*) Omigod! (*Pause, suddenly shakes her head from side to side, stops, puts her fingers to her forehead.*) Omigod! (*Collapses back into the sofa.*)

OLIVER *appears in the conservatory. He is carrying the coat and the mackintosh hat.* MOLLY *doesn't notice him.* OLIVER *clears his throat.*

MOLLY (*looks at him*). Oh hello. He sent them back, did he?

OLIVER. Yes Miss. He said to say he doesn't need them. And he says thank you, um, for —

MOLLY. What?

OLIVER. Well, Evie, Miss.

MOLLY (*smiles wryly*). Thank you. Well, sling them — sling them over there somewhere, would you?

OLIVER *puts them on the end of the sofa.*

MOLLY. And how's everything in the garden?

OLIVER. I got the weeds on the compost, I'm going to start on the hedge.

MOLLY. How lucky — to have something you've got to do.

OLIVER. Yes Miss.

*Slight pause.* OLIVER *goes into the conservatory, clatters about, just in sight.* MOLLY *looks towards the conservatory, watches.*

OLIVER. Just getting the shears, Miss. (*Holds them up.*)

MOLLY. Come in for a moment, Oliver, please. (*With authority.*)

OLIVER *enters, carrying the shears.*

MOLLY. Two, Oliver.

OLIVER. Miss?

MOLLY (*holds up two fingers*). You took two of my cigarettes, Oliver.

OLIVER. I didn't! Miss, I swear —

MOLLY. Oh Oliver, don't, please. It makes you sound like a goose when you protest — you honk.

OLIVER. But — (*Stops.*)

MOLLY (*gets cigarettes, holds package out to* OLIVER). Here, have another one.

OLIVER. No thank you, Miss.

MOLLY. Oh go on. You mustn't mind my knowing about you

being a liar, I lie all the time, all the time, about lots of things, about cigarettes too. I promise I won't smoke more than five a day, my husband thinks it's bad for my health, but of course I sneak extra ones, like now with you, he'd have a fit if he could see me puffing away. Do you know what he'd do? He'd put me across his knee and spank me, Oliver. Yes, he would. What do you think of that?

OLIVER. Well Miss — (*Gives a strange half laugh.*)

MOLLY. Now I've told you all that, you've got to take one, haven't you?

OLIVER *hesitates, then takes one.*

MOLLY. I bet your Dad doesn't put you across his knee and spank you, at least not any more, does he?

OLIVER. No Miss. (*Laughs again.*)

MOLLY. You did take them, didn't you?

OLIVER. Yes Miss.

MOLLY. There, now we've both confessed. But I'm very sorry Oliver, now I shall have to punish you. You do realise that, you can't pinch my cigarettes and then lie and bluster about it and not expect punishment, can you? (*She allows a long pause.*) Sit down please, Oliver.

OLIVER, *after a moment, sits.*

MOLLY. Do you know what I'm going to do to you?

OLIVER *shakes his head.*

MOLLY. I'm going to teach you a lesson, Oliver. I'm going to make you sit here and talk to me. (*Laughs.*) Just for a little, do you mind?

OLIVER (*smiles*). No Miss. Except there's the hedge and she goes on at me.

MOLLY. Oh, *her*! Don't worry about her, Oliver, I'll protect you from her! (*Pause.*) Tell me, do you think it's going to rain?

OLIVER. Yes Miss.

MOLLY. Oh don't say that, why?

OLIVER. Because it feels like rain. And my Dad said it would.

MOLLY. And is your Dad always right?

OLIVER. Usually Miss.

MOLLY. About everything, or just about the weather?

OLIVER. Well, about the weather, anyway, Miss.

MOLLY. How does he know, by sniffing the air, or holding his finger up or rising at six for shepherds' warnings?

OLIVER. No Miss.

MOLLY. How then?

OLIVER. He listen to the radio Miss, at breakfast. (*There is a pause.*)

MOLLY. Well, clever old Dad. (*Laughing.*) I bet you don't dare lie to him.

OLIVER. Oh no Miss.

MOLLY. What about?

OLIVER. Miss?

MOLLY. What do you lie to him about?

OLIVER. I said I didn't, Miss.

MOLLY. Yes that was a lie to me. What do you lie to him about? Come on, Oliver, do tell me. Please, pretty please. Because I know you do.

OLIVER. How, Miss?

MOLLY. Because if we didn't lie to people we love and live with, we wouldn't be able to love and live with them. See.

*Gets up, goes to cocktail cabinet, pours herself a gin, studies* OLIVER.

OLIVER (*after a pause*). Well, only about Guildford. What I do over at Guildford. That's all.

MOLLY. And what *do* you do over at Guildford?

*During this scene, and by imperceptible degrees, the stage darkens to suggest the sky darkening.*

MOLLY. Oh of course, you've got a girl there. (*Drinks.*)

OLIVER. Well — (*Shrugs.*)

MOLLY. Haven't you?

OLIVER. Not any more. There was a girl. I used to have tea with her sometimes.

MOLLY. Only tea?

OLIVER. Yes. She worked in a tea shop.

MOLLY (*drinks again*). And is that all you did with her?

OLIVER. We went to the films sometimes.

MOLLY. Were you lovers?

OLIVER. What?

MOLLY. Lovers.

*There is a pause.*

MOLLY. Here — (*pours a drink of gin, brings it to* OLIVER) have a sip of this.

OLIVER. What is it?

MOLLY. A truth drink. To help you tell me whether you were lovers. It's all right, I swear I won't tell your Dad if you promise not to tell mine. Husband. Sip and tell, Oliver.

OLIVER (*sips*). Well — (*Sips again.*) No Miss.

MOLLY. No, won't tell, or no, weren't lovers?

OLVIER. Weren't — um, lovers.

MOLLY. Oh dear, oh dear, why not?

OLIVER (*laughs embarrassed.*) Don't know anything about any of that.

MOLLY. Any of what? (*Goes over to him, takes the shears off his lap, puts them on the floor.*) There. Any of what?

OLIVER. My Dad wouldn't stand for any of that. He'd kill me if I did anything like that.

MOLLY (*standing close to him*). Then what happened between yourself and this girl, what was her name?

OLIVER. Rosie. Rosie Hitchens. Well — just one day she turned around when I went over and said her Mum didn't want her to see me any more.

MOLLY. And she didn't?

OLIVER (*after a pause*). No.

MOLLY (*after a pause*). Poor Oliver. Poor Rosie Hutchings, come to that.

OLIVER. Hitchens. Her name was.

MOLLY. Is your mother dead?

OLIVER. Yes Miss. When I was born.

MOLLY. You're terribly fond of your Dad, aren't you? Tell me, what do you do together? I mean in the evenings, or the weekends?

OLIVER. Well — we go shooting.

MOLLY. Do you, oh, dear, what do you shoot?

OLIVER. Only rabbits.

MOLLY. *Only* rabbits? Oh Oliver. And do you kill many of them?

OLIVER. Quite a few. My Dad's a good shot. I'm not bad.

MOLLY. What do you think, when you see them dead?

OLIVER. That they're dead, Miss. Dead rabbits. For pie.

MOLLY. Have you got a dog?

OLIVER. We had one once, Miss.

MOLLY. What happened to it?

OLIVER. It got run over.

MOLLY. And what did you think, when you saw it dead.

OLIVER. It was in the middle of the Guildford road, where all the lorries run. My Dad took me down to see it, lying there squashed, I was only six about.

MOLLY. Why did he do that?

OLIVER. To show me what happened if I was careless on the road.

MOLLY. Omigod, Oliver! And what did you say, when you saw it there?

OLIVER. I said (*thinks*) were we going to have it for lunch.

MOLLY. You didn't!

OLIVER. No Miss. We had it for supper.

MOLLY (*after a moment, laughing*). You're making fun of me! That's nice. (*Pours more gin into* OLIVER's *glass.*) There! You see how it helps. And me. (*Pours some into her own.*) Because now I'm going to tell you why I hate to think of shooting only rabbits even, and you mustn't laugh at me, promise?

OLIVER. Miss.

MOLLY. You see, I hate anything being killed by people. Ever since I heard about something very dreadful — about how

these great Canadian men with their red necks and tartan caps
on their heads drive down to the beach in their trucks and
they catch the seals, the mother seals and the baby seals, and
they beat their heads in with clubs and hammers. (*Sits down
beside him.*) Yes they do, Oliver, and sometimes the mothers
stay a little way out in the sea, watching, while these — these
men! — skin their babies while they're still alive often, skin
them for their furs. Dreadful. Dreadful. They have such big
eyes and they stare at their babies — D'you see, Oliver. (*Looks
at him intently.*) I wrote a song about it. It was broadcast on
the radio over there, and played right across Nova Scotia. But
it didn't stop them. That's when I knew I couldn't live in
Canada any more, amongst people like that. So don't shoot
any rabbits ever again. Please don't, Oliver. Pretty please.
With sugar on it. (*There is a pause.*) Oh I know, you've got to,
for your Dad's sake. You'll just have to try to miss them, that's
all. For my sake. Aim — (*raises her arm at* OLIVER, *jerks at
the last second*) sideways. (*Laughs.*) But don't hit your Dad.
For his sake. Are you happy with us?

OLIVER. Oh yes Miss.

MOLLY. I watch you sometimes, Oliver. Did you know that?
When you're in the garden. As busy as bees. Mowing the lawn
yesterday. I watched you from an upstairs window. And then
on your knees weeding this morning. But I haven't seen you
recite poetry to the flowers. No. And sometimes you even look
a trifle — sulky. There. I've said it. As if you weren't truly and
really deeply happy with us. Why not, Oliver?

OLIVER. I am, Miss. (*Pause.*) Well.

MOLLY. No, go on. On.

OLIVER. She gets at me a lot, Miss.

MOLLY. Oh, she gets at us all a lot, pay her no mind, we don't.
When she gets at me I pay her out my very best smile and say
forgive me, Evie, pretty please, with sugar on it. You can try
that. Because then you can ignore her and be rude to her or
whatever you want. What else is wrong?

OLIVER. Nothing, Miss. Well.

MOLLY. Oh, Oliver. On.

OLIVER. Well, only about the car, that's all. I mean I was taken
on to do the car, but now I've got it fixed up I've only taken it
out twice, the rest of it's been gardening and painting the

garage, and the other day it was sash cords even she made me
do.

MOLLY. I'm so glad you've told me this, Oliver. I'll have a word
with Teddy when he gets back. (*Pours herself another drink.*)
I promise you more outings in the car. I never break my
promises you know.

OLIVER. Oh, I don't really mind. It's just that that's what I
thought I was being taken on to do mainly and, well, they
make jokes about it at Sprinkley's and up at the pub, because
my Dad told them all I was going to be a chauffeur and they
say if you're a chauffeur where's your uniform. My Dad doesn't
like that.

MOLLY. If your Dad doesn't like it, that settles it. Although I don't
know about a uniform — I don't know if I'd like you so much
in a uniform. Will you teach me to drive, Oliver, and keep it a
secret from my Dad. Will you?

OLIVER. Yes Miss.

MOLLY. And then when you've taught me I'll show him I can.
Eh? Oliver? (*Laughs.*) If you promise to teach me then you
shall have a uniform — even though I like you just as you are,
Oliver. I like you very much. You do know that, don't you?

(*They stare at each other.*)

MOLLY. Do you like him?

OLIVER. Who?

MOLLY. Teddy.

OLIVER. Yes Miss.

MOLLY. So do I. Even though he calls you boy and Ollie and
Oliver Treefsir?

OLIVER. Oh, I don't mind that. It's just his way.

MOLLY. Because he's deaf, you see. It's so sad. Because people
when they're deaf can't have normal friendly conversations
with each other, as we're having, so they have to find little
tricks of their own to show normal friendliness, and to hide
their deafness too. And he's very friendly. More than
normally.

OLIVER. He doesn't really —

MOLLY. What?

OLIVER (*hesitates*). Put you over his knee, does he?

MOLLY (*stares at* OLIVER). D'you mind?

OLIVER. Miss. (*Laughs.*) He doesn't! Does he?

MOLLY. I'm so worried, Oliver, about his getting his ears wet.
And your saying it's going to rain — (*Goes over to the
window, looks out.*) It's darker, getting darker. It *is* raining
a little. Oh damn! Oh, poor Teddy. But it's delicious, too, isn't
it, the two of us snug inside, talking and drinking, while
outside — (*shivers*) delicious. (*Takes a gulp of gin.*) Do you like
me, Oliver?

OLIVER. Miss?

MOLLY. Or do you think I'm just a silly old vamp, do you?

OLIVER. No Miss.

MOLLY. What then? Say it. You must say it. I said it to you.

OLIVER. Like you, Miss.

MOLLY. But I don't frighten you, do I?

OLIVER. No Miss.

MOLLY. We'll have another cigarette, shall we?

> *Goes with cigarettes, offers one to* OLIVER, *lights it for
> him. She is staring at him. Takes a step around the side of the
> sofa, puts her foot on the shears, stumbles, cries out.*

OLIVER (*gets to his feet*). What is it, Miss, what is it?

MOLLY. I've cut myself — my foot — (*Tries to see the sole of her
foot.*) Can you see?

> OLIVER, *bending some yards away, stares.*

MOLLY. Look properly — take it — (*Stretches out her leg.*)

OLIVER (*takes her foot gingerly*). I can't see any cut, Miss.

MOLLY. But it's wet — I can feel the bleeding —

OLIVER. No Miss — that's your drink — I can smell it — that's
all —

MOLLY. But it hurts, oh God, it hurts — (*Loses balance, hops.*)

OLIVER. Miss — Miss — (*Lets go of* MOLLY's *leg.*)

> MOLLY *stumbles towards* OLIVER, *who puts out his arms to
> catch her.*

MOLLY. Oh Oliver — (*clinging to him*) it did hurt — it did —

OLIVER. Miss. (*In alarm.*)

MOLLY. Oliver — don't be frightened. Don't be.

OLIVER. Miss?

> MOLLY *begins to kiss* OLIVER, *ravenously.* OLIVER
> *clumsily responds. Lights down to sound of rain. Rain
> continues through the darkness.*


## Scene Three

*About an hour later. Lights up to greyness. Still raining heavily.
OLIVER is sitting on the sofa, putting on his socks. He has already
put on his underpants. The raincoat is spread under him, across
the sofa, the waterproof side up, there are cushions on the floor.
MOLLY is in her underpants, doing up her bra. She is standing
some way from OLIVER. She is dressing quickly.
OLIVER stops dressing, watches MOLLY. His face works. He
turns, rolls into the sofa, puts his arm over his face.*

MOLLY (*not noticing*). Oh that rain, that bloody rain — but
   they'll have found somewhere in the village — or a tree — the
   poor man — next time I'll check the weather with your Dad or
   the wireless — (*Dressing through this, turns, looks at* OLIVER.)
   Oliver — (*Goes over to him.*) Oliver, darling, what is it? (*Sits
   down on the sofa next to him, tries to remove* OLIVER's *arm
   from his face.*) Oliver — don't — you mustn't — here, here —
   (*Pulls his arm away.*) Why are you? Is it because you're unhappy?
   Are you unhappy?

OLIVER (*shakes his head*). No Miss.

MOLLY. Because you're happy then?

> OLIVER, *crying, turns his face away.*

MOLLY (*taking his face in her hands*). Because you're happy?

OLIVER. Miss. I don't know Miss.

MOLLY (*cuddles him*). There Oliver, nothing to cry for, nothing
   to cry for. I'm glad, I am, yes I am, and I want you to be
   happy, but you mustn't cry —

OLIVER (*embraces her with sudden and desperate passion*).
Please Miss please Miss please Miss —

MOLLY. What darling? What?

OLIVER. You won't send me away Miss.

MOLLY. No, no — of course not — just for now — just for a little
while — but there'll be other times. I promise you. Lots of
other times, but we mustn't let them find out, must we? They
wouldn't understand, and I wouldn't want to hurt Teddy, he
loves me, you know, and I must care for him too, mustn't I,
and not let him be hurt, so now I've got to put everything
right and you must finish getting dressed, darling, and help me
by being as quick as you can, darling, before they come back —
do you understand, darling? Do you?

OLIVER *nods.*

MOLLY. Go on then. Go on, my darling — (*Gets up, finishes
dressing.*)

OLIVER *goes on dressing, sniffing.*

MOLLY (*comes over, buttons his shirt*). Now you go now, my
darling — (*leads him to the door left*) there's a good boy —
(*Kisses him.*)

OLIVER *goes out left, there is a pause. He comes back, rushes
over to* MOLLY, *throws his arms around her.*

MOLLY (*strokes his head*). I'll see you soon. I promise. And I
never break my promises.

*They separate.* OLIVER *stands looking at* MOLLY.

MOLLY. Go, Oliver. (*Gently, leads him out left and sounds of her
saying goodbye quickly at the front door. Front door closes,
off,* MOLLY *enters left as* TEDDY, *followed by* EVE, *enters
the conservatory, right.*

TEDDY *is soaking, mud-stained. Followed by* EVE, *also
soaking.*

MOLLY (*stares, shocked*). Omigod — darling, what happened?

TEDDY. Well, here I am, Moll, back from a stroll in your nice
quiet countryside, right in the middle of the fields, eh Evie,
then wham, right from out of your nice quiet clouds, wham,
wham, wham! (*Laughs.*)

MOLLY. Darling, you must get into some dry clothes. (*Getting up,
going to him.*)

EVE. And a hot bath!

TEDDY *has gone to cocktail cabinet, pours himself an enormous Scotch.*

TEDDY. And there we were, Evie and me, (*gulping the Scotch*) licking across the field in the dark, sheets of it coming down, and there was this tree Evie saw, on a bank and a ditch running under it, anyway wouldn't pass in Novia Scotia for a river (*laughs*) and I swayed on the edge, eh, Evie?

MOLLY. Darling, tell me afterwards, get changed now!

TEDDY. Felt like minutes, rocking and swaying, and Evie had hold of my arm pulling me back, but a hand shot out of nowhere and down I went.

MOLLY. A hand?

TEDDY. And down I went, right Evie?

MOLLY. You were pushed?

TEDDY. And down I went, right, Evie, Evie almost coming with me. (*Laughs.*) So don't you two talk to me about your friendly English countryside again, we've got bob-cat, bear and skunk in Nova Scotia but we don't have anything you can't see or hear or understand come up behind you and tumble you into the mud for no damn reason — (*gulps again*) raining inside my skull — (*pulls out the hearing aid*) damn thing, damned thing, battery soaking — get it fixed, fixed tomorrow — (*Takes another gulp, stands staring at* MOLLY.) Hey, Moll!

MOLLY. He's trembling — darling! He's feverish — come on, darling, we must get you to a bath and bed — come along. (*Pulls* TEDDY *towards the door.*)

TEDDY. I'm all right — I'm all right — (*Goes out.*)

MOLLY (*before she closes the door, turns, stares at* EVE). I told you to make him take his raincoat and his mackintosh hat! I *told* you! (*Goes out.*)

EVE *stands for a moment. Then bends, automatically. Picks up* TEDDY's *hat.*)

EVE (*in an emotional voice*). It's jolly well not fair! (*Suddenly takes in the chaos of the room, glasses, cushions, etc.*)

*Lights.*

*CURTAIN.*

# Act Two

## Scene One

*A week or so later. The sun is shining. It is mid-afternoon. EVE is sitting with some knitting on her lap. She is staring ahead. There is the sound of a door closing, off, up left. Then quick footsteps, EVE starts knitting.*

MOLLY. Hello darling, seen my handbag?

EVE. On the sofa.

MOLLY. You are clever. (*Going to the handbag.*)

EVE. You usually leave it on the sofa. Have you got Teddy's drops?

MOLLY. Oh yes, here they are. (*Fishes them out of the handbag, puts them on the table.*)

EVE. He always needs them first thing, when he wakes.

MOLLY. I know, poor darling. Isn't that growing — Teddy'll be so thrilled. I wish I could knit.

EVE. Do you? It's not difficult.

MOLLY. No, I suppose it can't be, as so many dolts can. It's one of those activities I always thought I'd find myself doing when I grew up — like putting on grey hair and wrinkles.

EVE. Indeed?

MOLLY. Oh darling, I didn't mean — (*Laughs.*)

EVE (*smiles coldly*). Are you going out?

MOLLY. Yes, I've got an appointment with Oliver for a driving lesson. What about you?

EVE. Oh no. I don't think Teddy should be left alone at the moment.

MOLLY. But darling, he's asleep, I've just checked.

EVE. Yesterday when you were having a driving lesson and I was down here he woke up and thought he was alone in the house. He was quite fretful for a good half hour.

MOLLY. I must say, darling, that doesn't sound like a good half hour to me. (*Hesitates.*) In that case why don't you go out and I'll stay in, it's your turn.

EVE. No. I'd as soon get on with this. Besides Oliver will be expecting you.

MOLLY. Oh, I can always find something else for him to do.

EVE. I'm glad he's settling down so well. Since you moved him into the house.

MOLLY. Hasn't he been a Godsend.

EVE. Yes. Mrs Shepherd says he's funny in the head. She came around yesterday morning. She'd heard he was living in so she came around especially to warn us. She said he was funny in the head. That's why they dismissed him. Her husband caught him in their bedroom, going through her underwear drawer.

MOLLY. Oh, don't you worry, darling. Your underwear drawer is quite safe. Oliver's told me all about it.

EVE. I see. You don't think it peculiar even then?

MOLLY. Nothing like as peculiar as Mrs Shepherd, trekking all the way up here to tell us about it.

EVE. Oh well, as long as *you* don't mind —

MOLLY. No, I don't mind, darling. Not at all. And if you're not keen to go out I'll get some fresh air. (*Gets up, goes towards the conservatory.*)

EVE (*watches her, and as* MOLLY *gets to the conservatory door*). Oh by the way, Molly, as soon as Teddy's better I shall be leaving. (*Little pause.*) I thought I should tell you now, so you'd have time to find someone more suitable.

MOLLY (*takes out a cigarette, lights it*). More suitable to what, darling?

EVE. To what's going on in this house.

MOLLY. What *is* going on in this house?

EVE. Wasn't Oliver in your room last night?

MOLLY. Yes, he did look in to say goodnight and to ask how Teddy was.

EVE. He stayed the whole night.

MOLLY *makes to exclaim.*

EVE. Please don't lie to me, Moll, I couldn't bear it. I heard Teddy stumbling down the hall at midnight. It was only by the grace of God that I managed to stop him opening the door on the two of you. He'd had a nightmare, and wanted comforting. Thank God *he* couldn't hear what I heard.

*There is a honk from outside, right.*

MOLLY. Omigod! Thank you, Evie!

EVE. Oh it wasn't you I was thinking of, it was Teddy.

MOLLY. I know. Thank you. Teddy and I don't sleep together, surely you've realised that.

EVE. But — but he's still your husband. You married him.

MOLLY. Yes. And I do my best to make him happy, haven't you noticed? I get drunk with him, and cuddle him, and let him slap me on the bottom — all — all that. It's enough for Teddy. It's not always enough for me.

EVE. You mean — you've done this before?

MOLLY. From time to time. Though not as often as I want to.

EVE. Oh, you sound so hard — so hard.

MOLLY. Do I, darling? Sorry. You've been companion-housekeeper to a wicked woman, darling, you see. I need my sex. There. I've said it.

EVE. Then you had no right to marry Teddy.

MOLLY. Hadn't I? He wanted me to.

EVE. But what did you marry him for? His money?

MOLLY. I admit I wouldn't have if he'd been an impoverished — (*Gestures.*)

EVE. Garage hand. Like Oliver Treefe, you mean?

MOLLY. Well, unlike Oliver, Teddy would have been a sixty-year-old impoverished garage hand when I married him, so I probably wouldn't have married him, no.

EVE. I don't understand.

MOLLY. What, darling? What don't you understand?

EVE. You who could have married anybody —

MOLLY. Not when I married Teddy. Don't forget he *was*
sixty, and I was *all* of thirty — and he was quite a dynamic
Halifax businessman and I was one of those, you know,
glamorous English divorcees that end up in countries like
Canada on spec.

EVE. I didn't know you'd been married before.

MOLLY. Gets worse and worse, doesn't it, darling. Yes.
Married before. Sorry. There were no children though, other
than the two of us. Then he began to grow up, and left me for
someone who would look after him properly. I've never been
very good at getting meals on tables and organising homes and
curtains and housekeeping — all the things you're so good at
doing. He's a solicitor in Harrow now, I think it is, with no
doubt children and all the rest of the things — (*gestures*) he
couldn't imagine me providing him with. (*Pause.*) Actually, I
did almost manage a child, but it miscarried. He blamed me for
that — my fecklessness — because we'd been to a party and I
drank a mite too much and slipped and fell down the stairs. He
rather hated me — (*Pause.*) So after I'd set him free I took a
plunge, and went off to Canada, where I just managed to keep
my head above water doing lady-like little jobs and being
glamorous and English — all the right things to be if one
wanted one of those ghastly Canadian men as a lover, you
know, balding and fattening, but no good for husbands,
because they were already. Until Teddy came along. I was
working as a part-time receptionist sort of person who did
a little piano playing and drinking in the hotel and he was the
first eligible male I've infatuated. Except there is just this little
thing wrong with him, I don't know what, but he doesn't have
sex, I don't believe he ever has. But apart from that and already
beginning to deafen he was quite dynamic and infatuated. There.
Now do you understand, Evie?

EVE. I suppose I might, oh I wouldn't approve but I might understand
if it were some — some man you'd — you'd — but Oliver Treefe!
Can't you see what he is?

MOLLY. What is he, darling? Other than peculiar in the head?

EVE. Well, for one thing he's — he's twenty years younger than
you.

MOLLY. Is that worse than being almost thirty years older?

EVE. But he's — he's completely uneducated. He's not even particularly nice to look at. Even I can see that. He's a common, loutish —

MOLLY. Stop it, Eve. Please. The truth is, Ollie and I —

EVE. Ollie and you! Ollie and you! No, I can't stop it, I jolly well think it's disgusting. Disgusting!

MOLLY (*in a sudden scream*). We're all disgusting!

*There is a pause.*

EVE (*gets up*). Well *I'm* not, Molly Treadley. No, *I'm* not!

OLIVER *enters through the conservatory. He is wearing a chauffeur's uniform, carrying a cap and gauntlets.*

OLIVER. Oh, excuse me, Miss, I've been honking for you outside.

MOLLY. Honking for me?

EVE *exits, left.*

OLIVER. She in one of her bad moods?

MOLLY. A touch edgy, perhaps. (*Little pause.*) Look darling, I'm sorry, but I'd better not come this afternoon, after all.

OLIVER. Why not?

MOLLY. Why don't you give your Dad that ride you've been promising him. He's scarcely seen you this last ten days.

OLIVER. He's working.

MOLLY. Well darling, anything you want to do — do. (*Smiles at him.*)

OLIVER. I want to go out with you. You promised me, Moll. To make up for all that hanging about outside Gracey's this morning.

MOLLY. I know darling, I'm sorry, but really I can't.

OLIVER. It *is* because of her, isn't it?

MOLLY. I suppose so. Because of her and him and you and me — it's all very complicated and I'm not up to explaining it and you wouldn't like it if I did, darling, but what it comes down to is that it would make everything worse if we skipped off right now.

OLIVER. It's not fair. I've been sitting out there, honking and

waiting and honking and waiting and I've changed the oil even,
and now you tell me you can't come out and won't tell me
why, but it's because of her and him — I know it is.

MOLLY. Oliver!

OLIVER *makes to say something else.*

MOLLY. No, don't say another word Ollie. Not now. Just go.
For your sake, darling.

OLIVER (*looks at her, turns, makes as if to exit through the
conservatory, stops*). It's true what they say, isn't it? That you
hooked him for his money and car and that. That's what
Sprinkley said from the beginning, the first time he saw you,
and my Dad's said something about you and him, he thinks
it's wrong, and Bob Howells making jokes in the pub, if he
pays you for every go or how many times a week you have to
let him do it, they were all laughing at his jokes in the pub
about him and you. All of them. That's what I have to sit and
listen to.

MOLLY (*goes to* OLIVER).Who is Bob Howells, darling?

OLIVER. He's Sprinkley's cousin, he —

MOLLY *slaps* OLIVER *across the face.*
OLIVER *stands for a moment, then runs over to the sofa, falls
onto it.*

MOLLY (*looks at him, goes over to him*). If you ever — ever —
talk to me like that again, it's back to Bob Howells and
Sprinkley's for you, my boy.

OLIVER. You wouldn't. (*In a whisper.*)

MOLLY. Yes, I would, my lad. You can add some jokes of your
own and lead the laughter, but you'll never see me again,
except from a great distance.

*There is a pause.* OLIVER *sits upright, staring at* MOLLY.

MOLLY. Oh Oliver, why do you get like this?

OLIVER. But I love you, I love you.

MOLLY. That's all right darling. You may love me. I want you to.

OLIVER. But I can't stand it when I'm not with you, when you're
in here talking to her, or go into his room to talk to him, and I
don't know what's going on, but I think of you and him
touching you and I don't know, what am I to do, Moll. You
see, before it was like — it was like I was stuck somewhere

underground and — and you took me out — and now I want to
be out all the time, but when you're not there it's like being
stuck back down again. (*Little pause.*) Last night you said I
was your husband even. But I'm not, am I? He is, isn't he? He
has you most.

MOLLY. But you have far more of me, especially now. He
doesn't kiss me where you kiss me, he doesn't hold me as you
hold me — we mustn't grudge him anything, Ollie. Not
anything. (*Little pause.*) Darling.

OLIVER (*looks at her*). I'm sorry for what I said. I didn't mean
it.

MOLLY. I know. (*Puts her arms around him.*) Oh my Ollie.

OLIVER. You still love me then, don't you?

MOLLY. Of course I do.

OLIVER. You won't ever send me away, will you?

MOLLY. When Rosie Hitchins from Guildford comes to claim you
back.

OLIVER. Never!

MOLLY. Well, not if I can help it.

OLIVER. Then I've got you, then, haven't I? (*Jubilant.*) Got you!

*They embrace. MOLLY kisses him tenderly, as if he were a
child. She wipes his cheeks with her fingers, then kisses him
again. The kiss becomes passionate. OLIVER puts his hands on
MOLLY's breasts, sighs.*
*MOLLY responds.*

OLIVER. Please Moll. Come out.

MOLLY (*steps away*). You're quite impossible, Oliver Treefe.
(*Laughs.*)

OLIVER. You will, won't you?

MOLLY (*hesitates*). Oh why not — yes — let's —

*There is a knock on the door, left. MOLLY looks at the door.
Another knock.*

MOLLY. Come in

EVE (*enters*). Excuse me. I wasn't sure whether you'd gone.

MOLLY. Oh, that's all right, darling. We're just off.

EVE. I wondered if I could have a few words with you.

MOLLY. Of course. Oliver, wait in the car, would you. I won't be a minute.

OLIVER *glances suspiciously at* EVE, *exits.*

EVE. I think it would be better if I left as soon as possible. So I'd be grateful if you got back by five. I'd like to catch the six o'clock train.

MOLLY. Would you like Oliver to drive you to the station?

EVE. No thank you. I'll call for a taxi, if I may.

MOLLY. Where are you going?

EVE. To Gosport.

MOLLY. I didn't know you had anyone in Gosport.

EVE. A niece.

MOLLY. And does she have children?

EVE. Yes.

MOLLY. You'll be able to help her with them, I suppose.

EVE. They're quite grown up.

MOLLY. Those are the ones that really need your help. (*Smiles.*)

EVE. If Teddy wakes I shan't say anything, I'd rather you explained.

MOLLY. He'll miss you dreadfully. So will I, of course.

EVE. I'll pack now. (*Goes towards the door, left.*)

MOLLY (*hesitates, then*). Evie.

EVE *stops, turns.*

MOLLY. Evie, please don't go! (*Runs across to her, embraces her.*) I need you so. I do.

EVE *stands stiffly for a moment, then turns, embraces* MOLLY.

EVE. Oh Moll!

MOLLY. You won't leave me, Evie. Will you?

EVE (*after a moment*). No Moll. Not if you really need me.

MOLLY. Oh thank you darling. Thank you. Thank you.

*There is a sudden thumping from above. There is a pause. There is a honk from off, right.*

TEDDY (*off, above*). Hey  Molly, Eve — hey!

>    MOLLY *looks at* EVE *appealingly.*

EVE. You'd better go. But I can't tell lies for you, Molly Treadley. I can't do that.

MOLLY. No, darling. I know.

>    *Goes out through conservatory.*
>    EVE *watches her go through conservatory, stands for a moment. Puts her hand to her forehead.*
>    TEDDY *enters, left. He is wearing dressing-gown, slippers, but is without a hearing-aid.*

EVE (*turning*). Teddy — You shouldn't be up.

TEDDY. Where's Moll?

EVE (*slowly and loudly*). She's gone out.

>    *Sound of the car screeching down the drive.*

TEDDY. She went out this morning — where's she gone to this time?

EVE (*hesitates*). Oh, just for a drive.

TEDDY. What?

EVE. To get your drops. Teddy, you mustn't stay down here — (*Goes over to him.*)

TEDDY. What? (*Irritably, pulling his arm away.*) Did she forget them this morning, then?

EVE. They had to make up a fresh batch — it's too cold for you down here, Teddy.

TEDDY. Not going back to bed with a stuffed nose — like being in a damned prison. (*Goes over, pours himself a Scotch, slops the drink, pays no attention, takes a gulp.*) Can't taste the taste, only the heat. (*Sits down.*) Go in the car?

EVE. Yes. (*Goes back, sits down.*)

TEDDY (*after a pause*). Saw them coming around the side of the house the other afternoon. Looked out of my window and there they were, around my side of the house, right beneath me. Like a pair of ghosts. (*Attempts to sniff.*) Don't worry, not delirious, Evie. Like ghosts because I couldn't hear them. Couldn't have smelt them either, come to that. Lost my hearing, now I lost my smelling, what goes next, eh? (*Laughs.*)

She was laughing. He had his mouth open. Maybe shouting a joke or something. Anyway, his mouth was open.

EVE. I think he has adenoids.

TEDDY. Great sense of humour?

EVE. No, adenoids.

TEDDY. Knocked on my window, but they didn't hear. Went right on round. A moment later they were back again, on the other side, gravel showering every which way. Too damned fast. (*Pause.*) Too damned fast. God knows what he gets up to when I can't see him. (*Pause, sniffs.*) Why didn't you tell her yesterday I was running out, you could see I was, couldn't you?

EVE. I'm sorry.

TEDDY. What you knitting there, a coloured ladder?

EVE. A scarf.

TEDDY. What?

EVE (*explosively*). A *scarf!* It's going to be a scarf.

TEDDY. Like having him around the house all the time?

EVE. Who?

TEDDY. What's he like?

EVE. Oh, I expect he's a normal boy.

TEDDY. What?

EVE. A normal boy.

TEDDY (*after a pause*). Hey Evie — (*pause*) last night — (*sniffs*) you tuck me up in bed? Or was it a dream?

EVE. I made your bed comfortable for you. The covers had slipped.

TEDDY. Oh. (*Little pause, then vaguely.*) What? (*Attempts to blow his nose.*) Damn! Damn! (*Sits, sunken in misery.*)

EVE (*looks at* TEDDY, *goes on with her knitting, looks at* TEDDY, *then suddenly*). Get rid of him, Teddy!

TEDDY (*looks at her. Pause*). What?

EVE *gets up, goes over to him, takes out the bottle of drops, hands it to* TEDDY.

EVE. I can't bear to see you suffering like this.

TEDDY. That's all right, Evie, anyone can make a mistake.
(*Takes the bottle, administers the drops, two to each nostril.*)

EVE *goes back, sits down.*

TEDDY. Tell me something, Evie — that scarf. Is it for me?

EVE. Yes.

TEDDY. Thank you Evie.

*There is a pause.* TEDDY *sits staring ahead.* EVE *goes on with her knitting.*

TEDDY. What? (*Dimly.*)

*Lights.*


## Scene Two

*A couple of hours later.* TEDDY *is sitting, staring ahead, as before.*
EVE *is knitting.*
TEDDY *gets up, goes with his glass over to the cocktail cabinet, pours himself another large Scotch.*
EVE *looks up towards him then goes on with her knitting.*
MOLLY *enters through the conservatory, followed by* OLIVER.

MOLLY (*stops, stares at* TEDDY, *looks at* EVE). Darling, should you be up, Gracey said a few more days in bed —

TEDDY. Got tired of being stuck up there in bed — thought I'd come down, I'm fine — hello there boy, how are you?

OLIVER. Sir.

TEDDY. What?

OLIVER. All right, thank you, sir.

TEDDY. What about a drink? Moll? (*Dashes some gin into a glass, hands it her.*)

MOLLY. But darling —

TEDDY. Where you been?

MOLLY. Oh, just out for a little drive —

TEDDY. What?

MOLLY. For a little drive.

TEDDY. Get my drops?

MOLLY. No, I got you a fresh bottle this morning —

TEDDY. Don't need them anyway, Evie had a bottle all the time — nice drive?

MOLLY. Except for a horrid little scene on the way back.

TEDDY. What?

MOLLY. A horrid little scene.

TEDDY. You and him?

MOLLY. No darling, two louts shooting in the field past the bridge. I made Oliver stop the car and when we went over there was a rabbit, they'd only wounded it and tied its legs, can you believe? and a beastly little dog —

OLIVER. A terrier.

TEDDY. What?

OLIVER. A terrier, sir.

TEDDY. No good boy, yours is the voice I'll never catch.

MOLLY. Anyway, they just stood there while Oliver had to kill it with a stick.

TEDDY. Killed the dog with a stick.

MOLLY. No, a rabbit, darling —

TEDDY. Rabbit, eh? Bet she didn't like that, eh boy?

OLIVER. No sir.

TEDDY. Doesn't like animals being hurt, do you Moll? Ever told you about the seals at Nanaimo, she wrote a song about it, got done across Nova Scotia because Bob Hoskins was a friend of mine, I asked him to do it for her. A good friend. (*Laughs.*) Eh Moll? But she'd never ever been to Nanaimo, eh Moll, but somebody told her about the seals and she made up a song out of her head, and that's how it got heard right across Nova Scotia. Nanaimo's in British Columbia, four thousand miles away — What do you think of that, eh Ollie — these ladies, seals, rabbits, songs — all the same to them, hey boy? Out in Nova Scotia we only shoot rabbits when we can't find any Catholics. We like to shoot Catholics. (*Laughs.*) Ever told you about that Moll? When some damned fool out hunting saw the bushes move, fired into them, wounded another damned fool hunting. Nova Scotia paper headlined the story, 'Father of

Nine Shot. Mistaken for rabbit.' Hey. Nine kids, that's how
we knew he was a Catholic. (*Laughs*.) Wish we'd had you
around, boy, to beat him to death with a stick.

MOLLY *has lit a cigarette.*

Hey girl, come over here. Come on.

MOLLY *looks at him.*

Come on, girl. Here, I say.

MOLLY *goes over to* TEDDY.

How many's it been, eh? How many seen her smoke,
boy? Two hundred, three hundred, since I was laid up — say
five, let you off with five, Molly, eh — one — two — three —
four — five — (*Smacking at her bottom.*) There, letting you off
lightly, eh girl.

OLIVER's *face is set.*

MOLLY (*seeing* OLIVER's *face*). Evie, is there some tea for Oliver.

EVE (*gets up*). Come with me, Oliver. (*Goes out, back.*)

TEDDY. Hey boy, something I've been meaning to ask you —
that hedge you started, remember seeing you at it on my way
to the ditch I fell into — how's it going, got it level?

OLIVER. Well, I've been doing a lot of driving. Haven't had a
chance to get back to it yet.

TEDDY. Don't know what you're saying, boy, but I can see from
your face it's an excuse, where's Mr Goldberg's Alvis, put it
away?

OLIVER. Sir.

TEDDY. Where?

OLIVER. In the garage, sir.

TEDDY. Give me the keys, boy.

MOLLY. Darling, I did say Oliver could give his Dad a run later
this evening —

TEDDY. The keys. (*Holds out his hand.*)

OLIVER *takes the keys out of his pocket, glaring at* TEDDY.

TEDDY. That's the boy. Now why don't you go trim the hedge
until the sun sets — eh? (*Gives him a friendly cuff on the
shoulder.*)

MOLLY. But he hasn't had tea —

TEDDY. What? (*Turns around, gives her a malevolent stare.*)

MOLLY. He hasn't — (*Stops.*)

TEDDY. Well? (*Looks at* OLIVER.)

OLIVER *turns, blunders into the conservatory.*

Hey, just a minute —

OLIVER *picking up shears.*

There's another thing, don't need you around the house at night any more, you can go back to your Daddy now, best if you move out this evening, eh?

OLIVER *stands staring at* TEDDY, *then turns, goes off.*

(*Turns.*) Tell you the truth, Moll, don't like him. Foxy little face. Have you noticed his foxy little face?

MOLLY. No.

TEDDY. Just what you said when we took him on — furtive, pasty, crooked —

EVE (*appears at the back*). Oliver's tea is ready.

*There is a pause.*

TEDDY. Oh, hey Eve, that boy, he's not going to be around at night — just told him to go home to his Daddy.

EVE. Oh.

TEDDY. Come and have one of your dry-as-dust sherries, Evie. (*Goes to the cocktail cabinet.*) Things are getting back to rights here, going to get Moll to play us one of her tunes in a minute —

EVE. That'll be nice — (*Advancing.*)

MOLLY (*to* EVE). Would you please leave us. (*Low.*)

TEDDY. What?

EVE *goes towards door, left.*

Hey, Evie, where are you going?

EVE *exits.*

What's the matter with her?

*There is a pause.*

TEDDY. Hey Moll? Hey?

*They stare at each other.*

MOLLY. Why did you do that?

TEDDY. What?

MOLLY. I've never known you humiliate a child before.

TEDDY. What?

MOLLY. Never known you humiliate a child before. (*Loudly, fiercely.*)

TEDDY. Oh. (*Pause.*) Never had one to humiliate before. (*Laughs, then turns, goes and sits down.*)

MOLLY (*watches him, then runs to him*). Oh Teddy — what is it, what is it?

TEDDY *looks at her, turns his head away, mutters something.*

MOLLY (*kneels, takes his hand*). You're still not well, you shouldn't be up, darling — please come to bed —

TEDDY. What? What? What? (*Pause.*) Faces are different when they shout at the deaf. Ever thought of that, what I have to see in your faces — swelling, with effort and — contempt. And a little trickle of noise comes out I have to make sense of. Most often I get it wrong. I can see that in your faces too. Bellowing, contempt and boredom. That's all I see on your faces, all there is to see, isn't anything else, I see what's there. Everything. All I have of my own is — is the smell of fish. Fish. Know what's ahead of me — think I don't. I've seen old men. Hate this country of yours. Small and damp like a prison. Shambling, shambling about — cocktail cabinet to arm-chair, arm-chair to cocktail cabinet, pyjamas bagging out around the arse, crutch stained with pee dribble, cocktail cabinet to lavatory to arm-chair, to — to — Eve tucking me in, like I was a kid — teeth out in a glass — and all the time your faces swelling and bellowing, boredom and contempt, hate it, hate it, hate you all — what you've done to me — why didn't you leave me alone, never needed you, don't need you, natter, natter, natter — (*Sits staring ahead.*) Brought me here to die. Know you. Know what you are. (*Sits staring ahead, shrunken and malevolent.*)

MOLLY. Omigod!

TEDDY. What? (*Laughs.*) Ha! Look — there he is — back — look

at him — little — (*Gets up, goes over to the conservatory.*)
Get up!

OLIVER *rises. He is holding the shears.*

Hah! You're fired boy! Fired! Mine. Belongs to me. Mr
Goldberg's Alvis too — do what I like with her — everything —
you're fired, fired — (*Spits into* OLIVER'*s face, laughs, turns,
goes to chair, sits down with his back to* OLIVER, *looks at*
MOLLY *laughs.*)

OLIVER *stumbles towards* TEDDY.

MOLLY. Don't, don't, omigod — don't — don't —

OLIVER *thrusts the shears into* TEDDY'*s neck, again and again.*
TEDDY *lurches back, blood spouting.*

MOLLY. Omigod — omigod — (*Goes to* TEDDY.)

OLIVER. Didn't mean it, didn't mean it, Miss — he made me —
made me — what'll I do — (*pause*) Miss!

OLIVER *drops the shears, turns, runs out through
conservatory.*

MOLLY (*Looks at* TEDDY). Poor Teddy. Poor old man. (*Pause.*)
Omigod! Omigod! (*Goes to him, puts her arms around him.*)

Eve! Eeee-eeve! Eee-ve!

*After a pause,* EVE *enters.*

MOLLY. Eee-eeve! (*Sees her.*) He's alive, he's still alive; get
help you fool! Get help!

*Lights.*

## Scene Three

*About an hour later.* TEDDY'*s body has been removed.*
GREAVES *and a PC are standing, whispering.*

EVE (*enters, left*). It's just as I said. She's asleep. Dr Gracey gave
her a very strong sedative. There's not the slightest chance
you'll be able to see her until the morning.

GREAVES. Then perhaps you'll answer a few questions, Miss Mace.

EVE. I'm afraid I can't. I must get back to Mrs Treadley.

GREAVES. But if she's asleep?

EVE. Dr Gracey asked me to sit by her. She was in a state of shock. And if she wakes —

GREAVES. Miss Mace, I don't quite understand your position in the household.

EVE. I'm — the companion-housekeeper.

GREAVES. I see. And are you the only staff?

EVE. Well, there's a boy from the village, to help with the gardening and drive the car from time to time.

GREAVES. And was he here when the accident happened?

EVE. No. He'd gone home.

GREAVES. So there was just you, and Mr and Mrs Treadley?

EVE. Yes.

GREAVES. And did you see the accident?

EVE. No. I was in the kitchen.

GREAVES. So Mr and Mrs Treadley were alone in here?

EVE. Yes. Now I really must —

GREAVES. Where are the shears?

EVE. The shears?

GREAVES. Dr Gracey said the wound had been caused by gardening shears.

EVE. Oh. Oh yes — they're in there. On the second shelf under the potato sacking.

GREAVES. Why?

EVE. Because that's where they belong.

GREAVES. But they must have been covered in blood.

EVE. Of course they were. I washed it off.

GREAVES. But that was important evidence.

EVE. Evidence of what? It was an accident. Now I really must go to Mrs Treadley — you can come back tomorrow.

MOLLY (*enters, in night-dress and dressing-gown*). Ee-eeve — (*Stops.*) Oh, who are you?

EVE (*crosses to her*). Molly — you shouldn't be up, you must get back to bed.

MOLLY. Who are they?

GREAVES. Police, Mrs Treadley, I wonder if we could —

EVE. They were just leaving. Now come along —

MOLLY. The police. Oh I'm so glad you've come, I want to make a complaint.

EVE. Molly —

MOLLY. No, darling, I'm going to. About those ambulance men. They were rough — far too rough — I told them to be careful, but one of them pushed me away, yes, actually *pushed* me, didn't he Evie, when I was trying to help them lift him — and then they said he was dead but he wasn't, not until they came and heaved him about and wouldn't let me — he was alive, wasn't he Evie. I know because I held him you see, and I could feel something pumping under his blood, quite strongly, there was life in him and then they came — it must have been them, something they did — and they were very rude too, weren't they, Evie, do you know they refused to let me ride to the hospital with him, my own husband and they refused — so I want to report them, will you report them for me?

GREAVES. I shall certainly question them, Mrs Treadley.

MOLLY. Will you? Oh thank you — thank you, you're very — would you like a drink?

GREAVES. No thank you, Mrs Treadley.

MOLLY. What about you, I'm sure you'd like one, wouldn't you?

GREAVES. We're not allowed to drink on duty, Mrs Treadley.

EVE. Now come my dear — back to bed —

MOLLY. No, no, just a minute, Evie, I'd like a — I can't sleep you know — it's no good — I've tried and tried — you're sure you're not allowed — will you excuse me if I just have a little, teeny weeny — (*Goes to drink.*)

EVE. You really mustn't drink — Dr Gracey gave you a sedative —

MOLLY. Well, it hasn't worked darling, has it, I mean here I am full of beans, God knows what he gave me, unless it was beans of course — (*laughs*) and wasn't he so incompetent, he really was, not that I want to get him into trouble, he's old and easily upset, all he could do was shake those dreadful wattles of his, he had no idea, no idea at all. I can't help thinking if we'd got a younger man Teddy might still be — someone who could stand up to those ambulance bullies and — but all poor Gracey could do was shake his wattles and try to get me to bed, oh — (*laughs*) I don't mean — of course not — (*stops*) but I don't want to get him into trouble. Certainly not. He was very good to Teddy's ears. (*There is a pause.*) Oh, I do feel — feel — drinking by myself — do excuse me, but it's been a bit of a — a bit of a —

GREAVES. Would you mind telling me how it happened, Mrs Treadley.

MOLLY. What?

EVE. You can't possibly ask her questions — you can see the state she's in. Now come, Molly, I insist —

MOLLY. Oh tush tush, Eve, tush, I'm perfectly all right, perfectly. And I want to — to help these men — now what was it you—?

GREAVES. How did it happen, Mrs Treadley?

MOLLY. What?

GREAVES. How was Mr Treadley killed?

EVE. Molly, don't —

MOLLY. But it was an accident. Surely you know — haven't you told them, Evie, it was nobody's fault — except those men who were rough and poor old Gracey, it just — just happened you see, didn't it, Evie?

GREAVES. But Miss Mace wasn't in the room at the time.

MOLLY. What? Oh — no, no, you weren't were you darling, she generally comes in later, to clean up our messes for us, don't you darling? (*Laughs.*)

GREAVES. You and Mr Treadley were alone.

MOLLY. What?

GREAVES. There was just you and Mr Treadley.

MOLLY. Oh. Yes. Yes, that's right. Me and Mr — Teddy. And the cocktail cabinet, of course, that's always there, to make a third.

EVE. Molly — (*goes to her*) don't talk now. Don't talk now.

MOLLY. What, why darling, there's nothing to be afraid of, is there?

GREAVES. No, Mrs Treadley.

MOLLY. You see, it was just an accident. They understand that. That's all there is to it. (*Turns on radio. There is music playing.*)

EVE. Now Molly you're going to come with me —

GREAVES (*goes to* EVE, *and very quietly*). Miss Mace! Mrs Treadley has offered to help us in our enquiries. If you persist in interrupting. I shall have to ask you to leave the room.

MOLLY. What? (*Looks at* EVE.)

GREAVES. You were telling us what happened, Mrs Treadley.

MOLLY. Well, it was — something ghastly happened, you see. He had an accident. I — I didn't really see it, my back must have been turned or I was looking away for a moment but — but then there he was. Spurting — spurting — do you see?

GREAVES. One moment he was alive, and the next he was dying?

MOLLY. Yes — well, he had these sudden changes of mood recently, didn't he Evie? (*Laughs.*)

GREAVES *looks at* MOLLY. *There is a pause.*

MOLLY. Just a minute — need to — another little — a truth drink so you'll know I — (*Laughs, going to pour herself another drink, unsteady on her feet.*)

EVE (*goes over*). No, Molly — no — (*Attempts to take the bottle from her.*)

(*There is a short, absurd wrestle.*)

MOLLY. Bugger off, bitch!

EVE *recoils.*

MOLLY. Sorry Evie — sorry. Forgive please. Pretty please with sugar on it. (*Laughs, pours, then to* GREAVES.) That's all I have to say —

EVE (*to* GREAVES). This is disgraceful, disgraceful. I'm going to phone Dr Gracey and tell him —

GREAVES. That's your privilege, Miss.

MOLLY. What, she's got a pash on me, haven't you, Evie —

EVE *exits, left.*

MOLLY. Yes, she has, do you know about the pashes ladies have on ladies, ladies like her on ladies like me, are you married?

GREAVES. Yes.

MOLLY. Is she pretty, your wife?

GREAVES (*crosses to the radio, turns it off. Silence, then intimately.*) You were going to tell me the truth, Mrs Treadley.

MOLLY. What?

GREAVES. The truth.

MOLLY. What about?

GREAVES. Your husband's death. He was murdered, wasn't he?

MOLLY. Murdered? (*Pause. She yawns.*) I'm sorry — sorry — what?

GREAVES. Did you do it?

MOLLY. What?

GREAVES. You did, didn't you?

MOLLY. What — what do you do to people, when you — you catch them?

GREAVES. That's for the courts to decide.

MOLLY. But if they're children?

GREAVES. But there aren't any children, are there, Mrs Treadley?

MOLLY. Oh yes. Yes. We're all children in this house, all of us. That's what caused it, you see. But nobody meant — oh please believe — it wasn't mean't. He — he brought it on himself! He did! He did! An old man, come to the end, he wanted to die, he wanted to — full of hate — I couldn't bear his hate — and he knew — you see he knew — he was right, about his old man's smells, his deafness and the boredom, the boredom and the bellowing and the contempt and the pee-dribble and his pyjamas arsing — and — and —

GREAVES. And is that why you killed him, Mrs Treadley?

MOLLY. What?

GREAVES. Did you kill him?

MOLLY. I —

*Pause.*

EVE (*enters*). I've spoken to Dr Gracey. He's coming over —

MOLLY. It was her! She did it! She did it! (*Pause*.) No, no, sorry
Evie, sorry darling — it was me. Yes. I killed him. I killed him.
I took the things and I — I — (*Makes thrusting movements,
stops abruptly*.) And now you all hate me, don't you, like the
ambulance and Gracey and all — all hate me — well, here I am,
look at me you — you — (*runs to* PC) what do you see, an old
vamp, is that what you see, but you'd roger me, too, wouldn't
you, I could make you love — I'm still — look — look — (*Makes
to lift her night-dress to him*.)

EVE *strides across, grips* MOLLY *by the arm, pulls her away.*
MOLLY *collapses against* EVE.

MOLLY. Bed now, Evie, bed please. Bed darling — —

*Lights.*


**Scene Four**

*Some months later. Afternoon. The room fills with light, steadily,
to bright sunlight. There are dust sheets over the sofa, the chairs.
On the sofa,* MOLLY's *scarf, handbag. The door, left, is open.* EVE
*enters from the left, wearing a light raincoat. She goes to the
handbag, begins to go through it.*
MOLLY *appears at the door, back. She is also wearing a light
coat. She stands watching* EVE, *then comes across, takes the
handbag from her.*

MOLLY. Thank you, darling. I do wish people would stop
rummaging through it, it's been emptied and refilled by so
many different ladies recently, police ladies, prison ladies,
hospital ladies, (*takes out a cigarette*) it doesn't feel mine any
more. (*Lights cigarette*.) What were you looking for, darling?
The sleeping pills?

EVE. I couldn't remember whether we'd brought them.

MOLLY. Do we need them, though? Surely we don't mind being
awake on an August afternoon? (*Takes a bottle out of the
pocket*.) Do you want to look after them?

EVE. No, of course not, Moll.

MOLLY. Oh, you might as well, darling. I'm not going to try

again. For one thing, I don't seem to be very good at it, and I do hate the way they drag one back, with stomach pumps and sermons. Do take them, darling. There.

EVE (*takes them*). I'll make up a bed if you still want to lie down.

MOLLY. Lie down?

EVE. You said you had a headache.

MOLLY. Did I? Well then it's gone.

EVE. Oh. Oh good! Well, what about our walk then?

MOLLY. Our walk?

EVE. You were looking forward to a walk.

MOLLY. I think I'll leave it until tomorrow.

(*Pause.*)

To tell you the truth, darling, I'm a bit confused at finding everything so familiar.

EVE. It's my fault. I shouldn't have agreed to let you come back — at least so soon.

MOLLY. So soon? But I haven't been here for a long time. After such an eventful spring, and a summer wasted in — in institutions — I'd have hated to have missed the old haunts in their autumn colours. I long to see them.

EVE. You do want a walk then?

MOLLY. What do you want, Evie?

EVE (*intensely*). I want our old Moll back again.

MOLLY. Do you really? Our old judge found the old Moll a trifle too degenerate for his taste. Quite disgusting, in fact. Quite disgusting. Disgusting.

EVE. He had no right — no right to say those things. They had no right to make you go through that trial, not after — after the truth had come out. I shall never believe in British justice again.

MOLLY. Poor Eve! Still, think what we would have lost. The sight of old Treefe, for example, touching his forelock to thank everyone for all the trouble they were putting themselves to, to hang his son. Who's only just come of hangable age. (*Pause.*) Can I have a drink? No — no more drinks for me.

EVE. You must stop blaming yourself, Molly. You stood by him right to the bitter end.

MOLLY. Not quite, darling. His bitter end comes on Monday week, at six in the morning, isn't it? He's going to that without me. (*Pause.*) Looking across as if he believed I could just come out of my box and into his, and cuddle him through it. His peaky face, and the spot blooming on his nose. Do you think he'll expect me on Monday week, too, right to the very last, as a child expects his Mummy to come and take him away. (*Turns away.*) I'd have made a good mother, wouldn't I?

EVE. He did do it, Moll.

MOLLY. Of course he did. (*Pause, makes a violent gesture.*) So hang the little beggar! By the way, darling, I haven't thanked you properly for bringing him to book. Thank you. If it hadn't been for you —

EVE. I couldn't let you sacrifice yourself. I couldn't, Moll.

MOLLY. No. No. I don't suppose you could.

EVE. We have to do right by those we care about.

MOLLY. Yes. Yes we do. You love me Evie, don't you?

EVE. Yes.

MOLLY. Thank you.

EVE. Oh Moll — (*Gives a sudden shy smile.*)

MOLLY. It *is* a lovely afternoon, isn't it? Would you like a walk?

EVE. I'd love one.

MOLLY. Right. Off you go then.

   *They stare at each other.*

   Darling, we really must start doing our separate wants, or how shall we two live together? Please go darling. (*Pause.*) Please.

   EVE *exits through conservatory.*

MOLLY (*after a pause*). Pretty please (*pause*) with sugar on it.

*Lights.*

*Curtain.*

# MAN IN A SIDE-CAR

# Author's Note

I've forgotten every stage of writing *Man in a Side-Car* except its
initiating image: the photograph in a newspaper of a young, pretty
and already celebrated lady novelist, with her husband behind her
elbow and a baby (or a cat) at her feet; that, and a subsequent
report in probably the same newspaper that the marriage had
broken up amicably. I suppose there were the routine drafts on
drafts, but I don't recall even the usually memorable moment of
completion. There was some fuss, though, when the play was sent
out. Kenith Trodd, who had been involved in all my previous
plays, first as script editor, then as producer, had left the BBC,
probably in one of their periodic purges of talent, and no one
there was sufficiently taken by *Man in a Side-Car* to offer it,
except in a cursory way, to this or that director until Anne Scott,
who had worked with Kenith Trodd and myself, rescued it from
another producer's desk and brought it to the attention of James
MacTaggart. To Anne Scott, then, my double thanks.

Because, in retrospect, the most important fact about *Man in a
Side-Car* (for me, anyway) is that James MacTaggart directed it.
We'd already worked together, some years before, on a small play
of mine called *Pig in a Poke*, and got on sufficiently well to hope
that we would again, some day. With *Man in a Side-Car* we went
from getting on to friendship — we drank quite a few drinks
together; had one or two small quarrels; and laughed a great deal
— and professionally, had moved from clearly defined roles as
author and director to rather more than trusting collaborators. So
when I read through the play the other day to check it out for
publication, I was still quite unable to separate the text from my
(seven or so years later) vivid recollection of James's realization of
it. In fact, it now seems so inextricably his work as well as mine,
that in offering it up I feel that I am withholding rather more than
simply his half. But then Gerald Savory or someone like him
wiped the tape, of course. And now James is dead; and all I can do
is dedicate the lesser half to his memory, in gratitude and
continuing admiration.

MAN IN A SIDE-CAR was first broadcast by the BBC as Play for Today on 27 May 1971. The cast was as follows:

| | |
|---|---|
| EDITH | Gemma Jones |
| GERALD | James Laurenson |
| TOMMY | David Collings |
| MRS MERCHANT | Sheila Beckett |
| DAVID | Geoffrey Matthews |
| HELEN | Yvonne Gilan |
| DR SLOKUM | Walter Horsburgh |
| GILES | Jonathan Lawson |
| WAITRESS | Tessa Lander |
| MEN IN COFFEE BAR | Roger Minnis, Steve King, Colin Richmond, Paul Barton |
| GIRLS IN COFFEE BAR | Monica Wilding, Rosemary Turner |
| THREE MEN IN HOSPITAL | Len Sanders, Bert Simms, Ernest Jennings |
| TWO NURSES | Constance Reason, Iris Fry |
| WARD ORDERLY | Leonard Kingston |

*Directed by* James MacTaggart
*Producer* Graeme McDonald
*Script Editor* Ann Scott
*Designer* Stuart Walker

**1. Interior Edith's Study. Day.** *It is a sparsely furnished room, with one picture, mediaeval and devotional, on the wall. There is a desk beside a window. The window looks out onto a path which is, in fact, a narrow drive. The drive curves around a bend and then onto a country road. The desk is an old-fashioned school desk, with a sunken ink-well and a ridge for a pen. EDITH is writing into an exercise book at the desk. She uses a fountain pen that she dips into the ink-well. To her left is a pile of five exercise books, filled. Beside her, and behind her, past the window, is a bookshelf on which are arranged exercise books and novels. She is dressed in a long (as opposed to fashionably maxi) skirt, has hair swept down the side of her face, and in her cell-like room gives off a distinctly nun-like effect. She is in her early thirties. She is writing quickly and neatly onto the page, and at regular intervals is dipping her pen into the ink-well.*
EDITH's *voice over, as she writes:*

EDITH (*voice over*). Mathilda began to discover that she had many
    things against Simon, and consequently and quite consciously
    began to develop a proportional esteem for herself. For
    example, Simon had begun to take instruction with a view to
    conversion. He approached his studies — for that was what he
    had made of the matter — with an academic devotion that was
    as inelegant as it was thorough, and spoke of the impending
    moment at church as if he were about to be awarded a prize
    for an achievement, an advanced degree for example. Mathilda,
    who had gone over to Rome at the age of thirteen because she
    was in love with a girl, half Italian, half Irish, wholly beautiful
    and almost twelve, at her second boarding school, took her
    own Catholicism so much for granted that she could afford to
    be witty at its expense. Poor Simon was frequently shocked by
    her little jokes, and the resulting strain between them — a
    strain that confirmed Mathilda in her growing sense of
    independence — led to some strange failures in bed. These

failures were, of course, entirely Simon's. Mathilda, secretly enjoying them, marked them up as victories. Simon might well entitle himself to an adjoining pew, but his head would soon rest uneasily on the adjoining pillow.

EDITH *smiles as she writes the last few sentences.*
Cut to *her face, then as the smile stiffens*, cut to *the window beside her.*
GERALD, *in goggles, a flowing scarf, gauntlets, and a very distinctive and expensive-looking leather coat with enormous buttons, is staring in at her. He turns, walks away.*
EDITH *turns slowly, as if sensing him there, a second after he has disappeared, frowns slightly, then goes back to her writing.*

It turned out, in fact, that Simon, who in the early days of their relationship, had so amused himself by making fun of her own small aspirations, was unable to see the comedy of his own, larger ones. She came to the conclusion and not at all reluctantly that her husband was a fraud. She saw, with only enough pain to spicen the recognition into anticipation, that there was little prospect of their marriage lasting the course. She was too clever by half. Indeed, she was too happy by —

*Her voice is interrupted by the explosive sound of the motor-bicycle starting.*
EDITH's *shoulders jump, her pen waits above the paper as the motor-bike roars off.*

*Her voice over, writing.*

— by more than half.


2. Exterior. The path from the cottage. Day. GERALD *on his motor-bicycle, which has an old-fashioned side-car. It roars around the bend, and out of sight, and as it does so:*
MRS MERCHANT *wheeling a pram*, comes into shot. *She is staring after the motor-bike.*


3. Interior. Edith's Study. Day. EDITH *is now nearly at the bottom of the page. She writes:*

EDITH (*voice over*). She knew the day would come when she would say to her child-bridegroom — 'If you were half a man, you would go.' And she equally knew that, being half

a man, he would. So many divisions could be made to make a
very simple sum.

*She turns the page, shot of the blank page, her pen hovers, then
writes:*

But Simon, if he was not capable of success, was finding the
consolations of malice. He —

EDITH *smiles, screws the top back on her pen, puts it in the
ledge, closes the ink-well, blots the page, closes the exercise
book, then goes out of the study.*
Follow her *as she enters:*


**4. Interior. Gerald's Study. Day.** EDITH *enters* GERALD's
*study. There is a desk, a typewriter, a camp-bed, unmade, books,
papers, etc, scattered everywhere.*
*There is an ash-tray full of cigarette ends, a pair of spectacles, a
pipe half-smoked, an open box of cheroots, and beside the
typewriter various sheets of papers, some with fragments of
typing on them. There is a sheet in the typewriter.*
EDITH *makes a face, goes to the window, opens it, then goes out.
Comes back in, looks down at the page, reads a few lines, goes out
again, and* follow her *to the kitchen.*


**5. Interior. The kitchen. Day.** *First* come in on MRS MERCHANT's
*face, smiling, then* cut back to EDITH, *smiling, and she blocks the
view for a second, then turns around, having lifted GILES out of
his highchair, and is now cuddling him.*
GILES, *who is about nine months old, not seen until that instant.*


**6. Exterior. A Railway Station.** *The motor-bike.* GERALD
*appears with* TOMMY.
TOMMY *is wearing a slightly ludicrous, very long, tatty overcoat.
He is carrying an equally tatty overnight bag.*
*They come to the motor-bike;* GERALD *fishes into the side-car,
hands* TOMMY *a pair of goggles and crash helmet, they get in
and on respectively.*


**7. Exterior. Country Roads.** GERALD *is driving as:*
Credits.

Follow them through country roads, and on them in different shots, some of GERALD in close-up. Some of TOMMY, some from in front, some from behind, fading on the two of them in shot advancing as credits fade.


**8. Interior. The kitchen. Day.** EDITH *is holding the bottle for* GILES, *while also drinking a cup of tea.* MRS MERCHANT *is eating a proper lunch, as the noise of the motor-bike outside.* EDITH *glances up, then goes on feeding* GILES.
*Sound of voices and* TOMMY's *laughter outside the back door, then* GERALD *and* TOMMY *enter, still in goggles and helmets.*

TOMMY. Well, hello then.

> *He comes around, gives* EDITH *a kiss, bends down, clucks at* GILES.

> GERALD, *meanwhile is taking off his gear, smiling at* EDITH. GILES *begins to cry.*

EDITH. Your goggles.

TOMMY. Oh.

> *He takes his goggles off.*

GERALD. No, it's because you've taken the bottle away.

> EDITH *glances at him, puts the bottle down on the table.*

TOMMY (*to* GILES, *who is still crying*). What is it, Giles, what's the matter, don't you recognise me then, you only saw me yesterday.

EDITH. Yes, but he cried then, too.

> *She picks* GILES *up, looks at* MRS MERCHANT, *who gets up; they go out together.*

TOMMY. It was wind yesterday.

GERALD. Don't worry, I don't believe they *know*.

> TOMMY *sits down, cutting himself some bread.*

TOMMY. He never cries at me, normally.

> *He shakes his head, worried.*

GERALD. For Christ's sake — he's not going to throw you out. Well?

TOMMY. What? Oh, well like I said, they're interested Gerald,

certainly, the only thing that's holding them back, likely, is
they're waiting to see the second act complete. (*He eats
ravenously*.) That's all.

GERALD. Did they have any constructive suggestions?

EDITH *comes back into the room.*

TOMMY. I hope you don't mind, Edie — (*Holding up the bread.*)

EDITH. Please.

*Neutrally, she begins to clear up.*

(*To* GERALD.) Do you want anything?

GERALD. Just some sense.

TOMMY. Well — well, no, well he liked it, Gerrie. (*To* EDITH.)
That's Humphrey Jones, Edie, I worked with in Cardiff I
mentioned to you who's got hold of that new theatre club in
Chiswick, he's a smart bastard — no, all he said (*back to*
GERALD) was he liked its *tone* and that when we got it
worked through to the curtain to let him be the first to refuse.

GERALD *laughs.*

You know what I mean, first *refusal* he wants, it's the next
thing to an option. Edie, could I have one of those yogurts if
you've got one?

*He turns around in a practised way, opening the fridge, takes
out a yogurt.*

EDITH. But he's not taking an option?

TOMMY. Well I couldn't insist on it could I as — I'm a friend, see.

EDITH (*ironically*). Well, that's all right then.

GERALD. What does that mean?

TOMMY *is spooning down the yogurt at great speed.*

EDITH. The director of a new theatre's likely to find himself
with a lot of new friends as well. Or would he make it a
principle to buy options on the work of strangers only?

GERALD. Where's Giles?

EDITH. Having his nappy changed.

GERALD. Mrs Merchant doing it?

EDITH (*pretends to think*). Unless he's doing it himself.

TOMMY. But what really matters is that I could see he was
excited by it, he wouldn't pretend over that, you know —

*He is watching* GERALD, *who gets up, picks up the over-
night bag, and goes out.*

(*To* EDITH.) He's not a complete bastard.

EDITH. Merely a clever one.

*She looks at* TOMMY *who is smiling slightly shiftily. There is
a pause.*

TOMMY. Um, I was wondering, could you spare — ?

EDITH. Please.

TOMMY *turns around, opens the fridge, takes out another
yogurt.*

What is it about?

TOMMY. What? Our play? Hasn't Gerrie told you?

EDITH. No. Nor have you.

TOMMY. Well, you never asked before. (*Laughs.*) I mean, I
assumed . . .

*He opens the yogurt, begins eating.*

EDITH. Well?

TOMMY. Well. (*Laughs.*) It sounds very modish in outline, you
know. (*Pause.*) Well . . . (*He laughs again.*)

EDITH. I like quite a few of the current modes.

TOMMY. Well, in fact it's about these four queers who ran a
butcher's shop. Two of them draggy queens, see, and two of
them butch —

EDITH (*poker-faced*). Butch Butchers.

TOMMY (*laughs desperately*). That's one we did cut out, no,
you see, it's the sort of sexual and emotional permutations and
combinations — well, it's all in the dialogue and the tone, see,
there's no plot as such, but if it's played in the right style it
could be something special. (*Little pause.*) A cross between
Racine and Orton. (*Little pause.*) Not just another commercial
camp-up, Edie.

EDITH. Ah. An uncommercial camp-up?

TOMMY. Oh, Edie! (*Little pause.*) Why are you being so
depressing then?

EDITH. Self-protection.

TOMMY. For Gerald you mean?

EDITH. Actually, I meant for myself.

TOMMY. I'm sure it'll come off.

EDITH. Yes. Almost at once. If it gets on.

TOMMY. Well, I'm very hopeful.

EDITH (*stares at him unwinkingly*). Good.

TOMMY (*finishes his yogurt*). I must say, it's nice to be back. I've missed you all.

EDITH. You've only been away for the night.

TOMMY. Yes, well, it feels like a couple of weeks.

EDITH. Perhaps that's because it was going to be. A couple of weeks. We all adjusted to that prospect.

TOMMY. Oh? You didn't expect me back today then?

EDITH. No. Not actually.

TOMMY. But Gerald phoned last night — he left a message with Stewart to come back as soon as they'd read it at the theatre.

EDITH. Ah. In that case it must have been an emergency. (*She gets up.*)

TOMMY. Well, how's the novel going?

EDITH. I've done two days work, since you last asked.

TOMMY. Oh, good.

   As EDITH *goes out.*

   Humphrey Jones said he loved your last, to tell you especially.

EDITH (*reappears, smiles*). Oh, good. (*She waits.*)


TOMMY. Yes, he loved it. (*Rather feebly.*)

EDITH. Good.

   *She goes out, and as she does so* TOMMY *wheels round to the fridge.*


**9. Interior. Gerald's Study. Day.** *He is sitting before the*

*typewriter, spectacles on, staring down at the manuscript.*
*The over-night bag is at his feet.*
EDITH *stands at the door.* GERALD, *pointedly, doesn't look up.*

EDITH. Can I speak?

GERALD (*still looking down*). You can.

EDITH. You summoned him back, then?

GERALD (*still looking down*). Yes.

EDITH. Why?

GERALD. I was getting bored.

EDITH. We did agree that we might try two weeks without him.

GERALD. Not quite. *You* said *you* could do without him. You
asked me whether I could understand your feelings. I said I
did. There was thus agreement about your feelings. None at all
about policy.

EDITH. David and Helen are coming to dinner tonight. Or had
you forgotten?

GERALD. On the contrary. I specifically mentioned it to
Tommy, by way of an inducement.

*As* TOMMY *appears behind* EDITH.

Edith was wondering whether you could really face David and
Helen tonight. I've been reassuring her.

TOMMY. No, I'm looking forward to it, who are they exactly?

GERALD. Her publishers. Manic depressers. But never mind —
you'll have lots to eat. Edie'll make sure of that. And lots to
drink. I'll make sure of that.

TOMMY (*grins*). Ahh, just what I need.

*Close up of* TOMMY's *face, beaming, seen from* EDITH's
point of view, *then she goes out.*


**10. Interior. Edith's Study. Day.** EDITH *is at her desk, writing.*
*See her from side, including a shot of the window.*


**11. Exterior. Garden.** EDITH's point of view, *from her study
window:*
MRS MERCHANT *is sitting in a deck chair, reading.*

**12. Interior. Edith's Study. Day.** *Throughout this, there's also the sound of a distant typewriter.*

EDITH (*writes, as voice over*). He was turning into a way of life with a strong moral point of view. Mathilda would have found this boring if she hadn't known, indeed cherished the knowledge that this was merely a stage towards something even less consequential. During his time with her he had abandoned everything in turn. He had abandoned his art, for which he had no talent; and then his religion, for which he had had no feeling, and then his love making for which he had had no desire. Shortly he would abandon failure, for which he had no stoicism, in favour of a more sensational posture.

*There is the sound, dim, of* GILES, *crying.*
EDITH *frowns, makes to write another sentence, then turns to the window, raps on it, points.*

**13. Exterior. Garden.** MRS MERCHANT, EDITH's point of view, *gets up, goes off screen.*

**14. Interior. Edith's Study. Day.** EDITH *turns back to her writing.* Fade out.
In on EDITH *writing again.*

**15. Exterior. Garden.** MRS MERCHANT, EDITH's point of view, *playing with* GILES, *in his pram.*

**16. Interior. Edith's Study. Day.**

EDITH (*voice over*). Mathilda felt that although . . .

*The typewriter stops.*

. . . she had little time for Simon at the moment, she would manage to find some for his next phase. He promised, for a change, to be interesting. Also it would enable her to practise her newly acquired mercilessness, as well as to test her . . .

*All this over, as sudden shouts of laughter from* TOMMY *and* GERALD. *She frowns, goes on writing, as the shouts continue . . .*

**17. Interior. Gerald's Study. Day.** GERALD *and* TOMMY *are crouched on the floor playing tiddly-winks, with pennies and sixpences. Beside each is a pile of half-crowns.*
TOMMY *is playing.*
Come on them both from the door, then cut to:
TOMMY'*s face. Frowning in concentration as he is about to wink a tiddly into the pot. He does so, and then another one, very practised, extracts two half-crowns from* GERALD'*s pile, then moves back to do one a long way away, then shakes his head, moves forward to one closer in.*

GERALD. You're gutless, Tommy.

    TOMMY *pays no attention as he takes aim, very serious.*

    For a quid?

TOMMY (*looks up*). Let's see it.

    GERALD *reaches into his pocket, takes out a pound, puts it between* TOMMY *and the cup.*

    And if I miss?

GERALD. Oh, I never take anything from you, do I?

TOMMY. Done and done, boyo.

    *He crouches down, concentrating very hard.*
    *There is a sudden stillness, then he winks the tiddly in. He lets out a shout, reaches for the pound note.*
    GERALD *puts his foot down on the pound.*
    *See* GERALD'*s face smiling from* TOMMY'*s point of view.*
    TOMMY *crouching,* GERALD *standing above him.*

    Oh, come on, Gerrie, it's mine, I won it.

GERALD. Not yet.

    GERALD *bends down, extracts the pound from under his shoe, holds it up, and as* TOMMY *reaches for,it, flicks it away from his fingers.*
    *He keeps this up for some time,* TOMMY *clutching,* GERALD *whipping away, until* TOMMY *suddenly closes on* GERALD; *they begin to wrestle, crashing about, clutching at each other half-laughing, half-gasping, until they roll to the floor.*
    TOMMY *has* GERALD *pinioned and is reaching for the pound, when:*

EDITH (*voice over.* Focus on TOMMY *and the pound*). I hate to disturb you, but could you make less noise please.

*There is silence, then* TOMMY *gets up grinning sheepishly. He puts the pound note in his pocket.*

  GERALD, *still on the floor, turns his head, grinning, towards* EDITH.

TOMMY. Um. Oh I'm sorry, Edie, it was my fault entirely, we had this idea about a wrestling scene, see, you know male wrestling is all the vogue now, on stage and screen, of course, we'll have it done in the nude, but we wanted to get . . . wanted to get . . . (*He begins to laugh, helpless.*)

  GERALD *still lies smiling, staring up at* EDITH.

(*Helplessly.*) Get — get I'm sorry, Edie. Sorry.

  EDITH *looks at them both, turns, goes out.*
  On TOMMY *and* GERALD.
  TOMMY *is still laughing, his laughter dying down.*
  GERALD *gets up, smiling.*
  *There is a pause, heavy, empty, then* GERALD *turns, goes to the desk, sits down.*
  TOMMY *goes to the camp-bed.*
  GERALD *sits staring at the typewriter.*

GERALD (*after a pause*). What about a drink?

TOMMY. Oooh.


**18. Interior. The sitting room. Night.** *A table, laid for dinner.*
DAVID, HELEN, TOMMY *and* GERALD *sitting or standing, holding drinks.*
*But come in first on* TOMMY's *face, as he raises the glass to his lips.*
*He is already slightly tight.*
*Then take in* DAVID *and* HELEN, *sitting rather stiffy, and then* GERALD, *watching, smiling.*

TOMMY. No, no look (*expansively*) that the boys look like the girls and the girls look like the boys in Cannabis Street or Cannibal Street or wherever that doesn't matter, see, that just gives us twice as many to fancy, doesn't it? Eh? (*He laughs.*)

  HELEN *and* DAVID *join in.*

But you see uni-sex has been going on for years, yes it has, in the States they've had those creature-ladies and blue-ringed hair and goggles that are male martians, I'm sure of it, and in

Russia, you know, more elemental, they've gone in a straight line with pills and operations, like that, to get the best of both worlds, child-bearing muscle-men, what about, no I'm serious, all of those shot-putters or putt-shotters and javelin throwers and mile runners the authorities caught shaving in the bogs, eh? Well, that's all right, who minds a bit of cheating in the name of sport, but look, reverse it for a moment, think of it this way, supposing yes supposing our test team, our fast bowlers, were really women, eh? Supposing these South African apartheid blokes were destroyed by an opening pair of fast bowlers from Yorkshire who had little ladies' problems and had to be rested for them, eh, well, wouldn't that be lovely, we destroy the white man at cricket with our ladies like we destroyed the black man with our ladies, eh? So what happens then to white supremacy — like male supremacy, down the flush bowl with it — (*Laughing.*)

HELEN *and* DAVID *also laugh.*
HELEN *gets up.*

Where are you going, Helen?

HELEN. I'm just going to see if Edith needs a hand.

TOMMY. Oh yes, oh that's good, what about our World Cup side, eh, did it take a sex test, hormone count or whatever . . .

**19. Interior. Kitchen. Night.** EDITH *is mixing something on the stove.*
HELEN *comes in.*

HELEN. Can I do anything?

EDITH (*suppressing slight irritation*). Oh no thanks. I'm fine.

HELEN. I must say, we're enjoying Tommy. He's terribly funny.

EDITH (*neutrally*). Ah — yes.

HELEN. He lives with you, does he?

EDITH. In a sense. He has done, off and on, since we were students. We take him so much for granted we scarcely know he's around.

HELEN. Gosh, I'd have thought that was quite difficult.

EDITH. Yes. It is.

HELEN. He's incredibly Welsh, isn't he?

EDITH. Sometimes. When he's had enough to drink.

HELEN (*after a pause*). David's terribly excited about your new one. He says it's nearly finished.

EDITH (*brightening*). Yes. Next month if I can keep it up — God willing, etc.

HELEN. I don't know how you manage.

EDITH (*laughs*). By becoming extremely selfish.

*She takes a dish out of the stove.*


**20. Interior. Living-Room. Dinner table. Night.** *They are seated around the table, but* come in first on TOMMY's *face, he is blinking slightly, and tighter.*
*He raises the wine glass to his mouth, as* GERALD *says:*

GERALD. Nappies.

DAVID. What?

GERALD. Didn't we decide you'd call it nappies. You said, 'Let's be brutal, that's what it's all about.'

DAVID (*doubtfully polite*). Nappies?

TOMMY (*laughing*). Brutally would be crappy nappies.

EDITH. There isn't a title.

DAVID. I must say, I'm rather relieved.

GERALD. But darling, didn't you — ah no, it was Giles that was all about nappies, brutally. I'm getting your children confused. (*To* HELEN.) Do *you* have any children? I always forget.

HELEN. Yes two actually.

GERALD. Two *actually*! As opposed to metaphorically — like Edith's novels. Do you enjoy them?

HELEN. Yes, of course. They're brilliant. They're my favourites.

GERALD. It's nice to hear someone being honest about their own off-spring.

HELEN *and* DAVID *laugh.*

HELEN. I thought you were talking about Edith's novels.

GERALD. Oh, do you think of them as your children, too?

EDITH. Helen was talking about her actual children, actually. As I think you've grasped.

*There is a slight pause.*

GERALD. Well, I certainly have now, haven't I? What do you enjoy about them, Helen? All they do is eat, defecate and sleep. Extremely enjoyable for the baby, but slightly disgusting for the rest of us.

DAVID. On the contrary. Babies are —

TOMMY. Why does Giles get that rash on his bum?

GERALD. It's their urine.

> GERALD *passes* TOMMY *the wine.*
> *He fills his glass to the brim.*

Acid in their urine.

EDITH. Could the rest of us have some please.

> GERALD *looks at her, as if puzzled.*

GERALD. Oh the *wine* — I thought for a moment you meant —

> TOMMY *erupts with laughter, as* GERALD *pours the wine around.*
> *After another pause,* DAVID *says:*

DAVID. Tell me — I've often wondered — how do people write plays together. Do you alternate scenes, or what?

GERALD. Or what.

DAVID. What?

GERALD. Yes.

DAVID. I'm sorry.

GERALD. That's all right.

> DAVID *laughs, clearly getting angry.*

DAVID. I'm afraid I don't understand —

TOMMY. What?

DAVID. I said I didn't understand.

GERALD. I'm sorry.

TOMMY. Why?

GERALD. He didn't understand.

TOMMY. What?

GERALD. How we write plays.

> Cut to EDITH's *face*.
> *She is watching* GERALD *and* TOMMY *through this, almost as if studying them.*

DAVID (*controlling himself*). Anyway, what it amounts to is that you've given up writing novels.

HELEN. Oh, did you . . . ?

> *She stops.*

GERALD. Writing novels ? (*As if astonished.*) What novels?

DAVID. Oh come on, I read it.

GERALD. Ah, my *novel*. I gave up writing that some considerable time before it was published.

EDITH. It was a good novel.

TOMMY (*emphatically*). It was a bloody good novel.

DAVID. Yes, I liked it.

> TOMMY *vaguely, and with seemingly no sense of context, says:*

TOMMY. Christ.


**21. Interior. Living-room. Night.** *They are all sitting around having coffees, and brandies, but come in on* GERALD, *smiling, as* TOMMY *says:*

TOMMY (*voice over*). No well you see it was like this . . . (*Falteringly.*) I was — she was a demi-vierge, can you credit of forty-three and a half, I think it was, and I was a raw boy of thirty-one precisely, well I didn't know what I was saying, excuse me a minute.

> *The sound of* TOMMY's *feet, stumbling.*
> *A door slamming.*

> Still on GERALD's *face as we* cut to *a shot of the group as a whole, evidently embarrassed, and then* cut to:

EDITH (*perfectly collected*). She could have stayed up. Got a Fellowship at Newnham. It never occurred to me she had a novel in her. Is it any good?

DAVID. Well, very accomplished and acceptably derivative.

> *Dreadful sounds off of* TOMMY *being sick.*

EDITH. Really? Derivative from?

HELEN. From you. I'd call it plagiarism.

*More sounds from* TOMMY.

DAVID. Let's just call it flattery.

GERALD *appears at the door.*

GERALD. Darling. (*Cheerfully.*) Where's the mop?


**22. Interior. The Bedroom. Night.** *A double bed, with a bedside table on either side. On* GERALD's *a reading lamp, a bottle of sleeping pills, and a pile of paper-back books, littered. On* EDITH's, *a reading lamp, and a baby-alarm. Also one book, 'Persuasion', with a book-marker in it. But none of this seen as yet. Come directly in on* EDITH's *face, she is staring up at the ceiling.*
*The sounds of* GILES' *breathing through the baby-alarm are audible but not yet explained. There are sudden little cries, followed by the heavy breathing.*
EDITH *moves her arm, and turns down the baby-alarm. As she does so,* GERALD *enters.*

GERALD (*beginning to undress*). He's lying down. I thought he was heroic the way he came back in and told that story against himself, didn't you? Do you think he gave them pleasure?

EDITH. About as much as he gave me, I should think.

*Cut to her face, as* GERALD *goes on undressing, off-screen.*

When did you start getting him drunk? This afternoon? (*Little pause.*) You know, you do go very well together. You're so predictable, like a rather silly married couple that everyone else has outgrown. How do you see yourself? As a *succès manqué?* Does he represent your last hold on your old self, attractive dominating, etc, and so forth?

GERALD *climbs into bed, lies down beside her.*

The glamour is entirely in the vocabulary. A failure. An unhappy husband. A desperate man. Try — flop. Flop's the right word for you. No Graham Greene connotations, no dimmed brightness, no forlorn flickers of promise. Flop. You're a flop and Tommy's a miserable despairing parasite. What the Americans call a bum.

**23. Interior. Hall outside the bedroom. Night.** TOMMY *is standing outside the door, listening. He is in a state close to collapse, exhausted.*

EDITH (*voice over*). What was interesting *and* poignant, about his performance tonight, was its desperation. Didn't you feel it? (*Sharply.*) Don't do that!

GERALD (*voice over*). Why not? We always used to celebrate the guests' departure with a spasm of analysis and a bout of love.

EDITH (*voice over*). What I'm celebrating tonight has nothing to do with you. In fact, that *is* what I'm celebrating. I witnessed Tommy's desperation and your malice this evening without even embarrassment. He was sad and you were trivial, and really I quite enjoyed it. Like recognizing a perfect definition. You behaviour was definitive. I said don't!

TOMMY *puts his hand to his forehead.*


**24. Interior. Bedroom. Night.** GERALD *is leaning over* EDITH, *grinning,* EDITH *is staring up. The sound of* GILES's *breathing is audible.*

EDITH. Would you please turn out the light. Because if you're going to go on grinning anally down at me, I'd rather not see you.

GERALD *maintains his position.*

You don't really think they're going to do your play, do you? Surely you know Tommy better than that. I do, anyway. He never showed it to them.

GERALD *goes on grinning down at her.*

What you've written is a flop. A flop's flop. And Tommy knows it.

GERALD. Do *you* know what I've got against you? Your chin. You've got the chin of a boxer. The tension of not punching it is driving me mad. I'd like to have you in the ring, belting away at your chin. Your novels stink. They make you lots of money and you sell the film rights, but they stink.

*He rolls over, turns out the light.*
*There is a pause.*

EDITH (*in the darkness*). Yes, but Tommy still didn't show your play to anyone. Not even a Welshman. He'll be leaving in the morning.

GERALD. Oh no he won't.

EDITH. Do you want a bet?

**25. Interior. Gerald's Study. Night.** TOMMY *is sitting on the camp bed. He begins to take off his shoes and socks. He looks forlorn, beaten. His hand moves, and he picks up a piece of bread, puts it into his mouth, chews on it desperately, and on his face:*

**26. Interior. The Kitchen. Day.** Come in on TOMMY's *face, munching, as if carried over from last scene.*

EDITH (*voice over*). You're a pig.

TOMMY *looks startled, then* cut to EDITH *looking down at* GILES, *to whom she is giving a bottle.*

TOMMY. And he'll grow up to be a big strong pig, like me, see.

EDITH *looks at him coolly, goes on feeding* GILES.

(*Clears his throat apprehensively.*) Um, while we're on the subject of pigs, Edie, in relation to myself see, I — well, I've been awake all night, worrying and guilty — I thought — (*attempts a charming smile*) — I'd outgrown that kind of thing, it must have been the train journey and being tired with it, you know.

EDITH. From here to Waterloo is thirty-five minutes.

TOMMY (*laughs*). Yes, that's true, well you know British Rail. (*Laughs.*) Anyway, I thought I had an apology to make.

*Pause, he looks at* EDITH, *who addresses herself to* GILES.

I did like your friends, very charming I thought they were. (*Pause.*) I hope I'm forgiven then.

EDITH *looks at him, makes as if to speak as:*

MRS MERCHANT (*comes through the door*). Good morning.

EDITH. Good morning. He's just finished.

*Lifts him out of the chair, hands him to* MRS MERCHANT.

MRS MERCHANT (*taking him*). And how's my ba-ba today? (*Carrying him out.*)

EDITH *suppresses a grimace of irritation.*

TOMMY. It's funny the way she talks to him like a sheep, eh?
(*Laughs.*)

EDITH. You know I'm going to ask you to leave, don't you?

TOMMY *stares at her, licks his lips.*

It's time, Tommy. You've been with us since we started living
together — and that was a year before we got married. Four
years, interrupted by short breaks of three months or so,
and your six months spell in Cardiff. Now I want you to go,
and not to come back.

TOMMY (*staring at her helplessly*). But — Edie — because, you
mean because of last night? I'll never — never — I promise —

EDITH. You see, you talk to me as if I were your older sister, or
mother, someone you make promises to, that you're slightly
frightened of, that will look after you and make everything
all right again. (*She shakes her head.*) I don't feel
protectively towards you. Not any more.

*After a pause* TOMMY *nods his head.*

TOMMY. Could I stay then until we've completed the play? It'll
only be to impose on you another week or so? (*With dignity.*)

EDITH. Why? You know the play's no good. You didn't take it to
anyone in London.

TOMMY. Do you think I'd lie about a thing like that?

EDITH. Yes. (*Smiles.*) Don't look so incredulous. You lie a great
deal. About things like that, and more important things.

*She gets up, comes over, stands behind him, touches his
shoulder.*

Just go, Tommy. Like a good boy. (*Both tenderly and
ironically said.*)

TOMMY (*turns, clutches at her hand*). But what will I do — what?

*The door opens.*
EDITH *moves away from* TOMMY *as* GERALD *comes in.*

GERALD. Good morning.


**27. Interior. Edith's Study. Day.** EDITH *is watching* MRS
MERCHANT *and* GILES.

**28. Exterior. Garden.** MRS MERCHANT *is wheeling* GILES *in the pram down the path.*

**29. Interior. Edith's Study. Day.** EDITH *turns, sits down at her desk, opens the exercise book, unscrews the top of her pen, dips it in the ink, makes as if to write. Her pen hovering over the page, as she reads the previous sentence:*

EDITH. . . . could not deny that the excitement the process of cleaning up gave her (*begins to write*) . . . was oddly pleasant, and although cerebral in its planning was becoming — was becoming — was becoming —

*Lifting the pen up, she gazes down at the paper.*

— cerebral in its planning was becoming —

*She dips her pen into the ink, it hovers over the page.*

— was becoming —

**30. Interior. Gerald's Study. Day.** TOMMY *is sitting on the bed, hands clasped between his legs.*
GERALD *is sitting at the desk-chair, doodling.*

GERALD. Why?

TOMMY. Because she told me to.

GERALD. I haven't. (*Little pause.*) What will you do? Go home to Llannelly?

TOMMY. No, I'll go to London.

GERALD. You've been to London.

TOMMY. I can always wash dishes for a bit.

GERALD. No you can't. Not any more.

TOMMY (*after a pause*). No.

GERALD. Where will you live?

TOMMY. Well, I can — perhaps I can go and stay with someone for a time, until I've settled down.

GERALD. No you can't. They won't have you. Not any more.

TOMMY. No.

GERALD. It's all ended, all that, Tommy. They're all married, to one sex or the other, they've got houses or flats, children or positions, one or two are even dead. They'd like to see you now for ten minutes in a pub, from an accidental meeting, and even so they won't ask you your address or give you theirs. There's nothing for you in London.

TOMMY (*after a pause*). And do you know, I can't do it anymore, I can't Gerrie. I'll tell you something: it frightens me, London. Not just the people who don't want to hear my voice when I telephone them, or the pubs nobody goes to any more, no, it's the whole place, the whole feel of the place and all eleven million of them, however many it is, it makes me feel too little.

GERALD. That's because you're too old. So what will you do, Tommy?

TOMMY. I don't know. I don't know. Of course Edie's right. I can't go on like this, living off you.

GERALD. Why not?

TOMMY. Because — (*thinks*) — she won't let me. (*Laughs.*)

GERALD. Well, there's always this, isn't there?

*He holds up the manuscript.*

Perhaps this will save you, if Humphry Jones is to be trusted.

TOMMY. But there's still the second act —

GERALD. Is Humphry Jones to be trusted ? (*Little pause.*) Tommy?

TOMMY (*looks at* GERALD). No.

GERALD. You didn't take it to him then?

TOMMY. No, Edie's wrong about that, I took it to him, and I walked about for two hours while he read it, it was very kind of him, you know, on the spot he read it, and then I went back and he told me he thought it wasn't very interesting, straightforwardly and honestly, like a good friend should. So he's a good friend, you see. I've got a friend in Humphry Jones. He'll always turn me down on the spot.

GERALD. But it doesn't matter what Humphry Jones thinks, does it? *You've* still got confidence, haven't you? *You* still like it, don't you?

TOMMY (*after a pause*). No. I think it stinks, you know.

GERALD. So what will you do, Tommy?

Hold on *his face, staring at* TOMMY.

**31. Interior. Edith's Study. Day.** Come in on *her pen-nib, poised above the page. Then it stabs down, begins to write.*

EDITH (*voice over*). Positively sexual in its execution. (*Repeats.*) And although cerebral in its planning was becoming positively sexual in its execution. She had felt the same sensation when completing her General Paper for her Oxford Scholarship. She was in control, the prize was hers. In the very exactness with which she organized and made lucid her originality there was a respect for convention that could have been interpreted as contempt. So poor Simon's career as her husband was about to be brought to a neat finish, with, of course, a respect for the conventions that marked her contempt for him. Under these circumstances it would have been delightful to make love to him for a last time. She would see if it could could be arranged. The method of dispatch was so orderly, surely a bravura flourish could be permitted. She —

*She is interrupted by the roar of a motor-cycle from outside. She turns to the window, looks out.*

**32. Exterior. Garden.** EDITH's point of view *from window:* GERALD, *in his gauntlets, helmet and gloves, is starting the motor-bike, while* TOMMY *in his ludicrous overcoat, is getting into the side-car. The motor-bicycle roars off, up the path.*

**33. Interior. Edith's Study. Day.** EDITH *smiles contemptuously, returns to her exercise book, dips in her pen.*

EDITH (*voice over continued*). — now saw her mercilessness as a quality of mind —

**34. Interior. A Wimpy Bar in a small town. Day.** GERALD *and* TOMMY *are seated at a table.*

GERALD. Has it occurred to you that if she hadn't met us when she did, she'd never have written a word. Not a word. Except

possibly for a few academic reviews in academic journals. She
didn't aspire to creation. She had a first from Oxford and a
great gift for thinking dully about dull books. She only took up
novels because I was finishing mine and you were in the middle
of thinking about beginning yours. If I'd been a weight lifter,
she'd have gone in for that.

TOMMY. In the end, she'd have lifted heavier weights.

*A* WAITRESS *puts a coffee in front of* GERALD, *a Wimpy, a*
*piece of cake and a coffee in front of* TOMMY.

GERALD. It took me two years to write my novel, Tommy. Do
you remember?

TOMMY, *who is raising the hamburger to his mouth, nods.*

It was gestured at, at the bottom of long reviews on other
novels.

TOMMY. I remember.

GERALD. And in three years, she's written four novels —

TOMMY (*his mouth full*). Five almost.

GERALD. And she gets whole reviews to herself, with a photograph
inset that was taken when she was twelve. She gets interviewed
on average once every three months, with sometimes a
reference to myself in the text, or a picture of me striking a
husband's pose to the left of her elbow, or with an ear and half
an eye showing behind Giles' face. But that's not it, no, that's
not it. What it is, is that she sits there in her chaste little cell
over her bloody exercise books imitating a schoolgirl imitating
a nun, and she still doesn't know how to write a novel. She has
a special little gland that other people haven't got, that
functions away glandularly, and it makes her richer and richer
and more and more famous, and that's not it, either, no, that's
not it, it's not even the sum of the injustices of her victories and
successes, it is simply that she's killing me. Killing me, yes,
that's it.

TOMMY. Killing you?

GERALD. Oh, I don't mean that she's ending our marriage. She's
doing that. You today, me tomorrow. Your departure is the
means to my end. I mean, she's making me dead.

TOMMY. You hate her then?

GERALD. I'm in love with her. You know, the way one might be
with a schoolgirl or a nun, Aren't you?

TOMMY. What? In love — ?

GERALD. Oh come on Tommy. You've *always* been in love with her. I've only just started.

TOMMY *shakes his head.*

Why, you've slept with her, haven't you?

*As* TOMMY *stares at him, transfixed.*

That year when we were living together. All three of us. Didn't you sleep with her?

TOMMY. Look Gerald, I don't know what you're talking about.

GERALD. Didn't you fancy her, then?

TOMMY (*laughs*). Well of course, that's a different question, isn't it?

GERALD. No it isn't. Everyone was sleeping with everyone. I took it for granted you did with her.

TOMMY. Why didn't you ask me before, then, if you've thought that?

GERALD. I wanted to preserve the proprieties. It doesn't matter any more. So you can tell me. (*Smiling.*) How often did you sleep with my wife?

TOMMY (*laughs*). Well you know, I can't remember. You know, Gerrie —?

GERALD. You do remember, Tommy. Was it once — (*Holds up a finger.*) twice — (*Holds up two fingers.*)

TOMMY *holds up two fingers.*
GERALD *continues to hold up two fingers also.*
*They sit staring at each other, holding up two fingers.*
*Then* GERALD *smiles.*

Did you enjoy it?

TOMMY (*shrugs*). Well no, (*lowering his fingers*) it wasn't very successful, it was you she wanted, see.

GERALD. I'm sorry to hear that.

GERALD *begins to laugh.*
TOMMY *also laughs.*
GERALD *draws* TOMMY's *cake to himself, and while he is talking, covers it with various condiments, pepper, salt, mustard, tomato sauce etc.*

Sometimes when you're walking along a street you see a
schoolgirl with her satchel, her legs they go down very
vulnerable, almost pitiful, into their socks and shoes. Do you
know what I mean?

TOMMY *is staring in horror at the cake.*

And one in a hundred has a face, exquisite, sealed off, and you
put out of your mind what you know goes through theirs, and
you feel it inside you, caught between cherishing and despoiling.
(*Little pause.*) The desire to rape nuns is, of course, conventional
fantasy. I won't bore you with it. Here — you've had my cake.
Now eat yours.

GERALD *pushes the cake at* TOMMY.

TOMMY. Like hell I will, boyo.

GERALD. It's the price you have to pay, Tommy. If you're to
inherit my mantle.

TOMMY *shakes his head laughing uncertainly, and then stares
down at the cake, back at* GERALD, *and on his face:*


**35. Interior. Edith's Study. Day.** *Register the sound of her laughing
quietly, over the last shot of* GERALD.
EDITH *writing.*


**36. Exterior. Garden.** MRS MERCHANT *and* GILES *approach up
the path.*


**37. Interior. Edith's Study. Day.** EDITH *writing.*

EDITH (*voice over*). And so he departed, for the last time, from
their bedroom, with his tail between and not metaphorically,
his legs. With his clothes bundled in his arms and his face
bulging with unconsummated aggression, he was not a
particularly dignified spectacle. But he had pathos, of a kind
that Mathilda knew —

*She turns, looks out of the window.*


**38. Exterior. Garden.** EDITH's point of view, GILES *and* MRS
MERCHANT *now in the very middle of the path.*

### 39. Interior. Edith's Study. Day.

EDITH (*voice over*). — in the solitary (*writing quickly*) but by no means lonely years to come. She— she —

EDITH *stops, smiles at the page, then screws the top on to her pen, closes the ink-well, blots the page, closes the exercise book, stands up, stares, smiling, out of the window.*

### 40. Exterior. Garden. Day. *From* EDITH's point of view. MRS MERCHANT *lifts* GILES *out of the pram.*

### 41. Exterior. Country Road. Day. *The motor-bicycle is roaring at great speed along the road.*
Cut from GERALD's *face, impassive behind goggles, etc,* to TOMMY's *eyes staring in fright.*
TOMMY *attempts to attract* GERALD's *attention, the motor-bicycle roars on,* past the camera, see it from behind, *suddenly slowing and then stopping.*
TOMMY *scrambles out of the side-car and runs, clutching his stomach, to the bushes.*

### 42. Exterior. The Garden. Day. EDITH *is pushing* GILES *in the pram slowly up the path, towards* MRS MERCHANT.

### 43. The Road. Day. *The motor-bike roaring along the road,* cut from GERALD's *face,* to TOMMY's, *crumpled in misery.*

### 44. The Garden. Day. EDITH, MRS MERCHANT, GILES, *in the middle of the path as before.*
*Sound over of the motor-bike and as they look up, the motor-bike is roaring towards them, and cut to their reactions,* then to TOMMY's *face, stiff with horror.* Then GERALD's, *indecipherable behind the goggles, etc.*

### 45. Interior. Living Room. Day. Come in directly on GERALD's *face, now without goggles, helmet, etc. He is sitting impassively.* Then take in TOMMY, *sitting on the sofa, clearly shaken.*

*The door opens,* MRS MERCHANT *comes out, walks past*
GERALD, *stiff faced.*
GERALD *follows her with his eyes, then looks towards the door,*
*as* EDITH *comes out, closing it behind her.*
*Baby noise off from* GILES.

EDITH. You nearly killed us all. Do you realise that?

GERALD. It *was* a close thing, wasn't it? Old Tommy would have
thrown up his gâteau vinaigrette if he hadn't already thrown it up.

EDITH. Are you being defiant, or are you actually a little mad?

GERALD. A little mad actually. (*He gets up and goes to the door.*)
You've got a lunatic on your hands. I give you warning. (*He
smiles, goes out.*)

TOMMY (*to* EDITH, *who is staring after* GERALD ). Edie . . . .
um, you know, he's, well —

EDITH *turns, looks at him.*

It's — it's — look Edie, he isn't well, there's something wrong
with him, I don't mean he tried to run you over or anything
like that, see, but he might do something desperate, if you ask
me.

EDITH. And if I ask you, what would you suggest?

TOMMY. You shouldn't be alone together, not just now, Edith.

EDITH. Tommy, I asked you to go. Are you going to, please.

TOMMY. He hates you, you know.

EDITH. Of course he does. Why should he make an exception of
me. He almost certainly hates you too.

EDITH *goes out.* TOMMY *stands for a moment, on his face an*
*expression of rage.*


**46. Interior. Gerald's Study. Day.** GERALD *is lying on the camp*
*bed, smoking a cheroot.*
TOMMY *comes in.*

TOMMY. I'll stay if you tell me to . . .

GERALD (*looks at him*). *Tell* you to?

TOMMY. Yes.

GERALD. Well, I won't. I'd prefer you gone. I need you somewhere else, Tommy.

TOMMY, *after a moment, goes to his suitcase under the camp bed, drags it out, begins to shut it.*

Could I have my shirts back, please.

TOMMY. I've soiled them.

GERALD. The soil may belong to you, the shirts belong to me.

TOMMY *takes out the shirts, puts them on the bed, closes the suitcase.*

How romantic, to travel light. You don't mind if I don't take you to the station after all.

TOMMY (*looks at him, after a pause*). Will there be a train?

GERALD. At the station? Well, if you don't find one there, you won't find one anywhere.

TOMMY (*suddenly firm*). Could I have my coat please.

GERALD. It's behind you.

TOMMY. The one I inherited.

GERALD. Inherited?

TOMMY. The one I ate that cake for.

GERALD. Oh, you misunderstood me. I was speaking poetically.

TOMMY (*desperately*). What is it you want me to do, then? What?

GERALD. Go.

TOMMY *turns, goes out of the door.*


**47. Interior. Edith's Study. Day.** EDITH *is standing at the window looking out, and* from her point of view, *through the window, sees* TOMMY *plodding up the path.*


**48. Exterior. Garden. Day.** From EDITH's point of view, TOMMY *plodding up the path. He is carrying his suitcase, and wearing his ludicrous overcoat.*


**49. Interior. Edith's Study. Day.** *For a moment* EDITH *looks uncertain, as if perhaps on the verge of calling out to* TOMMY.

**50. Exterior. Garden. Day.** *There is the roar of the motor-bike and* GERALD *comes into view, stops beside* TOMMY, *talks to him.* TOMMY *gets into the side-car.*

**51. Interior. Edith's Study. Day.** EDITH *turns away to her desk. She sits down at it, stares ahead for a moment, then unscrews the top of her fountain pen, opens the exercise book, then sits staring at the page. On her face.*

**52. Interior. The bedroom. Night.** EDITH *is lying in bed reading 'Persuasion.' Beside her the baby-alarm is on. The sound of* GILES's *breathing. Hold on this, then the roar of the motor-bike, and immediately, from the baby-alarm,* GILES's *cry.* EDITH *starts, sits still, then makes as if to get up. The crying stops.*
*She gets back into bed, sits tensely.*
*A few snuffling noises from the box, then silence.*
*Sound of a door opening and closing, footsteps.*
GERALD *comes in, closes the door behind him. On his face is an expression so impassive that it is sinister. He begins to get undressed.*

EDITH. I think you'd better sleep in the study. As it's free now.

GERALD. No, I'll sleep with you tonight. It'll be the last time.

EDITH. Yes.

*There is a silence as* GERALD *goes on undressing.* Keep on EDITH's *face, watching him. It is very composed, but a hint of excitement.*

GERALD. By the way, Tommy informs me you've slept with him.

EDITH. Really?

GERALD. You did then?

EDITH. Tommy is a liar. I've never gone in for adultery.

GERALD. I wasn't asking after your religious habits. I was indirectly asking whether you and Tommy had ever copulated with each other.

EDITH. Are you hoping he did? Do you think that jealousy is less demeaning than envy?

*As* GERALD *gets into bed.*

I'd be grateful if you'd wash. You're dirty.

GERALD *lies staring up at the ceiling.*
EDITH *picks up 'Persuasion'.*

GERALD. There is, I suppose, the faint possibility that Giles isn't mine?

EDITH. Would it make any difference if he weren't?

GERALD (*reaches past her, turns off baby-alarm*). I'd like to think he'd disgust me just as much if I were sure he were.

EDITH. You are literally hateful. Full of hate. *Did* you try to harm him this afternoon?

GERALD *suddenly rolls over, looks down at her, then takes the book from her hand, and drops it over the edge of the bed.*
EDITH *laughs.*
GERALD *puts a hand on her breast.*

EDITH (*ironically*). Oh dear.

GERALD *slaps her.*

You don't have to do that. I'm yours.

GERALD *stares at her blankly, and* EDITH *smiles.*
*He begins to make love to her. As he does so,* EDITH's *hand comes out, turns on the baby-alarm. Her hand withdraws but stay on the baby-alarm. A few small cries come from it, and cries from* EDITH, *then on a full cry from* EDITH, *cut to:*
EDITH's *face, she is flushed and smiling. A small, triumphant smile.* Then take in GERALD *beside her. He is lying, staring up.*

(*She turns towards him.*) Oh dear. (*Pause.*) I'm sorry.

GERALD *goes on staring up. Then suddenly he begins to cry.*
EDITH *stares at him, her smile becoming suddenly uncertain.*

Gerrie — (*whispered*) Gerrie —

*And aghast she puts her hand to his head, stares into his face. He is still crying.*

Gerrie —

*He stares at her pathetically.*
*He rolls away, gets out of bed, picks up his clothes, goes to the door, turns, stares at her. On his face, an expression of dreadful malevolence. He goes out.*
EDITH *stares after him, makes as if to follow him, then lies*

*back,* hold on *her face, suggesting time passing. Her expression tense.*
*Then the roar of the motor-bike, the sound fading way.*

*A pause.*

(*Her voice slightly shaky.*) That's that, then. (*Little pause.*) Consummatum est. (*She laughs, still shakily.*)


**53. Interior. Gerald's Study. Day.** Hold on *the room, in its slovenliness. Then* EDITH *comes on camera. Purposefully, almost violently, she rips the covers off the camp bed. Then* a series of shots, montage, *of her cleaning out and cleaning up the room, with a kind of fanatical intensity,* culminating with two last shots, sustained longer than the others, *of her wrapping up* GERALD's *manuscripts in brown paper, tying them into a parcel, then putting the hood over the typewriter.*
Move back to *the door, where* EDITH *stands when she has finished.* Take in *the room, bare and as if purged. She turns, goes out.*


**54. Interior. Bathroom sink. Day.** On EDITH's *hands, as they are briskly washing themselves,* EDITH's *face in the mirror as she combs her hair.*


**55. Interior. Edith's Study. Day.** *She goes to the window, stands for a second, then turns to her desk, picks up the exercise books to the left, the ones filled, holds them almost devotionally, smiles. She puts them down, sits down, takes out her pen, opens the ink-well then turns the exercise book open. The page is blank. She frowns, turns back a page. Also blank. She picks the exercise book up, riffles through it, blank. In horror she picks up the filled exercise books, riffles through them. On the last page of the last exercise book, scrawled in large letters:* 'Go back to page one.'


**56. Interior. The kitchen. Day.** EDITH *is sitting at the table, staring ahead.*
*Her face is over-composed, as if against panic. She gets up, goes to the phone, opens the address book beside it, begins to dial. Then cut to shots of her finger on different telephone numbers, dialing*

*with the other finger, to suggest numerous phone calls being
made, then* cut to:
EDITH *sitting at the table again. There is the sound of a motor-
car outside, a honk.*
*She gets up, picks up a coat and handbag, already arranged on a
chair, goes to the back door, opens it. And finds herself facing*
MRS MERCHANT, GILES *in her arms.*
EDITH *blinks in a shock of recognition.*

EDITH. Um, um — I've got to go to London on — um,
  something urgent. Could you do Giles until, I um — if I'm
  late? It's terribly urgent.

MRS MERCHANT. Of course, it's nothing serious is it?

EDITH. Yes. (*Makes to go.*)

MRS MERCHANT. I'll tell Mr Dunlop you've gone.

EDITH. Oh, he won't be — yes, if he comes, tell him he must
  wait for me. He must. All right?

  *She looks at* GILES, *kisses him as if remembering, goes out.*


**57. Exterior. Garden. Day.** Shot of EDITH, *from* MRS
MERCHANT's point of view, *getting into a taxi.*


**58. Interior. David's Office. Day.** Come in on EDITH's *face,
seen from* DAVID's point of view. *She looks exhausted.*

EDITH. Credit where it's due. It's effectively humiliating. I
  spent the morning on the telephone to people I haven't seen
  for months, for years. Asking them if they'd seen my husband.
  They hadn't, of course. But they found the question interesting.
  One or two hinted that I'd dropped them with my success. I
  longed to say that I'd been merciful. If I'd dropped them when
  I'd been a failure they'd have had to attribute some fault to
  themselves. This way I gave them the opportunity to blame
  me. The afternoon I spent in familiar half-forgotten pubs, not
  knowing whose eyes to dodge and whose to catch. None of
  them looked as if they could have belonged to my past, but
  they might all have belonged to *his*. I don't know. I can't
  remember. How could I? (*Little pause.*) I should have thought.
  I should have *thought*. But it was the one unthinkable thing.
  (*Little pause.*) But he thought of it. Why didn't I? I should

have slept with them under my pillow, had them chained to
my wrist, hidden them under the floor-boards, until he'd
gone. (*Little pause.*) But I've worked out this much. He
wouldn't have put the blank ones there if he'd decided to
(*with an effort*) destroy the other ones. He'd have left torn
pages, or embers, or nothing. He *must* be going to use them —
as hostages, so to speak. (*She smiles.*) What shall I do? (*Lips
tremble.*) David?

*She attempts a smile. On her face.*


**59. Exterior. Drive. Day.** *Taxi coming towards the drive.* But
carry on shot of EDITH's face from previous scene, and then cut
to:


**60. Interior. Kitchen window. Day.** MRS MERCHANT's *face
staring out, desperately worried.*


**61. Exterior. Garden.** MRS MERCHANT's point of view. *A
taxi draws up, beside a car.*
EDITH *gets out, paying the taxi-driver hastily, looks at the car,
begins to run towards the house.*
MRS MERCHANT *hurries to the door, opens it, and see her face
worried, from* EDITH's point of view.

MRS MERCHANT. I don't know what's wrong, Dr Slocum's
with him now.

EDITH *runs past her.*


**62. Interior. Giles's Room. Day.** *Terrible cries coming from*
GILES. DR SLOCUM *is straightening up from the cot,
stethoscope dangling from his ears. He turns, stares at* EDITH,
*his face severe.*
EDITH *stares back at him, panic stricken.*
MRS MERCHANT *comes in behind her.*

EDITH. Oh God, what's the matter.

DR SLOCUM. I've not the slightest idea. His lungs are in
excellent shape, at least.

EDITH (*confused, shouting*). What?

> *She goes to the cot, looks down at* GILES. *She picks him up.*
> GILES *begins to calm down.*

DR SLOCUM. But whatever it was, I can't believe it was worth
calling me out for. We've got the summer 'flu epidemic on our
hands, you know.

EDITH. Called — who called?

> *She looks accusingly at* MRS MERCHANT.

MRS MERCHANT (*indignantly*). I didn't —

DR SLOCUM. The call was from your husband. (*Packing his bag.*)
He said your child needed attention. (*Straightening, and on his
face, cut to:*)

**63. Interior. Bedroom. Night.** EDITH *is in bed, reading. The book
held up to her face. She lowers the book. She is crying, silently.
She wipes her eyes with the sheets, lies still for a moment. Then
turns out the light, there is a pause.*
*The light comes on again. She lies staring ahead, as if trying to
remember something, then suddenly turns her head to the baby-
alarm which is silent. She stares at it in panic, then grabs it, turns
up the sound. Still nothing. She makes to get out of bed,
suddenly remembers the on-off switch. Fumblingly she checks it,
turns it to on. The sound of* GILES *breathing. She turns the light
on. Picks up the book, resolutely, begins to read.*

EDITH. The sod! The hateful sod!

> *Fade into a shot of* EDITH *asleep, the light on, the book open
> beside her.*
> *It is still night. There is over, the distant noise of the motor-
> bicycle, very muted, being driven at the lowest possible throttle.
> Her eyes flicker open. She stares ahead, then sits up as the
> noise goes on, slightly louder.*
> *The noise stops. Cut to her face, listening, waiting. Sounds of
> a key in the lock, a door opening, closing quietly, footsteps,
> other doors opening and closing. Then silence.* EDITH *gets up,
> goes to the bedroom door, opens it. Follow her through to:*

**64. Interior. Various Rooms. Night.** GERALD's *study. On to her
own study, the door is open. She goes to it.*

**65. Interior. Edith's Study. Night.** *What appears to be* GERALD's *back — it is, in fact,* TOMMY, *in* GERALD's *coat. His head is bent low as he fumbles inside* EDITH's *desk. Cut to her face, resolute as she walks quickly and softly over, puts her hand on his arm.* TOMMY *jumps, looks up.*
EDITH *stares into his face,* see it full in camera, from her point of view, then back to EDITH.

EDITH. What do you want?

TOMMY. Oh, I'm sorry Edie (*nervously*) I — I — was just — well, see the thing is Gerald asked me to get something for him.

EDITH. He's got them all. There aren't any more.

TOMMY. What? Sleeping pills? He says he hasn't, Edith, no look.

*He holds a bottle out in the palm of his hand.*

He said you kept an extra bottle in your desk —

EDITH. You came here for that?

TOMMY (*shrugs*). Well, he asked me to come and get them, Edie. He said he needed them.

EDITH (*after a pause*). What are you doing in his coat?

TOMMY. Well, he gave it to me in the end, you see. I won it in one of our bets. It was a cake I had to eat, he —

EDITH. Where is he Tommy? Where is he?

TOMMY. Well, I promised him I wouldn't say. He said you'd ask, he made me promise, Edie.

EDITH. He's got my exercise books, you know. My novel. I want them back.

TOMMY. Of course you do. Of course.

EDITH. He's not in London then?

TOMMY. No.

EDITH. Has it occurred to you that he's ill.

TOMMY *looks at her as if wavering.*
EDITH *goes to him, clutches his arm.*

Tommy, take me to him. (*Little pause.*) Please.

TOMMY *looks at her. She is pleading, but there is something deliberately sexual in her appeal.*

Please? (*Wonderingly.*) Don't tell me anything. Just take me to him. You didn't promise him you wouldn't do that, did you?

TOMMY. No. (*Little pause.*) Do you mean now?

EDITH (*gently*). Please, Tommy.

TOMMY (*after a pause*). But what about Giles, you couldn't leave him all by himself then, could you?

EDITH, *as if realising, shakes her head.*

EDITH. I'd — I'd — (*Stops.*) Well then, ask him to give me a ring, will you please.

TOMMY. Yes. Yes, I'll do that.

*He hesitates, then takes* EDITH *in his arms, kisses her gently on the mouth, then stands hesitant.*

I'll tell him to give you a ring then.

*He goes out. Keep on the door, sound of doors opening, then* EDITH *goes to the hall, and through to:*

**66. Interior. The kitchen. Night.** EDITH *goes to the window, looks out.*

**67. The Garden. Night.** *There is a figure on the seat of the motor-bicycle, in crash-helmet and goggles, indistinct. She stares towards it, through the window, assuming that it is* TOMMY.
*The figure raises an arm, in salute, then* TOMMY *appears, in goggles and helmet, climbs into the side-car. All this from* EDITH's *point of view.*

**68. Interior. The kitchen. Night.** EDITH *stares at the motor-bike, then realizing, runs to the kitchen door.*

**69. The Garden. Night.** EDITH *opens kitchen door, as* GERALD, *on the seat, kicks the motor-bike into life, it cruises up the drive. Cut to* EDITH's *face, and from that cut to:*

**70. Interior. Edith's Study. Morning.** EDITH *is sitting at the desk, she stares blankly ahead, then takes a fresh exercise book, opens*

*it. She picks up her fountain pen, lifts the lid of the ink-well. Dips
the pen in. Her pen hovers. She writes:*

EDITH (*voice over*). Mathilda felt that — Mathilda felt that she —
   Mathilda felt — Mathilda — Mathilda —

*Having stopped writing, she turns her head, looks out of the
window, and, from her point of view, cut to:*

**71. The Garden. Day.** Shot of MRS MERCHANT, *with* GILES *in
the pram, just leaving the house.*

**72. Interior. Edith's Study. Day.** EDITH *suddenly screws the top
back on her pen, snaps the ink-well shut, very quickly hurries out
of the room.*

**73. The Garden. Day.** Shot of MRS MERCHANT *and* GILES *as if
through the study window, as* EDITH *runs up to her, takes over
the pram, begins to push it.*
MRS MERCHANT *walks beside her, as, over, the sound of the
telephone ringing.*
EDITH *stops. Turns around, runs back to the house, all this seen
as through the study window, then* cut to:

**74. Interior. Kitchen. Day.** EDITH *hurrying to the telephone,
picks it up a fraction after it stops ringing. The dialling tone is
audible. She stands holding it, then puts it down. She stands
looking at it, then goes back to the open kitchen door.*

**75. Day.** *From* EDITH's *point of view at the kitchen door,* MRS
MERCHANT *and* GILES, *waiting.*

EDITH (*shouting*). I shan't be coming. You go on.

   MRS MERCHANT *turns, goes down the path.*
   EDITH *watches, then turns, goes back in, shuts the door.*

**76. Interior, Kitchen. Day.** EDITH *goes to the stove, puts on the
kettle, and* cut to:

EDITH *sitting at the table, drinking a cup of tea. The telephone rings. She leaps up, goes over to it, picks it up.*

EDITH. Hello. Hello.

> *There is a click of the receiver being replaced at the other end. She puts the telephone down, goes back to the table. Sits. The telephone rings again. She leaps up, it stops ringing. She stares at it.*
> *She sits down, almost gingerly. It rings. She gets up. It stops ringing. She remains poised between sitting and standing, staring at the telephone, and cut to:*

**77. Interior. Giles's bedroom. Day.** Come in on GILES, *nappy off,* then come in on MRS MERCHANT, *dropping the dirty nappy into a bucket. She smiles down at GILES and cut to:*
EDITH *at the door, comes in, stares down at* GILES.

EDITH. Hello darling.

MRS MERCHANT. I was just going to do his rash.

EDITH. Were you? I'll do it.

*As* MRS MERCHANT *opens the jar of ointment,* EDITH *dips her finger into it, takes sone ointment out on the end of her finger, when the telephone rings.*
MRS MERCHANT *turns towards the door, as if to answer the telephone.*

I'll get it.

*She pushes past* MRS MERCHANT, *handing her* GILES, *and leaves the room.*
MRS MERCHANT *looks at* GILES, *then puts her finger into the jar, as the telephone stops ringing. There is a short pause.*
EDITH *reappears.*
MRS MERCHANT, *not seeing her, is about to apply the cream.*

(*With a tight smile.*) I said I'd do it.

*She is still holding her fingers ahead of her. On them, Baby-cream.*
MRS MERCHANT *steps aside, offended.*
EDITH *advances towards* GILES, *as the telephone rings.*
EDITH *stiffens, then making an immense effort, goes on dabbing the cream.*
*The telephone goes on ringing. She goes on dabbing the cream,*

*finishes, wipes her fingers. The telephone is still ringing. She turns to* MRS MERCHANT.

Would you do his nappy, please.

*She walks out of the room, and* cut to:

**78. Interior The Kitchen. Day.** EDITH *walks steadily towards the telephone, picks it up. She waits a second, as if expecting a click. There is a pause.*

EDITH. Hello. (*There is a silence.*) Hello. Giles?

GERALD. Gerald.

EDITH (*smiles very slightly*). Gerald. Yes.

GERALD. You asked me to give you a ring.

EDITH. Yes. (*Ironically.*) Thank you.

GERALD. I've given you several. I shan't be giving you any more.

*Click, as he hangs up.*
EDITH *stands there, holding the receiver, then bangs it down, then picks it up and bangs it down several times, in a fury. Stops, begins to walk away.*

*The telephone rings.* EDITH *turns, stares at it, then picks it up.*

Edith? Gerald here. Hello again! Look old girl — it occurred to me you might want something. Is there anything?

EDITH (*controlling herself*). You know what I want. (*There is a silence.*) Don't you?

GERALD (*after a pause*). Me?

EDITH. I want my novel back. (*Long pause.*) Are you there?

GERALD. Yes — yes, I'm here. Is there anything else you want?

EDITH. I'd like to talk to you. Properly.

GERALD. Would you like to see my room? Where I'm living, and how I've settled down?

EDITH. Yes. (*Quickly.*) Where is it?

GERALD. Oh, better to pick you up, I think. If you don't mind riding in the old side-car, that is?

EDITH. No. That'll be all right.

GERALD. Say in an hour.

EDITH. Yes. Yes. In an hour.

GERALD. In an hour.

*Click as he puts the telephone down.*

EDITH *replaces the telephone, turns, sees* MRS MERCHANT *standing before her, holding* GILES. *Looks at her, looks at* GILES, *then, as if realising.*

EDITH. Oh. Mrs Merchant. Um, would you mind terribly holding the, um . . .

Cut to:

**79. Interior. Kitchen. Day.** MRS MERCHANT, *her face staring out of the window.*

**80. The Garden. Day.** From MRS MERCHANT's point of view. *At kitchen window see* EDITH *walking down the path to the motorbike. There is a man sitting on it in* GERALD's *coat goggles, etc.* EDITH *says something to him,* cut to:

TOMMY. All I know, Edie, is he told me to bring you. Isn't that all right?

EDITH, *after a pause, gets into the side-car, it roars off. And* cut back to:

**81. Interior. Kitchen. Day.** MRS MERCHANT *at the window, turning away. And* cut to:

**82. Exterior. The Hotel. Day.** *The motor-bike pulling up before a large shabby house converted into a shabby private hotel.* TOMMY *gets off.* EDITH *gets out,* TOMMY *takes* EDITH's *arm, they walk up the steps to the front door, and* cut to:

**83. Interior. The Hotel. Day.** *They go up grubby stairs, passing a lounge-type room. From which comes the noise of a television set. Then up more stairs past various doors with numbers halferased. They reach the last two doors, next to each other.*

TOMMY. This is his, Edie.

EDITH. I think I'd better do this alone, if you don't mind.

TOMMY. Of course, Edie.

*He turns, to go to the other room, stops as* EDITH *makes to knock.*

Look, I'll be in here if you need me. See.

EDITH *looks at him, then turns to* GERALD's *door, knocks. There is no reply.* EDITH *knocks again, then turns the handle. The door opens. She goes in. The light is on. The bed is unmade. There are clothes spilled everywhere, and a general sense of muddle and squalor. Propped against the mirror there is a note, on which is written: 'This is my room'.* EDITH *reads the note, turns, looks around. Makes as if to go out, then turns, goes to the chest of drawers, cupboard, bed, each one in turn, hunts rapidly through them, then stops, stares around, and cut to:*
TOMMY's *room. It is in the same condition as* GERALD's. TOMMY *is sitting in an arm-chair.* Come in on *his face, looking towards the door, then cut to:*

EDITH (*at the door*). He's not there. (*Little pause.*) Of course.

TOMMY. Oh.

*He gets to his feet, as if about to go and look.*

EDITH. He's not there. He never intended to be. Where is he?

TOMMY. I don't know. (*Little pause.*) Edie, I don't know. Look, he said I was to pick you up and take you to his room, seeing as you wanted to see it, that was all, Edie.

EDITH (*advances towards him*). You're lying. You're lying. (*Stands in front of him.*) All the money you've borrowed and never mentioned again — all the food you've guzzled — the drink you've got drunk on to give yourself the courage to bore and insult my friends — who do you think buys him those shirts you make dirty, his coat — that coat — *I* gave it to him, my books gave it to him, to you — you owe me, you owe me. (*Punching at his chest.*) Now you tell me, tell me, tell me!

*Her voice is rising hysterically, and cut to:*
*The Hall, before the front door.*
TOMMY *holds the door open for* EDITH. *She steps out, he follows, his hand on her arm. He closes the door, and from the doorstep,* their point of view, cut to:

**84. Exterior. Hotel. Day.** GERALD *in* TOMMY's *coat, on the motor-bicycle, driving away.*
TOMMY *and* EDITH *stand staring after him, and* cut to:

**85. Exterior. The drive. Day.** Come in on MRS MERCHANT, medium shot, *coming up the drive. Her walk — seen from in front is jerky, odd.* Hold, then cut to:

**86. Interior. Taxi. Day.** EDITH *is sitting forward, staring towards* MRS MERCHANT *who is walking towards them, she taps on the glass, stops the taxi. She opens the window and leans out of it.*
Close-up *of* MRS MERCHANT's *face, seen from* EDITH's *point of view.*
*Tears are streaming down her cheeks. She makes to open her mouth, closes it, clearly very distraught. But there is something sinister in the effect.*
EDITH *gets out, starts after her, clutches her arm.*
MRS MERCHANT *turns, says something,* EDITH *says something then turns, runs towards the house.*
TOMMY *has got out of the taxi, and is following slowly. He stops, turns back to the taxi.*

**87. Interior. Kitchen. Day.** EDITH *flings open the door* shot from inside the kitchen then a brisk montage *as she runs through the house, comes to* GILES's *room, goes in.* GILES *is asleep.* EDITH *turns, comes out, walks back to the kitchen.*
TOMMY *is standing just inside the door.*

EDITH. He's here somewhere.

TOMMY. Is he?

EDITH. He must have been. He's just sacked Mrs Merchant.

   *She goes to the door, looks out.*

**88. Exterior. Garden. Day.** *From* EDITH's *point of view at kitchen door, see taxi still there. There is a short, intense silence, then* GERALD's *motor-bike starts up (not seen) and roars around the house into sight, up the drive, past the taxi and away. There is a pause.*

**89. Interior. Kitchen. Day.** EDITH *turns, looks at* TOMMY.

TOMMY (*licks his lips*). I haven't got any money, Edith.

EDITH. What?

TOMMY. For the taxi. To get me back to Guildford, see.

EDITH *starts to laugh, stops, opens her handbag, fumbles in it. Then looks at* TOMMY.

EDITH. You've got to make him come here and talk to me.

*She takes a five-pound note out of her wallet, hands it to him.*

Will you?

TOMMY *looks at the money, then at* EDITH.

TOMMY. This is a fiver, did you know, Edie?

EDITH (*after a slight pause*). I haven't got anything smaller. That's all I have.

TOMMY *puts his hand into his pocket.*

TOMMY. Oh look, I've got a pound. I won't need this after all.

*He hands it back to* EDITH.

Thanks.

EDITH. Please, Tommy.

*Cut to her face.*

Please.


**90. Interior. Edith's Bedroom. Night.** EDITH *is asleep, 'Persuasion' lying open beside her. The lamp is on the floor, lamp-shade tilted, to soften the light. The baby-alarm is on. Gentle sounds of* GILES *breathing. Keep on* EDITH's *face. She sits up suddenly, stares around. Gets up, walks to the door. There should be something almost somnambulistic in her movements.*


**91. Interior. Living room. Night.** *She goes down the hall, opens the door to the living-room. Stands blinking. Then cut to* GERALD *sitting in a chair, in* TOMMY's *coat, facing her.*

Cut back to EDITH.

GERALD (*smiling, voice gentle*). I've come, you see.

EDITH. Yes. (*Quietly.*) Just a minute. I'm not properly awake. I've got to be awake to say the right words, haven't I? (*She smiles, goes out.*)


**92. Interior. Bathroom. Night.** Cut to EDITH *washing her face under the cold tap.*


**93. Interior. Living room. Night.** Then cut to EDITH, *drops of water still on her face, coming back to the sitting room. It is empty. She stares around as:*
GERALD *comes out of* GILES's *room, closing the door quietly.*

GERALD. It's all right, I haven't gone. (*He sits down.*)

EDITH. You've grown so expert in your games. (*Smiling, gentle.*) They're very literary. Literal, in fact. That's why I have to get the right words.

*She is walking slowly towards him, then crouches down at his feet, takes his hand.*

There. I've got you.

GERALD *puts his hand on hers.*

GERALD. I didn't realise you wanted me.

EDITH. Please Gerrie, could I have it back? Please.

*She smiles up at him.*

GERALD (*carefully*). Would you say you wanted it more than anything?

EDITH. Is that what you've been proving to me? I knew it already. I've known it since I started writing — since about the third paragraph of my first novel. It's the only thing nobody would ever have to prove to me. I'm not ashamed, either. I'm not ashamed.

GERALD. And what would become of me, if I gave it back? How would I sustain your interest? You've tried to catch my every move, these last few days.

EDITH. You could come here again, if you wanted. For as long as you wanted. And Tommy too.

GERALD. Would you love us?

EDITH (*after a pause*). I would do my best.

GERALD. I could make love to you?

EDITH (*with a slight, malicious smile*). You could do your best.

GERALD. Ah! (*He smiles. Touches the side of her cheek.*)
   And if it's too late? If I haven't got the exercise books any more?

EDITH *thinks, then very carefully.*

EDITH. I think I'd like to see you die.

GERALD (*nods*). Then it's too late for me. I haven't got them any more.

EDITH *stares up at him, frozen. Then slowly gets up, walks to a chair opposite, sits down, looks at* GERALD. *She tries to smile.*

EDITH. What did you do with them?

GERALD (*shakes his head*). It doesn't matter any more. Not to me. (*He puts his hand into his pocket.*) Did you find the right words, do you think?

EDITH's *mouth is trembling, but her voice is controlled, as if with a tremendous effort.*

EDITH. I shall start again. And once I've started, what you've done won't mean anything.

GERALD *is holding sleeping pills, not of course registered by* EDITH — *in his cupped hand.*

*He begins to pop them into his mouth, as if they were smarties.*

GERALD. You'll be able to say of me . . . (*Popping them into his mouth nonchalantly*) . . . that I was literal to the end.

EDITH. Perhaps doing it again is only right. It'll be different, there will be things to add — but above all — you won't be here. What you've done *will* mean something. But to me. Not to you. You're so much waste, got rid of. And there's nothing more you can do to hurt me, you see.

GERALD. I know. That's the appalling thing about you.

EDITH (*smiles*). Would you go now, please. (*Getting up.*)

GERALD. Oh. Aren't you going to stay. I thought you wanted to see me — um, die. (*Modestly*.)

EDITH *stares at him, aghast.*
GERALD *throws the last few sleeping pills into his mouth, swallows them down with a gulp. Then shows her the bottle.*

Isn't that what you wanted?

EDITH (*after a pause*). How many have you taken?

GERALD. Twenty-two.

EDITH. You're a child. A nasty child.

*Long pause, she stares at him.* GERALD *is staring up at her.*

GERALD. And my games are so literal. But the words *were* yours. Weren't they the right ones, after all?

EDITH (*after a pause*). Do you want me to telephone for a doctor then? If you do, say so.

GERALD. Oh, that's *your* business.

EDITH. I'll do what *you* tell me to do.

GERALD. Then — do whatever you think is best. You have your church, your art, and your education. If the maxims you derive from each should conflict, you will have to choose.

EDITH (*after a pause*). How do you feel?

GERALD. A trifle nervous. But physically tip-top. The system needs about twenty minutes to absorb them. After that it's down-hill all the way. But I believe the decline can be arrested until I go into a coma.

EDITH. In other words, you can reach the telephone unaided.

*She turns, goes out.*
*Cut to* GERALD's *face, he smiles, uncertainly. There is a pause.*
EDITH *returns, walks past him, into* GILES's *room. There is the sound of a protest from* GILES, *sleepy.*
*She comes out, carrying him. Walks past* GERALD, *and out of the room.*
*Cut to* GERALD's *face. He sits resolutely. Crosses his hands in his lap. Licks his lip. His face twitches slightly. He raises a hand, scratches at his cheek as if he had an itch there. Then lowers his hand, raises it, scratches again, blinks.*

**94. Interior. Bedroom. Night.** EDITH *is sitting up in bed, staring ahead.*
GILES *is lying beside her, asleep. She picks her watch up from the table, looks at it, puts it down.*
*She turns, looks down at GILES and, cut to his face asleep.*
EDITH'*s hand, shaking, goes to his hair, touches it and* cut from this to:

**95. Interior. Living Room. Night.** GERALD'*s face, eyes closed, mouth open in a yawn. His hand is resting against his cheek. His eyes blink open. He stares blearily around, heaves himself up, gropes forward, stands swaying, and* cut to:

**96. Interior. Bedroom. Night.** EDITH *is sitting up, staring ahead with great intensity. She closes her eyes, opens them.*
*Suddenly there is a crash, eerily distanced.*
*Her head jerks in alarm as the room fills with heavy breathing. She looks towards the baby-alarm.*
*The breathing is coming from it. She jerks her head away, stares ahead. Then reaches out a hand trembling slightly, to the alarm, turns it off. Then she sits with her head sunk on her chest, eyes closed.*
Fade out *on this, and* fade up *on* EDITH *lying, her face sideways on the pillow, her thumb in her mouth, staring into* GILES'*s face, also sideways on the pillow, thumb in his mouth, asleep. She straightens slowly, turns to the baby-alarm, still sucking on her thumb. She reaches out a hand. Turns on the knob.*
*The breathing is now stertorous, rasping. She turns the knob off quickly, blinks and as if coming to herself, swings her legs out of bed. She hurries out of the bedroom and* cut to:

**97. Interior. Hall. Night.** EDITH *is in the hall, and from her point of view.* Cut to *the door to* GERALD'*s study. It opens.*
EDITH *is staring at it, making incomprehensible noises of fear.*
TOMMY *is standing there, in* GERALD'*s coat, goggles pushed up on his forehead, helmet and gauntlets under his arm.*

TOMMY. I'm cold. (*Slightly whining.*) He told me to wait outside, with the bike, where is he then?

EDITH'*s lips move for a second. She gives a ghastly grin.*

EDITH. Asleep.

    Cut to:


**98. Interior. Giles's Bedroom. Night.** Come straight in on
GERALD, *lying on the floor, snoring heavily. The baby-alarm
microphone close to his face.*
Then cut to TOMMY's *face, shocked and bewildered, staring at*
GERALD.

    TOMMY. Ohh – Ohh – look now – look – Edie we've got to –
    look.

    (*Little pause.*)

    What are we going to do, then? What are we going to do?

    (Cut to EDITH's *face. She is staring at* TOMMY. *Cut to:*)


**99. Exterior. The drive. Dawn.** *In on* GERALD's *face, in close-up,
in goggles and crash helmet.*
Then draw back *to see him in the side-car, with his head back and
his mouth open, breathing deeply. Then his face is drawn slowly
out of camera and:*
Cut to:
TOMMY *and* GERALD, *on the motor-bicycle and side-car
respectively, pulling quietly down the drive,* from EDITH's *point
of view.watching from the window, then* cut to:
*Her face at the window, staring out.*


**100. Exterior. Field. Day.** *A path across a field. The motor-bike
travelling slowly and eerily across it, and from a distance, see the
motor-bicycle stopping.*
TOMMY *pulls* GERALD *out of the side-car, lowers him to the
ground, then* TOMMY *walks away, running, walking, running, and:*
Cut to:


**101. Exterior. Mrs Merchant's house. Day.** *The gate to the front
door,* MRS MERCHANT *standing before it, arms akimbo.* EDITH,
*with the pram.*

MRS MERCHANT. I've never been spoken to like that before. Never in my life.

EDITH. He'll never speak to you like that again. I promise.

(*Little pause.*)

He left me — just after he — he'd spoken to you. He said he wouldn't come back.

(*Little pause.*)

We've always had such a good relationship Mrs Merchant.

(*Little pause.*)

Please. We need you, Giles and I. We do need you.


**102. Interior. The kitchen. Day.** *Come in on* TOMMY's *hand, raising a cup to his lips, then to his face. He looks desperately tired.* EDITH *sits opposite, watching him.*

TOMMY. Could it be murder, Edie?

EDITH. It was suicide.

TOMMY. But legally? I mean, if the police —?

EDITH. He wanted to kill himself. He wanted to do it in the way that would hurt me most. He was determined to be hateful to the end.

(*Little pause.*)

He had the right to kill himself. I had the right to defend myself from the consequences of his doing it here.

TOMMY. You said yourself he was ill. He needed help —

EDITH *looks at him very coldly.*

EDITH. Well, you didn't give it to him, did you?

TOMMY. No. I gave it to you instead.

EDITH. Why?

TOMMY. You know why, now. Don't you?

EDITH. Are you in love with me?

TOMMY. I've always been, Edie. Always. (*Little pause.*) And did Gerrie ask you about it? About whether we'd ever slept together.

EDITH (*after a pause*). No. Anyway, it was a long time ago.

TOMMY. Still, he asked *me*. I was just wondering —

EDITH. What did you tell him? (*Little pause.*) *Did* you tell him?

TOMMY. Certainly not. No. I told him it was ridiculous.

EDITH. And so it was. It always is. Quite ridiculous. Everything is ridiculous. Gerald's death.

> *The telephone rings.* EDITH *and* TOMMY *stare at each other. She gets up, lifts the telephone from the receiver, staring at* TOMMY, *then turns away, puts it to her ear.*

Hello. (*Little pause.*) Yes, it is. (*Brightly smiling.*)


**103. Interior. Hospital Ward. Day.** EDITH *and* TOMMY *walking along it, past various beds, to a bed near the end, screened off. There is a* NURSE *with them. The* NURSE *pulls back the screen and cut from* TOMMY's *face and* EDITH's *face to a* MAN, *sitting up, grinning, his arm in a sling, having his pyjamas changed, and cut to:*
TOMMY *and* EDITH *walking on to the next bed, screened. The nurse opens the screen for them, and cut to* GERALD's *face on the pillow, eyes open, breath very faint, then:*
EDITH *is sitting in a chair beside him.* TOMMY *standing beside her. He looks down at* GERALD's *face, he makes a sound, turns his face away, clutches at* EDITH's *hand, and on the tableau:*


**104. Interior. Kitchen. Day.** TOMMY *and* EDITH *sitting at the table, a cup being raised to* TOMMY's *lips.*

EDITH (*almost desultory*). That's your fifth cup. You'll be ill.

TOMMY (*after a pause*). Four, I've only had four cups.

EDITH. That's still too many.

> *Little silence, as —*

> MRS MERCHANT *comes into the kitchen, walking on tip-toe. She stops by* EDITH, *looks down at her compassionately.*

(*Wanly smiling.*) I'll be all right. Really. Tommy's going to look after me, for a little.

> MRS MERCHANT *gingerly touches* EDITH's *arm, she goes out. There is a silence.*

EDITH. You had two cups in that ghastly room, and two in the hospital canteen. It's your fifth.

TOMMY (*thinks, nods*). Fifth. (*Little silence.*) I won't have any more.

EDITH. What are you going to do now? Are you going to stay here?

*After a pause,* TOMMY *nods.*

I won't want you here.

TOMMY. I know.

EDITH. But you'll stay anyway?

TOMMY. Yes I will, Edie. I don't mind being inferior, see. I don't mind.

EDITH *looks at him, with a weary smile.*

EDITH. I shall despise you.

TOMMY. Sometimes. Other times you won't notice me, even. And I'll be nice to Giles. (*Little pause.*) I have no shame.

EDITH. No. That's your strength, isn't it?

TOMMY. Of course people will despise you for living with me.

EDITH. I'm quite strong too. (*She gets up, goes out of the kitchen.*)


**105. Interior. Edith's Study. Day**. *She enters, turns on the light, goes to the window, looks out. Suddenly she crosses herself, closing her eyes and lowering her head. She smiles ironically, turns to the desk.*
*On the desk are the exercise books, neatly piled, and as the camera comes in on them:*
*Sounds of great chords of religious music, organ, which goes on as* EDITH *approaches the desk slowly, as if in a trance, picks them up as if holding something sacred, turns around, her eyes aglow. The music still going on, solemn and magnificent, and:*

TOMMY (*at the door*). So he put them back then?

*The music stops. There is a silence.*

EDITH. You see. You see. I was bound to get them back. I'm a novelist. (*In a whisper.*) That's all I am. That's all I want to be.

I shall go on writing novels until I die. If God is good to me, I shall die as I finish a sentence. His Will Be Done.

Cut to:

TOMMY's *face, staring at her,* stay on his face *as organ music, over, starts again, gently,* mixing into EDITH *at her desk.*


**106. Exterior. Garden. Day.** *The organ music going on, as through the window to her side we see* MRS MERCHANT *in a deck chair, holding* GILES *in her arms, in an accidentally religious posture, and kneeling beside her,* TOMMY, *beside whom is a small jug of soapy water. He has his hands to his face, as if in prayer, blowing a mighty bubble.*
This shot freezes into a still, *as the organ music continues, and:*

Titles superimposed.

Fade out.

**The End.**

# DOG DAYS

To Ian Hamilton, in whose *The New Review*
this play was first published,
my thanks for many other things.

# Author's Note

*Dog Days* was begun before the final draft of another play —
*Butley* — was in production, was continued at odd moments during
rehearsals and completed — frequently and variously — during the
next two years or so. It was just one of a number of plays I was
working on in an increasing state of muddle that was eventually like
a madness. There were moments when, nauseated into lucidity by
the piles of typescript that filled my drawers, my cupboard, an
antique chest and two pinewood coffins, I swore I'd never write again;
which I would have to amend, as I crouched a few minutes later at
my typewriter, into the more calming proposition that I would
merely never finish anything again.

So I went on and on, covering page after page. Characters from
one play would slip into another, change name, age, occupation and
even sex, before either slipping into yet another play or back into the
first. The same passages of dialogue cropped up in different scenes,
in different plays, sometimes in different scenes in the same play or
plays. At the end of each session I squirrelled the newly-written
pages away for tomorrow or next week; for whenever I might be
short. I was the Casaubon of show business.

I doubt if I could ever have stopped, if I hadn't had to go to
New York. In the ten days before my departure I wrote an entirely
new and above all freshly conceived piece that probably differed only
in the odd passage here and there from its first version, dropped it
off at my agent's on the way to the airport, and left him to decide
whether to pass it to a producer or return it to me. Both agent and
producer cabled me in New York. I remember settling into an
armchair in the lobby of the Algonquin and toasting their adjectives
— routinely intoxicating — in champagne, before going on to glare,
several stages later and through a brandy fog, at their noun; which
was 'draft'. As its implications became increasingly distinct, so did
my future as a writer. I would never finish anything again. I would
never write anything again.

Back in London I was given lunch with my agent by the producer in an expensive Spanish restaurant (a good omen, but not conclusive; an invitation to the Cafe Royal would, in a sense, have made the lunch unnecessary). A copy of *Dog Days* that the producer had had re-typed and bound (also a good omen) lay between us as we pursued the preliminary courtesies that always run, in these situations, from the first hand-shake through to coffee. They had both read the play again ('several times', but that was a metaphor) and were prepared to add a few more adjectives to their cabled lists. It seemed to them, too, to be far less of a 'draft' than they had first thought it. 'It was all there.' So much so, in fact, that we must think about a director, and could certainly talk about casting, dates, venues, etc. But perhaps a director first, with whom I could collaborate — 'if I were too close to the script to face it alone' — on whatever needed doing. What needed doing? Oh, a little work, no more — a revision in the second scene of the first act, did I think? the mildest of personality changes to the central character (a dash of motivation, perhaps) — and well, a touch of economy and a modicum of expansion — in different places, of course. Certainly nothing more than most plays needed in rehearsal anyway, for, after all, it was from 75 to 95 per cent *all there*. Good.

I took the producer's copy with me when I left — that night I threw it, along with everything I'd written in the two years since *Butley*, out with the other rubbish. Some day I might begin again. But not in my lifetime, as I saw it. At least, I hoped not.

It was extraordinary to be free. In my study now only the usual bottles, books, empty drawers and chests, a clear desk, a typewriter which could at last be put to proper use (abusive letters to friends, relatives and other strangers, for instance). It was as if I had rid myself of an aged and incontinent alter ego. Halved back to my only self, I could keep things clean.

My agent sent me his copy of *Dog Days*. I tossed it unopened into a chest. The Director of the Palace Theatre, Watford, telephoned to arrange a lunch. Over it he reminded me that I owed him a play. It had been promised years before, but he'd tactfully held back until I had nothing left to give. We went to my house and into my study and opened the chest. We met shortly afterwards to arrange a production.

Within two or three months I'd finished two television plays — *Plaintiffs and Defendants* and *Two Sundays* — and a stage play, *Otherwise Engaged*. It is possible that these three pieces evolved out of the unrelated labour that preceded them, but it is far more likely that I embarrassed myself into them at the prospect of *Dog Days* being performed.

My agent sent the two television plays to the BBC, and I hurried
*Otherwise Engaged* off to Watford. But the Director of its Palace
Theatre was by this time passionately committed to *Dog Days*, and
would accept no substitute. So *Otherwise Engaged* went to the
producer who had talked of doing *Dog Days*, and the Director of
the Palace Theatre, Watford, generously agreed to postpone his
production until the year after *Otherwise Engaged* had opened in
London.

*December 1975*

*Post script.* It was not, after all, to be so easy. I went on behaving
badly towards the Watford Palace Theatre and its director during
the year that followed the opening of *Otherwise Engaged*, pleading
that I wasn't yet up to discussions about a production of another
play, with all the concentration it demanded and all the prospects
(of casting, rehearsals, etc) it opened out, until he became
increasingly cynical about my intentions (while remaining admirably
a friend) and went off to the States on a year's visiting scholarship.
And that was that. Until some time later a sudden show of interest
from the Oxford Playhouse revived my own interest. I agreed to do
it there, and to direct it myself. The by now habitual reaction
followed. Almost at once I dispatched a grovelling message through
my agent withdrawing the piece. One of the Playhouse directors
came down to London to see me, we talked over lunch, and at its
conclusion I agreed to restore the play to him, with the
understanding that I shouldn't direct it myself (after such a display
of doubt how could I?) and that I shouldn't again change my mind.
I shan't. *Dog Days* will open at the Oxford Playhouse in October,
1976 — God and the other devils willing; and I shall find out for
myself at last what it is precisely I've been dreading all this time.

*August 1976*

DOG DAYS was first presented at the
Oxford Playhouse on 26 October 1976
with the following cast:

PETER                    Charles Kay
CHARLES                  Richard Wilson
HILARY                   Gayle Hunnicutt
JOANNA                   Emma Williams


Directed by Gordon McDougall
Set designed by Saul Radomsky
Lighting by David Colmer

# Act One

## Scene One

JOANNA *enters from the kitchen, tentatively. She has a folio under her arm. She puts it down on the table, sees the photograph, looks at it.*

PETER (*enters from the kitchen, carrying two mugs of Nescafé*). Only instant, I'm afraid. The trick is to pretend it's not coffee at all, but a quite other beverage. (*Takes a sip of his own.*) The next trick is to like the other beverage.

JOANNA. Oh this is great. I was just looking — (*Puts the picture down.*) Are they your parents?

PETER. Yes, in our old garden in Bromley.

JOANNA. Your Dad's a fine figure of a man, I love his balaclava, is it from the war or something?

PETER. Actually that's my mother in her gardening gear. But you're right, she was a fine figure of a man. That's my father there, on the edge of the picture as usual. In the fine figure of the little husband.

JOANNA. He's got a really nice smile.

PETER. Hasn't he? A positive advertisement.

JOANNA. For what, your mother you mean?

PETER. No, drunkenness.

JOANNA. Oh. Did he drink too much then?

PETER. He did, yes.

JOANNA. But he gave it up?

PETER. Oh, nothing so drastic. He got killed in a car crash some years ago.

JOANNA. Oh God, I'm sorry. How terrible.

PETER. For whom?

JOANNA. Well, your mother . . .

PETER. Not at all.

JOANNA. You mean she didn't mind?

PETER. She didn't have time to, as she was driving. She always insisted they do everything together, you see. Except drink. And sleep. That's me on his shoulders, by the way.

JOANNA. Oh. Oh yes. And who's this between your mother's legs?

PETER. My brother Charlie. He used to lurk there until quite late in life. He's something of a home body. He's got lots of children of his own now.

JOANNA. Really, how many?

PETER. Actually, I'm never quite sure, but it works on an opposite system to one's bank account. More than one remembered. He's half Catholic.

JOANNA. *Half* Catholic?

PETER. His wife is, and he's wholly married.

JOANNA. You're not married, though?

PETER. Certainly not. Charlie's done enough for two.

JOANNA. Then you have this place all to yourself?

PETER. Well, we're not allowed upstairs.

JOANNA. Who?

PETER. You and I.

JOANNA. Oh. Who lives there?

PETER. My landlady.

JOANNA. Is she in now?

PETER. No, she works. She teaches English to foreigners at one of those dingy academies off Oxford Street. Then she picks up her little boy from school. She's never back until four-thirty to five on Wednesdays, she has to do some shopping at Sainsbury's. So they won't disturb us.

JOANNA. Is *she* married?

PETER. Yes, she is.

JOANNA. What's he like?

PETER. Like any other landlord in the Muswell Hill area. He goes down as his property value goes up.

JOANNA. Down where?

PETER. Downhill. All the way to Islington, if he can make it. (*Puts his mug down, turns away.*)

JOANNA. I'm sorry, I always ask questions when I'm nervous. You're the first editor I've shown my work to, and I've been puffing myself up so much that now you're going to look at it I keep putting off the big moment. Well — (*Opens the folio, shows him.*) I know it's not your department, you do all the intellectual stuff I know, but I'd really value your opinion.

PETER. Ah, nudes. I like nudes. The one on the left though, the chap's a bit fat isn't he — oh, they're both chaps.

JOANNA. Well yes.

PETER. What's it for, a homosexual sex manual, nobody told *me* we were doing one.

JOANNA. No, it's that dieting manual. Those blokes are before and after.

PETER. I see. Before looks altogether nicer, I like that.

JOANNA. Do you think you people will go on using me, now you've started?

PETER. Oh once we people start using people, we never stop. In life, as in art. (*Goes over, grabs her, kisses her clumsily.*)

JOANNA (*struggles free*). Hey, you haven't even looked at it properly.

PETER. Well, I'm a little short of time.

JOANNA. Time for what? (*Pause.*) Oh, I get it, bed you mean?

PETER. It'll have to be the sofa actually. But if we take the slip-cover off and plump up the pillows it'll pass muster. (*Pause.*)

Well, the wooing *is* going on rather, isn't it, like one of those
hors d'oeuvres that stop you getting to the main course. (*Pause.*)
And I've got a sociologist called Nuzek coming in this afternoon
with his latest book. On *Protestantism and Pornography*. I'll see
if I can't get you the dust-jacket. (*Comes over to her, takes her
in his arms again, kisses her.*) Something on the lines of that one
would do very well — the thin nude could be Protestantism and
the fat one Pornography, or the other way around even. I could
get you lots more commissions — (*Kisses her.*)

JOANNA. Get off me! (*Forces him away.*) What sort of fool do
you think I am?

PETER. My sort, I hope . . .

JOANNA. You're married!

PETER. Good God, who to?

JOANNA. That landlady of yours.

PETER. Scarcely.

JOANNA. Scarcely what?

PETER. Scarcely eight years.

JOANNA. And that little boy's your son. Well, isn't he?

PETER. If I answer that question with too much confidence, I'll
destroy the premise of a whole tragic literature. Besides, he's *very*
little, if you stare straight ahead you won't even see him. (*Moves
towards* JOANNA *again.*)

JOANNA (*moves away*). I don't sleep with married men, I'm
afraid.

PETER. Of what? We're very well trained.

JOANNA. Jesus, what a prick!

PETER (*angrily*). What a *what*?

JOANNA. Prick, that's what you are, a prick!

PETER. Oh, thank God, I thought you said *prig*.

JOANNA. Is this the way out too? (*Gestures towards kitchen,
right.*)

PETER. Right into the boulevards of Muswell Hill. I'll go this
way (*Gestures to the left*) and wink at the neighbours.

JOANNA. And in your own home too. (*Turns, goes out with portfolio.*)

PETER (*stands for a moment, then goes to the window, leans out*). Hey — hey — what about *your* place then?

*Waits, gets no response, turns, goes to the drinks table, pours himself a stiff scotch, adds soda water, swallows it down, looks at his wrist watch, picks up his briefcase. Goes out, left.*

*Lights down.*

*Lights up.*

*The room full of sunlight. Outside the sound of children's voices at play. Toys and Sunday bits and pieces scattered around the room. After a moment, PETER enters, left, in weekend wear and very sloppy. He is smoking. He looks towards the window, winces, goes to the drinks table, pours himself a scotch, squirts in soda water, turns, goes to the sofa.*

CHARLES (*off, outside the window, right*). Nindy, what a clever girlie, did you do this just for Daddy, thank you darling, thank you. Now you go and watch the big ones play football while Daddy takes this in and looks for Uncle Peter.

PETER *listens to this, then turns over on the sofa, cupping his cigarette and drink.*

CHARLES *enters, carrying a plastic pot. He goes through and out, left. He's also in weekend wear, but neat, short-haired and springy of step.*

PETER *adjusts himself more comfortably, sips from his drink, puffs on his cigarette.*

*Sound of tap running, lavoratory flushing, left.*

PETER *takes up his defensive position, back to the audience.*

CHARLES *re-enters, left, carrying the pot. He hesitates, goes to the drinks table, then puts the pot down on it as he squirts himself an enormous soda water. Begins to drain it off, becomes aware that somebody is on the sofa. Goes over, looks down at PETER.*

CHARLES. Pete!

PETER (*rolls over*). Hi Charlie.

CHARLES. What on earth are you doing?

PETER. Practising.

CHARLES. Practising what?

PETER. Secret drinking.

CHARLES. Oh, I see. Not feeling very sociable, eh?

PETER. On the contrary, but it's such a rare feeling I like to savour it on my own. (*Gets up, goes to the window.*)

CHARLES (*watches him*). I must say, you've been acting very strangely today. We've scarcely seen you, except at lunch. Is something the matter?

PETER. No.

CHARLES. Frankly some of your remarks were a bit off.

PETER. Really? (*Staring out of the window.*) Probably because I've kept them in too long. Did you know that Alison's joined the boys in football. Is that wise at seven months gone? I should warn you that Jeremy's got a powerful shot for a five year old *and* has a nasty English habit of going over the top.

CHARLES. Oh, she'll be all right, you know how active she is during her pregnancies. Peter . . .

PETER. And between them too, to get to them so quickly. When do you intend to stop exactly? I realise Alison's a practising Catholic but this'll make six in five years . . .

CHARLES. Four, actually. In six years. As I'm sure *you* realise. And you also realise, because I've told you often enough, that we *both* happen to believe in letting them come as they please.

PETER. Well, you certainly do please them, from the speed at which they keep coming.

CHARLES. The important thing is that they please *us*. Anyway, now that you've chosen to raise the subject, Alison and I sometimes wonder what you two have got against having more.

PETER. Contraceptives, and they work miracles.

CHARLES. Oh ha ha. But has it ever occurred to you that it might

turn out a little hard on Jeremy himself? He'll be the one
that'll have to cope with being an only child.

PETER. If I can cope with being an only father, when we need
two or three, he can cope with being an only child when we
don't need any more.

CHARLES. Something's the matter, isn't it?

PETER. With what?

CHARLES. With you. For one thing you're smoking and drinking
far more than usual.

PETER. Oh that's quite usual with smoking and drinking.

CHARLES. But Pete, think of your health! I'm sure you would
feel much better if you cut down.

PETER. Ah, but then I wouldn't have the scotch and fags I need
to help me endure it.

CHARLES. Endure what?

PETER. My health. (*Toasts himself.*) I notice you've cut down
though. To the very bottom. And the last time you were here
you'd fought your way up to five a day wasn't it?

CHARLES. Only because I was under some stress.

PETER. What stress?

CHARLES. I was still waiting to hear whether I'd got it.

PETER. Got what?

CHARLES. The Assistant Headmastership at Ampleside.

PETER. And did you?

CHARLES. Not only did Alison phone Hilary as soon as I'd
phoned her, but before lunch today Alison actually described a
sort of informal interview she'd had with Headmaster.

PETER. Oh, that was with Headmaster!

CHARLES. Who did you think it was with?

PETER. Her gynaecologist.

CHARLES. *That* was during lunch.

PETER. She had an interview with her gynaecologist during
lunch . . .

CHARLES. Oh ha ha.

PETER. Well, anyway Charlie, congratulations. I know how much you respect that Headmaster of yours. It'll be wonderful to work so closely with him, won't it?

CHARLES. Yes, it will.

PETER. He's a great influence over your life, isn't he?

CHARLES. In some things, perhaps, I don't deny it.

PETER. How can you, when there's scarcely a decision, large or small, on which you don't consult him — where he leads, you follow, eh?

CHARLES. I wouldn't go that far.

PETER. Really? How far has he gone?

CHARLES. It's no good, you won't get at me through Headmaster, you know.

PETER. Does he smoke?

CHARLES. He's got far too much sense.

PETER. Does he drink?

CHARLES. Yes, he does.

PETER. What does he drink?

CHARLES. The odd wine, why?

PETER. That wine you brought along for lunch was odd, was it one of his?

CHARLES. It was a retzina.

PETER. Home-made though, wasn't it?

CHARLES. How on earth would one make retzina?

PETER. Exactly as the Greeks do, I should think. By boiling up some tree bark.

CHARLES. Didn't you make it clear enough at lunch what you thought of it — sniffing at your glass and making faces to yourself? I got the message, Pete!

PETER. You've got that smirk on, Charlie.

CHARLES. *What* smirk?

PETER. Your lying smirk.

CHARLES. Lying—what lie, for Heaven's sake! (*Little pause.*) I never said it wasn't home-made, I just wanted to make sure you really guessed. I had a little bet with Alison when we decanted it into that bottle that you wouldn't. Which I'm now perfectly prepared to admit I lose, all right!

PETER. Who gave you the recipe?

CHARLES. It's a traditional one from Cyprus, that's been handed down.

PETER. To whom? Headmaster?

CHARLES. His wife, actually. Now I really think I ought to go out and help Alison and Hilary entertain the children—are you coming, or are you going to stay here?

PETER. They're vegetarian too, aren't they, Headmaster and wife?

CHARLES. Yes they are, *so what?*

PETER. And that's why you and Alison have given up meat, is it?

CHARLES. Given up meat? Didn't you see me put Hilary's casserole away?

PETER. Yes, into your handkerchief. You used to employ the same technique with Mummy's Friday night fish stews—until she asked you to explain why your trouser pockets smelt of haddock.

CHARLES (*after a long pause*). Yes, well I do apologise for that. The truth is, as we'd forgotten to warn Hilary, and as we realised she'd gone to a lot of trouble to cook for us, we felt it a matter of common courtesy to go through with it. Frankly, we knew the children would more than make up for us. (*Little pause.*) I do hope she didn't notice, though.

PETER. Oh, you were as skilful as ever. The funny smile, the elaborate chewing, the dabs at your lips. You may have made her casserole look inedible, but you did look as if you were managing to eat it. Is it still in your pocket?

CHARLES. Yes.

PETER. Well, you can chuck it into the garbage now, I won't sneak.

CHARLES. Actually, I'd rather keep it.

PETER. Keep it!

CHARLES. Yes.

PETER. In your pocket?

CHARLES. For the time being.

PETER (*after a pause*). Oh I see, no cloistered and fugitive virtue for you, eh Charlie? You like to carry your vice around with you, to fight every moment of the day. A handkerchief full of temptation! — I just hope you don't spill it out in front of Headmaster when you have to blow your nose. He mightn't believe your story.

CHARLES (*slowly*). Ha. Ha. Ha. I happen to want it for a dog.

PETER. You haven't got a dog.

CHARLES. No, but the school has. Alfonso — at least that's what I call him. He's a sort of stray that's always in and out of Headmaster's garden. Somebody's got to feed him.

PETER. And you've chosen my wife? Why can't Headmaster do the job, it's his garden. Or doesn't he like animals?

CHARLES. I'm sure he loves them. And I *know* his wife does. So I expect they do feed him. But I also expect he'd be grateful for any little tid-bits. Does that clear that up? There can't be any further questions Pete — now that you've managed to embarrass me, after all.

PETER. Well, just one.

CHARLES. I don't think I want to hear it.

PETER. OK. (*Goes and stands by the window.*)

CHARLES (*stands uncertainly, then goes to the soda water, takes a swift draught from his glass, looks at* PETER). All right, what is it?

PETER. Mmmmm?

CHARLES. Your last question?

PETER. Mmm. Oh yes — Did you give up meat, cigarettes and alcohol — except for boiled tree bark, that is — *before* your appointment as Assistant, to ingratiate yourself with Headmaster? Or *afterwards*, on his orders? Or did you do it *during* the interview, in a series of dramatic renunciations?

CHARLES. I didn't give up, or have to give up, anything to get the Assistantship. Alison and I merely observed how well Headmaster and his wife looked on their regimen and drew a sane conclusion which would doubtless have escaped you. Furthermore, far from feeling ashamed of it, I don't mind telling you that I, personally, feel absolutely marvellous for it. As if I were fifteen again!

PETER. I'm sorry to hear that. You were particularly ghastly at fifteen. Even Mummy thought so.

CHARLES. At least *I* see the world properly, in its vivid details. And most of what I see, I like. What do *you* see at the moment, Pete?

PETER. Nothing much to like, I admit, Charlie. (*Little pause.*) Actually, from my recollection of Alison's gynaecological anecdotes, delivered during the lunch she was presumably pocketing in her pregnancy trousers, you don't have to give up anything to get the vivid details. As long, that is, as you don't give up Alison.

CHARLES. Right! That does it! I spent the whole morning trying to overlook your bloody nasty remarks—

PETER. Spoilsport.

CHARLES. But don't worry, I'm not going to overlook that one. You jeer at my feeling fifteen, but you must have gone right back to the nursery to insult my wife like that.

PETER. You didn't have a wife like that in the nursery, Charlie. Or are you about to spring into the Freudian open by naming Mummy? Come to think of it we didn't have a nursery either. We were allowed the run of a box-room in a semi-detached in Bromley which *she* called a nursery for the same reason that she used to call that ghastly institution she made the drunken mouse buy us into a public school.

CHARLES. Wundale is a Public School! (*Pause.*) *What* did you say about Mummy? (*Pause.*) And Daddy?

PETER. That you're fulfilling her ambitions to the hilt, Charlie. And I can't say worse than that, can I? You may have risen a notch in greasing your way into the Assistant Headmastership at Amplesides, but then she got you to plan *your* public school early, didn't she, in the Wundale Remove at thirteen. And you don't intend to stop until you get all the way to Eton in your

mid-forties, when you'll be the first real old, or at least
middle-aged, public school boy in the family.

CHARLES. Why, you little— (*Makes as if to hit* PETER, *checks
himself.*) You have the nerve to talk about snobs—a man whose
sole ambition was to end up editing books he's discovered too late
he despises and so is stuck as a Junior Editor—and for life, the
way you're going on. And quite rightly given your attitude. A
muddled little Oxford pseud, whose only way of elevating
himself is to sneer at other people. I'd hoped you'd grown up a
little since marrying Hilary, but you haven't have you? That's
what you've really reverted to, isn't it—a cheap little
undergraduate.

PETER. Not at all cheap. I cost the State quite a lot of money.

CHARLES. You little— (*Pulls himself together, and with dignity.*)
If it weren't for Hilary's feelings, and Jeremy's—I wouldn't set
foot in this house again. (*Turns, goes toward exit kitchen,
right.*)

PETER. That's where a graduate of Oxford and a graduate of
Reading have more in common than either of us thought,
Charlie. Because those are my own sentiments exactly. (*As*
CHARLES, *unhearing, exits, collapses on sofa.*)

*There is a lighting change, to suggest time passing.* PETER
*lights a cigarette. Much activity from the kitchen, right.*

HILARY (*enters, looks at* PETER, *and as she begins to clear up
toys and bits and pieces*). Jeremy is in bed, I trust.

PETER (*not stirring*). Yup.

HILARY. And did you bother to get him to read to you?

PETER. Until we both realised he still couldn't.

HILARY. Of course he can.

PETER. Then we have a wonderchild who can read with his eyes
shut. My own view is that he was reciting.

HILARY. You probably made him nervous.

PETER. Not as nervous as he made me. 'This is Janet. This is John.
That is Janet. That is John.' (*In a sing-song.*) I thought he was
trying to put me under a spell. I was reading at four. So were

you. So was everybody in our day, except Charlie, and he made it by five and a half.

HILARY. And except those who'd never read. Because they were never taught.

PETER. Oh, I recognise the modern system is more democratic. Now everybody gets taught but nobody reads.

HILARY. What would *you* know about the modern system, as you don't even go to the lectures the school lays on to explain it.

PETER. I went to the first, if you remember; in which case you'll also remember that it was doubtful whether the lady who gave the lecture could read, she could scarcely talk. But don't worry darling, it's all being attended to. We publishers are working hand in hand with the Department of Education. They're making it their job to ensure that our Jeremy won't read when he grows up, and we're making it ours to ensure that if he grows up there are no books around worth his reading. I promise you our son shall not feel deprived! What's left can be read by those foreigners you teach, most of whom seem to be writing them anyway, judging by the standard of the English I'm called on to edit.

HILARY *has gone to the door, toys etc in her arms. Turns, glares at him.*

By God, I believe that's what's known as a level look, or would be if it weren't for your slight squint, now you're tired.

HILARY (*sees the pot, manages to pick it up*). Do you mean you've just lolled there, letting it stare you in the face?

PETER. I did try staring back, but it remained unmoved.

HILARY. Could you at least open the door, please!

PETER *gets up, saunters over, opens the door, swivelling at the same time to pick up the scotch. As HILARY exits, pours himself a glass, lights a cigarette. Goes back to sofa, after a pause.*

HILARY, *off, calls something.*

PETER. Wah—?

HILARY *calls again.*

Right, fine, fine. (*Goes back to the sofa, settles onto it.*)

HILARY (*enters, stage left*). God, I wish you'd at least answer me when I call.

PETER. I did.

HILARY. And what did you say?

PETER. Wah—? Right, fine and fine.

HILARY. And what sort of answer is that?

PETER. What sort of question was it?

HILARY. That typescript that's been lying in the lavatory since Thursday, how important is it?

PETER. To Nuzek, the Polish socio-prophet, very. Because he wrote it. To me, not at all. I'm merely its editor.

HILARY. So you won't have to read it then?

PETER. Nobody who buys it will read it, why should I?

HILARY. And those reviewers you used to worry about so—won't they notice if it's not edited?

PETER. Oh, they can write their reviews from my blurb.

HILARY. And what will you write your blurb from?

PETER. Their last reviews. It's what's known in publishing as a benign circle. Nuzek's reputation depends on nobody reading him. His prose guarantees that nobody will. You're taking an unusual interest in the mysteries of my little trade, darling, how come?

HILARY. Only to find whether wha—? right, fine and fine were reasonable answers to my question. (*Goes over to the desk, picks up a brief-case beside it, takes out some papers.*)

PETER. And how did I do?

HILARY. All right, it appears. (*Beginning to sort through.*) As it clearly doesn't matter that either Jeremy or one of your nephews blocked the lavatory with it this afternoon.

PETER. Christ, they didn't!

HILARY. I thought you said it didn't matter.

PETER. But he's coming to our six simultaneous publications party in a couple of weeks. He could ruin it if he finds out about this. We've already asked the Brendan Behan of Women's Lib along to do the swearing and fighting. Ah well, I'll just have to tell him our son mistook it for a bottom copy. (*Gets up, goes to the drinks table.*) Drink?

HILARY. No thanks.

PETER (*pouring himself a large one, adding soda water*). Ah, I've been looking forward to this all day.

HILARY. Really? What's so special about the fifth or sixth?

PETER. It's backed up by four or five others. By the way, how do you think your casserole went down with Charlie and Alison? (*Sitting down again.*)

HILARY. You needn't bother.

PETER. What?

HILARY. Alison confessed in the garden.

PETER. Oh. (*Little pause.*) In the garden she confessed, did she? She really does practise away at her Catholicism, in Church, in the open air, in bed — I must say, she's pretty swollen, even for nine months, swollen older Alison. Do you think that gynaecologist of hers has taught her how to begin the next before delivering the last? She surely doesn't bother with such fripperies as labour any more — just a brief muscular spasm something like a hiccough. Oh, I remember when she was a mere slip of a lump of a thing — studying Charlie and English at Reading, who would have believed — Why even prophetic Nuzek will be a mite perplexed to hear — that because my brother happened to marry a lump of a slip whose reproductive organs might have been plumbed by the Vatican itself, his *Protestantism and Pornography* is currently washing through the sewers of London . . .

HILARY *has got together her papers, and is on her way out.*

What about some supper, I'm peckish. (*Taking her by the wrist.*)

HILARY. Are you? Then you'll have to get it yourself.

PETER. Why?

HILARY. Because I've got to finish these tonight.

PETER. Why?

HILARY. So that I can brush up on some phonetics tomorrow before taking Jeremy to school.

PETER. Why? Is his classless accent slipping?

HILARY. Unless of course you take him for once. Can you?

PETER. Darling, I don't drive, remember. You do.

HILARY. It's within walking distance. He could easily manage it.

PETER. But I couldn't. Besides, he'd use up my whole day's supply of artless prattle, which I'm going to need for my work. (*Little pause.*) Surely even in these glum days a wife can rustle up a sandwich and cocoa for hubby, before hurrying off to her diversions.

HILARY. Diversions! My diversions! Do you mean these! (*Shakes essays at him.*)

PETER (*pretending to peer closely*). If those include the essay I glanced at last night, on *Lady Windermere's Fan.* By some Swiss or Swede or Frog. Or Hun or Finn or other Wog. He concludes that Oscar Wilde was a bit of a humbugger. You know darling, they really shouldn't have to pay you for reading, you really ought to pay them for writing, lines like that. (*Reaches behind, pours scotch into his glass.*)

HILARY. Is it any good telling you you'll be sorry in the morning, if you drink that.

PETER. I'll be sorry now, if I don't.

HILARY. Not too nice though, for Jeremy, at breakfast.

PETER. Then I shan't let him have it for breakfast.

HILARY (*makes to go to door, stops, comes back*). Just because *you've* started being contemptuous of your work, don't you dare start showing me your contempt for mine. Because not only am I not contemptuous of it, no I'm not, but also—

PETER. Perhaps you should practise a *little* contempt for it. Taking it seriously is beginning to affect your conversational style. That last sentence was like the other half of a simultaneous translation.

HILARY. I started to tell you something and I'm going to finish.

PETER. OK. But keep your head. Now—'not only do you have a

job which not only are you not contemptuous of, no you're not,
but also—' Can you pick it up from there? But also?

HILARY. But also I have this home to run, and I'm sick to death
of your contempt for that too. It's a difficult enough proposition
at the best of times, but it's virtually impossible since you've
taken to sneering at me for trying to do it while refusing to make
even a gesture towards actually helping.

PETER. Actually helping in what?

HILARY. Everything. As for instance taking Jeremy to school *and*
fetching him. Every day. With four hours' hard teaching in
between. Then there's the ironing, some of which you actually
used to do at one time, remember, the *twice*-a-week drag
through Sainsbury's now that you refuse to accompany me for one
*big* load on Saturdays, then the cooking for Jeremy at tea-time,
and preparing something for you later on, with tomorrow's
teaching to get ready in the evening. On top of which I still do
my best to look attractive—

PETER. On top of which on top of what, out of that assortment
of recriminations and accolades? I know what else you've been
doing, you sly-boots you, you've been mugging up on the rhetoric
of the new woman. A tirade in the form of a *curriculum vitae*.
Wherever have you found the time? (*Pause.*) Actually, now you
mention them, some of those meals you've been preparing
recently were first prepared by Indians or Chinese, in those
take-away restaurants. All you've had to do was to bring them
home and then take them away. Usually uneaten. Before
throwing them out. Why, if Charlie's doggie knew about your
catering arrangements, he'd give up Headmaster's garden and
lope straight up Muswell Hill.

HILARY (*after a long pause*). Tell me—how long *do* you intend to
keep this up?

PETER. What up?

HILARY. This—this pose of yours.

PETER. What pose of mine?

HILARY. I don't know what you're aiming at, but the result is
somewhere between Falstaff and a spiteful woman columnist.

PETER. Falstaff? But I was only aiming for the spiteful woman
columnist. (*Shakes his head effeminately.*)

HILARY. God, I wish you knew how you looked.

PETER. A wish you're about to make come true, from the look of you. (*Settles back as if comfortably.*) Well?

HILARY. You've got a — what? — two-day stubble over your face, your eyes are blood-shot, you've got a smoker's cough, which I've been hearing develop almost by the week. (*Pause.*) Like your paunch.

PETER. You've been hearing my paunch develop? So that's why you've been sleeping so far down the bed, eavesdropping?

HILARY. No, keeping away from your breath. Which reeks of nicotine and booze.

PETER. Now that's dandruff, bad breath, smoker's cough, stubble and paunch. (*Ticking them off on his fingers.*) But those details apart, do you find me as winsome as ever?

HILARY. I find you quite disgusting.

PETER. Careful sweetling, or in a second you'll say something you'll regret.

HILARY. I regret not having said it to you weeks ago. I don't know what's the matter with you, but I can't stand it any more. Not the sight of you, nor the nagging it provoked from me at first, nor the contempt I've felt for you recently. Because *that's* what my contempt has been for, *you.* We haven't been to a dinner party recently at which you haven't ended up drunker than anyone else, or any social occasion at which you haven't contrived to insult half the people in the room. I've been ashamed.

PETER. Well, some of those rooms were pretty large. Look at it this way, if they'd been half the size I'd have managed to insult the lot.

HILARY. But you haven't done it with style, Peter, don't delude yourself.

PETER. Quantity these days darling, a lot of those people I scarcely knew.

HILARY. But why? Why? (*Pause.*) Today, with *your* brother and his family around — I don't know what you said to him when he came in here, but he was in a dreadful state when he came out — and before that at lunch, the way you sat lolling forward, your eyes glassy with too much drink and too much food —

PETER. And too much boredom! Don't forget the too much boredom!

HILARY. The real bore was you! Stirring yourself only to bait Charlie, completely ignoring Alison —

PETER. Not fair! I tried to bait Alison too. She chose to ignore it.

HILARY. I can't go on like this!

PETER. Really? I thought you were just warming up.

HILARY. You're poisoning my life. And Jeremy's. He doesn't even want you to read to him in the evenings any more. He actually cried when I said tonight you might be doing it. Or does that make you pleased with yourself too? (*Pause.*) Neither of us can bear you as you are.

PETER. Well, neither of you will get me as I might have been, because that's over. And as for how I *was* —

HILARY (*after a pause*). Well?

PETER. That's over too, so far over I've forgotten how I did it.

HILARY. Very well. (*Turns, goes towards the door.*)

PETER. Oh, just a minute darling! (*Gets up, goes towards her, stands staring at her, then begins to unbutton her blouse.*)

HILARY. What are you doing?

PETER. Stripping you down. (*Stops, then puts his arms around HILARY, pulls her to him, kisses her.*) Before having you off.

HILARY *beats him off savagely.*

Hey — hey — (*Defending himself*) this is fun! (*Advances on her again.*)

HILARY (*strikes out at him again*). Stop it, stop it, stop it!

PETER *backs away. They stand, breathing heavily, staring at each other.*

How dare you!

PETER. How dare I what?

HILARY. Grab at me as if I were — I were — (*Slight pause, then witheringly*) like some dirty old man.

PETER. But you're not at all like some dirty old man. If you were I'd grab him instead. (*Little pause.*) Well, it *is* Sunday, isn't it? And therefore about the hour for our Sunday evening sex. Distinguishable from our Wednesday evening sex by its venue. Wednesday evening's workaday sex, upstairs in bed after a dinner out. *If* we can arrange a baby-sitter *and* you have no marking to do. Sunday evening's Sabbatical sex down here on the sofa in a spontaneous tussle *after* you've shyly slipped off the sofa cover. (*Little pause.*) At least so it used to be not too long ago.

HILARY. Well, not any more.

PETER. Now let's see — that's no cooking any more and no lovemaking any more —

HILARY. Love-making? You haven't made love to me for months. You just use me as a stage towards one of your post-coital cigarettes. That is, when you've been conscious. Otherwise you merely roll on top of me yawning and away from me snoring —

PETER. What do you do between my yawn and my snore, I wonder, in the short period when I tend to be quite active? Draw up your Sainsbury's shopping list or practise one of those pronunciation classes you give to Spanish nuns and other lay-abouts? I recall catching the odd murmur, though your limbs remain supine.

HILARY. It wasn't a murmur. It was a mutter.

PETER. But what? Directions? Encouragement?

HILARY. Hurry up pig, or get it over with. That sort of encouragement.

PETER. I see. Less of an effort then than actually resisting.

HILARY. At least quicker than all the rows and explanations that dragged on until dawn.

PETER. Which you now, you ageing paradox you, seem bent on having. Well then, let's discuss your past bedtime *froideurs* — the ones that led to the rows, and for which everything from Victorian headaches to brutally contemporary ailments were offered in explanation.

HILARY. The most usual explanation was that I was tired after a day out at work and a day of domestic duties. A simple matter which you were incapable of understanding —

PETER. Which, I suppose, is why you had to put more effort into a normal marital fuck.

HILARY. Do you honestly mean that you're going in for all this —
smoking and drinking and spite — to make up for your sex-life?

PETER. My lack of it, perhaps.

HILARY. How childish you really are.

PETER. Well — well — do you think it's been fun sharing a bed with
you.

HILARY. Then don't. (*Pause.*) Will you stay down here, please.

PETER. Certainly not! *You* stay down here, I'm off to the
conjugating bed, as one of your Frogs or Wogs would doubtless
put it.

HILARY. If you prefer. I just didn't think it would be fair to
separate you from your bottle.

PETER. Or yourself from Jeremy. Having two males beside you in
bed has given you delusions of old-fashioned womanhood. But
what lures him to slide between us most nights is only a nightmare
after all. As he'll find out post-puberty.

HILARY. Which is it to be? Down here or upstairs?

PETER. I'll take down here. In my suddenly converted Muswell
Hill maisonette bed-sitter, thank you.

HILARY. Right. (*Turns, goes out of the door, left.*)

PETER (*following her, shouts up after her*). So. You're replacing
mechanical sex with spontaneous frigidity. (*Waits. There is a
slight pause, then*)

*Sounds of* JEREMY *crying.*

PETER *stands listening with growing uncertainty.*

HILARY (*re-appears*). You've woken him. Does that complete your
day's work? (*Goes out again.*)

PETER *surges across the room as if to shut the door with a slam.
Holds his hand, listens.*

HILARY (*off*). It's all right, darling, nothing to be frightened of.
Mummy's coming.

PETER. Sounds bloody frightening to me. (*Closes the door, goes to the drinks table, pours himself a large scotch, squirts soda water into it, drains it off. At the top of his voice*) I consider myself free at last! Absolutely free! (*Hurls the glass against a wall.*)

*Lights.*

## Scene Two

*A small and depressing bed-sitter in, say, Chalk Farm. Bathroom off.*

*A cupboard-type kitchen on, concealed by a curtain. A chair by the bed, a desk, a tatty armchair. Books and magazines scattered about, and on the wall some Marxist-type posters. Ancient copies of the* Daily Worker *and more recent ones of the* Worker's Press.

*It is about eleven in the morning.* PETER, *dressed except for his shirt, emerges from the bathroom, in which he has evidently been shaving. He is carrying a tin mug of Nescafé, from which he sips. He sits down on the bed to put on his shoes.*

*There is a knock at the door.*

PETER. Christ! (*Looks at his watch.*) Just coming! (*He pulls on his shirt, buttons it up, knots his tie, runs his hands through his hair, races over to the bed, pulls up the covers, makes a futile attempt to clean up the mess.*) On my way! (*Gives up, goes towards the door, stops, looks at his shoulders, brushes dandruff off them.*) You're nice and early. (*Opening the door.*) Oh.

CHARLES. Can I come in?

PETER *steps aside with reluctance, lets* CHARLES *in.*

I didn't really expect to catch you in. I thought you'd be at work.

PETER. I didn't really expect you to catch me in. I thought you'd be at work.

CHARLES. Actually, I've got a free morning. At least until lunch, when I have to see Headmaster.

PETER. Have to, do you, Charlie?

CHARLES. *Want* to, actually, Pete. It's a personal matter.

PETER. Really? What?

CHARLES (*after a little pause*). I don't mind at all telling you. Bursar says there's a house opposite the school, quite a large one. And as Alison and I realise we need a larger place, I thought I'd ask Headmaster about the chances of getting it.

PETER. Rent free, would it be?

CHARLES. A nominal rent.

PETER. Well, I can see that if you don't believe in contraceptives, you've got to go in for family planning.

CHARLES. Perhaps I simply take my responsibilities seriously. To my family as well as my work. Or are you giving that up, too?

PETER. Isn't there some Froggy epigram to the effect that we don't give up our vices — they give us up?

CHARLES (*shocked*). Do you mean you've been sacked?

PETER. Why should I be sacked, I haven't done anything. For weeks. Oh don't worry Charlie, we're having our six simultaneous publications party today. By two o'clock they won't remember that they didn't see me at ten o'clock, by three o'clock they won't even remember that they did see me at two. Drink?

CHARLES. At this hour?

PETER. Ah, but I've got some — (*Taking a syphon of soda from behind the curtain, holding it out temptingly. Then a bottle of scotch for himself. As he does so*) Like it, my bachelor pad?

CHARLES. Isn't it a bit out of date for a bachelor?

PETER. Yes, but then so am I. It belongs to one of our middle-aged Northern working-class authors. (*Squirting soda for* CHARLES, *pouring scotch and squirting soda for himself.*) I had him commissioned back to Wigan Pier, wherever that is, for a few months. To flatten down his prose and fire up his politics after his long stint as beer correspondent, or something, for the *Worker's Press* or whatever. (*Hands* CHARLES *his glass.*) I suppose Hilary sent you?

CHARLES. No. She didn't want me to come.

PETER. Although telling you where I was to be found, eh?

CHARLES. No, she refused. I happened to stumble on that extraordinary post card you sent her.

PETER. It was a perfectly ordinary change of address card.

CHARLES. With an obscene drawing on it.

PETER. Well it was done from memory. And where did you happen to stumble on it, Charlie? In her handbag?

CHARLES. No, in the waste-paper basket. Hilary has no idea I'm here. (*Little pause.*) Is it any use asking you to explain.

PETER. Explain what?

CHARLES. Why you've left Hilary.

PETER. Certainly, as it's easily explained. She asked me to leave her bed and I kept on going — right out of the house. All right?

CHARLES. No, it's damned well not all right — for one thing, what about Jeremy?

PETER. Oh, she won't be turning *him* out of her bed for some years yet, if then.

CHARLES. Look Pete, I've been thinking — is it because of her job? You don't resent that, do you? Because you feel less important now that she's meeting new people — her colleagues — ?

PETER. Oh, they don't sound particularly new. In fact, most of them sound old and weary, except for the students, who just sound foreign.

CHARLES. Oh come on Pete, come on, I don't believe it's as simple as it seems. You didn't just start going to seed and then turning nasty, and then walked out or were asked to leave — not just like that. There must be something really terrible between you suddenly, after so many years of happy marriage. What is it?

PETER. Oh, perhaps just so many years of happy marriage between us, eh Charlie? And perhaps so many turned out to be more than our fair share.

CHARLES. And that's all you'll say?

PETER. What does Hilary say?

CHARLES. Nothing. Except that it's for the best.

PETER (*after a pause*). Well there you are. In accord to the very end.

CHARLES. And so what now? What do you do now? (*Angrily.*) This—this bachelor pad and a return to your old ways.

PETER. What old ways?

CHARLES. Your promiscuous old ways. Do you really think at your age you can just go back to a life of short affairs and—what was that hideous phrase you used to use—easy lays. Well, you're not an Oxford undergraduate any longer Peter, you won't find it easy with the Gertas—

PETER. Gerta? Who's Gerta?

CHARLES. Frieda, whoever she was, that German ballerina.

PETER. Oh, Gretel it was. Wasn't it?

CHARLES (*contemptuously*). And that Italian painter who was old enough to be your mother. Do you think it's going to be like that all over again. And that wretched business with André Gide's daughter.

PETER. André Gide's daughter! (*Laughs.*) Charlie, I assure you, André Gide never had a daughter.

CHARLES. Well some French writer who was in vogue a dozen years ago. Well you're a married man now, that's what you are.

PETER. Am I? Charlie, you know nothing about any of it.

CHARLES. Don't I? I remember the states you used to get into. It's a lucky thing for you you married Hilary when you did— your bachelor days nearly killed you.

PETER. Now I've got them back, perhaps they'll finish the job. You're not still jealous, are you Charlie, of those old passions of mine?

CHARLES. Jealous? What should *I* be jealous of?

PETER. Well you never slept with a woman before you married Alison, did you? You had no premarital sex at all, did you? Well, did you?

CHARLES. As a matter of fact I did, yes.

PETER. You didn't! Christ, who with?

CHARLES. Alison.

PETER. Why, you *rascal!* You used to boast that yours was a *real* wedding night, in the old-fashioned sense of the term. Which I always took to mean a disaster, by the way.

CHARLES. It only happened the once. One Sunday in my room in Reading we went — without meaning to — we went all the way. Afterwards we talked the whole thing through and decided that what with Alison's Catholicism and Mummy's desperation about your behavior *and* my own — no doubt from your point of view, simple-minded — principles, I'd have to control myself a little.

PETER. A *little?* That's not very flattering to either of you. Anyway, Charlie, you see how unqualified you are to judge other people's sexual lives. Your own having consisted of ten years of marriage to Alison, preceded by two or three years of light to heavy necking with Alison (apart from that interrupting coitus) preceded by (*Little pause*) Jane Russell, wasn't it? Into a jam-jar.

*There is a pause.*

CHARLES. How did you know that?

PETER. What?

CHARLES. About the — the —

PETER. Jane Russell jam-jar? Mummy told me you'd confessed.

CHARLES. When?

PETER. After she'd interrogated you about the jam-jar and the Jane Russells she found under your floor-boards.

CHARLES. But when did she tell you?

PETER. Oh, immediately after I'd confessed. Which was after she'd interrogated me about the old sock and the Betty Grables she found on top of my cupboard. But why look so troubled, Charlie, everybody wanked at Wundale, including most of the staff, from a memory of their complexions. That scandal when it was discovered that some of the older boarders had established it as a competitive sport and were awarding House Colours?

CHARLES. It's not that. It's just that she promised me she'd never say a word about it to anyone, especially you.

PETER. And I promised her I'd never tell you she told me. So now we're all square, two decades on. What exactly did she say to you?

CHARLES. That if I went on doing it, I'd never get into the Wundale First for soccer.

PETER. And she was quite right, you didn't. Although I suppose you didn't go on masturbating, either?

CHARLES. What did she say to you?

PETER. That I'd ruin my eyes, lose my concentration, and wouldn't get a scholarship to Oxford. Of course, I didn't know then what Oxford was like, or I'd have settled for spectacles and a few O-levels.

CHARLES. You were bloody lucky to get into Oxford.

PETER. Really? Your line used to be that Reading was just as good.

CHARLES. Indeed it was. And is. You were lucky to get into Oxford because you'd never have got through the interview at Reading. You were far too pretentious for us at eighteen — especially the way you worked at it.

PETER. I know. That's why I worked at it.

CHARLES (after a pause). Anyway, how dare you confuse my attitudes to sex with Mummy's. Do you seriously believe I'd make that sort of mistake with *my* children? You wouldn't find a more enlightened attitude to masturbation than Headmaster's and mine at Amplesides.

PETER. Except possibly at the cinemas and theatres.

CHARLES. I'm not against sex, I'm very much for it — *good* sex, that is. Which is what one has, lovingly, with those one loves.

PETER. Such as oneself?

CHARLES. Oh ha ha. Anyway, this is all a waste of time — as I take it you haven't left Hilary because she won't allow you to masturbate. Not that I don't know what you're up to, oh I knew straight away really, and so did Alison. She said the only question was whether you'd started sleeping around again, or whether there was a particular girl. Although, as she also said, the girl wouldn't be too particular to want you as you are now. (Pause.) Well, which is it? (Pause.) For how long and with how many have you been committing adultery?

PETER. Committing— (*Laughs*) *committing* adultery. Oh Charlie. (*Shakes his head.*) One isn't *allowed* to commit it these days, it's stopped qualifying as a sin. Why, for lots of blokes in publishing it's become such a habit that half of them don't even enjoy it. For instance, it's an open secret that one of our Senior Editors always takes his lady authors to bed instead of to lunch, so that he can spend the expenses another day on his grown-up daughter by his first marriage. Three marriages back. That's all that's meant by a permissive society now, Charlie, an arrangement with a restaurant. I believe he has some deal with his male authors too, but that secret's closed. Good God, brother, all our friends, Hilary's and mine — and *her* colleagues too, at that language school, I'll bet — they're all having affairs or have had them and are moving on to separations and divorces, which, by the way, sound far less hum-drum than the adulteries that led up to them. There's only one marriage I can think of that's survived as long as yours and mine — and that's Jeff and Davina Wainwright's.

CHARLES. The Wainwrights! You mean those ghastly people you had us to dinner with — he was drunk, as I remember, and she was crying in the lavatory, Alison discovered, over some long-drawn-out affair he was having, you told us so yourself, afterwards. Is that your idea of a good marriage?

PETER. No, only of a settled one. If his mistresses left him, his wife would go too. She couldn't stand the conversational vacuum — or having him home so early in the evenings.

CHARLES. I remember distinctly your telling me you'd stopped liking the Wainwrights.

PETER. But that was years ago.

CHARLES. And now you like them again?

PETER. God no. I've merely realised that they're among our oldest friends, and that old friends are like old habits. It doesn't matter whether you like them, they're what you've got. Until somebody introduces a really useful trade paper at least — new friends wanted, old ones offered in part exchange.

CHARLES. What have the Wainwrights got to do with all this anyway?

PETER. Absolutely nothing, as they're still together. But the rest of our friends, Charlie, over the eight years during which Hilary and I have idled and dallied together, have been busy splitting up and re-grouping. Why, in at least three cases we've actually been lapped. Double divorces are becoming as fashionable as separate holidays.

CHARLES (*with total contempt*). So you've left Hilary to be fashionable, have you?

PETER. Possibly. Or possibly to be free of something that neither of us could stand any longer.

CHARLES (*gestures around the room*). Free! You call *this* free.

PETER. Yup. Not even a nominal rent, Charlie.

CHARLES. You know why you're a bloody fool, Peter? Not for moral reasons, or conventional or *unconventional* ones, as they are nowadays, to do with the sanctity of family life and the squalors of easy sex — not those. But simply that you're on your way to losing your wife and your son, both of whom you love. You can't go back to your pre-married life, and you can't behave like all these others you cite — and I'll tell you why. At bottom your nature is as affectionate as mine. So one day, probably very soon, you'll go back to Hilary, and it'll be too late. The damage will have been done. (*Pause.*) It's true, isn't it? You *do* love Hilary?

*There is a knock at the door.*

PETER. Ah, excuse me, Charlie, can we leave that question hanging while I open the door. (*Opens it.*)

JOANNA. Hello. Sorry I'm late.

PETER. Oh don't worry — I was in no danger of giving you up. This is my brother Charlie.

JOANNA. Hello.

PETER. Joanna's one of our free-lance cover designers. I've asked her to accompany me to the party.

JOANNA. It'll be the first real publishing do I've ever wormed my way into.

PETER. Then we mustn't miss a minute of it. Shall we go?

CHARLES. Just a minute — (*Takes a photograph out of his pocket, hands it to* PETER.) Something I was going to leave for you if you weren't in.

PETER. Ah, a *memento mori*. Well, as I *was* in, you can take it away again.

CHARLES. It belongs to you.

PETER. Did you retrieve it from the waste-paper basket too?

CHARLES. No, it was on our piano. Alison took it last summer.

PETER. I don't want it, Charlie.

CHARLES. Why not? Does it upset you?

JOANNA. God, what's it of, anyway?

CHARLES. It's a photograph of my brother's wife and child. (*Hands it to* JOANNA.)

JOANNA (*studies it*). Taken with an instamatic, right?

PETER (*takes the photograph back, hands it to* CHARLES). It belongs to Alison, I believe we've established. Can't she find room for it in her waste-paper basket. (*Holds the door open for* JOANNA.)

JOANNA *and* CHARLES *stare at each other.* CHARLES *coldly,* JOANNA *puzzled. She goes out.*

PETER *keeps holding the door open for* CHARLES, *who doesn't move. Then he goes out.*

CHARLES (*stands trembling for a second, then goes to the soda syphon, squirts himself some*). The little — the little — (*Gulps down the soda water, pulls himself together, then goes over, places the photograph on the table, by the bed. Exits.*)

*Lights half down.*

*Lights up.*

PETER *enters, followed by* JOANNA. *They are both slightly drunk, and laughing.*

JOANNA. Christ, no truly, you were devastating. I've never heard anyone put so many people down before. But then I've never seen so many intellectuals before — are all publishing parties like that?

PETER (*who is getting out the scotch*). It was a special occasion.

We were launching a coffee table book on Sir Alf Ramsey Must
Go. One of six simultaneous cultural publications. If you buy
the lot we throw the coffee table in free, along with a ghosted
autobiography of the late Lord Chamberlain and a portfolio of
photographs of Henry Cooper's greatest defeats.

JOANNA. Henry Cooper the boxer? Was he the bloke that made
the speech?

PETER. No, that was the new Chairwoman of the Arts Council.

JOANNA. It wasn't!

PETER. No it wasn't. I'm just fantasising to distract our attention.

JOANNA. What from?

PETER. The party. Drink? (*Pours himself one, squirts in soda
water.*)

JOANNA *lets out a peal of laughter.*

Something?

JOANNA. No, just remembering the way you put down that
specimen who was praising up somebody's books—

PETER. Nuzek's?

JOANNA. Nuzek's, right. 'Why Cyril, I didn't know you had a
lisp,' you said.

PETER (*laughs, stops*). But he hasn't got a lisp, old Cyril. Has he?

JOANNA. No, he hasn't, that was why you said it. Because *he* said
if Nuzek's latest was like his last it was bound to be full of pith.
Then you said, why Cyril—

PETER. Got it. Got it, got it.

JOANNA. It took *me* two minutes to get it at the time.

PETER. Then Cyril was a mite quicker than you, if memory serves.
Which it suddenly insists on doing, now you've set it in motion.
Like some uncontrollably obsequious waiter . . . (*Sits down.*)

JOANNA. He didn't know which way to turn when you'd finished
with him, who was he?

PETER. One of the Sunday reviewers. Unlike his colleagues, he'll
know which way to turn come Nuzek's Sunday, a year hence.

JOANNA. And that lady—she marched out when you were telling everybody that story about some creep who takes writers to bed instead of lunch—I thought it was brilliant, who was she anyway?

PETER. What did she look like exactly?

JOANNA. Tall and grey haired with a hat and a see-through.

PETER. Our Senior Editor's third wife.

JOANNA. And that little creep with the goatee and the beady eyes—

PETER. That was the Senior Editor. His eyes aren't usually beady. They're usually twinkly.

JOANNA. Well, they were beady from the moment we arrived and you told that joke about Nu Nude—what was it again?

PETER. Nuzek. Nu-zek.

JOANNA. His bottom copy going on a five-year-old bottom, so the paper hadn't been wasted after all. It nearly brought the house down.

PETER. It still might.

JOANNA. Most people really enjoyed you, except those and that little roly-poly bloke—the one with the foreign accent standing next to me for a bit—he really hated you. Who was he?

PETER. A roly Pole called Nuzek. Nu-zek. Oh Christ.

JOANNA. What's the matter?

PETER. Nothing. Absolutely nothing.

JOANNA. And the Horatio Bottomley of Women's Lib—I never thought I'd see *her* cry, I mean I'm on her side really, and that man that was with her—

PETER. Look, look, I don't really nead a list, thanks very much. The names are winging in, in flocks and unaided.

JOANNA. Hey, you're not sorry or anything, are you?

PETER. Sorry! (*Laughs.*) No, no, it's only that it's a long time since I struck out without making sure of hitting only air or a loved one. (*Goes over to her.*) Besides, haven't we better things to do (*Lurches slightly*) than reminisce over my past before it's properly begun. (*Puts his arms around her, kisses her. Whispers in her ear. Pause, looks at her apprehensively.*) Eh, what do you say?

JOANNA. All right. Great. (*Goes over to the bed, sits down, begins to undress.*)

PETER *looks towards her, then also begins to get undressed.*

JOANNA (*who has been staring at the picture as she undresses*). How old's your wife anyway?

PETER. What? (*Sees the picture*). Oh. Um, thirty-one and a half.

JOANNA. Your boy's what, five?

PETER. Nearly six. That was taken a year ago.

JOANNA (*picks up the picture*). What's she look like? It's hard to tell because she's out of focus.

PETER (*going over in trousers and shirt*). Can we keep her that way, do you mind? (*Taking the picture from* JOANNA.) To avoid pre- and even post-coital depression. (*Comes back with the picture, drops it on the floor.*) I'm free now, you know.

*They go on undressing, on opposite sides of the room.*

*Lights.*

*Curtain.*

# Act Two

## Scene One

*The bed-sitter. Some time later.* JOANNA *is sitting on the bed in her under-pants, doing up her bra.* PETER *is on the chair, in vest and trousers, pulling on his socks. He stops, sits staring blankly ahead, then fumbles in the pocket of his jacket (which is slung over the back of the chair) for his cigarettes. Takes one out.*

JOANNA (*who has been watching him*). I've got some pot, if you want. (*Taking a small box out of her handbag, beside the bed.*)

PETER. What? (*Sitting down, not looking at her.*)

JOANNA. Do you want a joint?

PETER. No thanks. I find these much more exciting. (*Lights up, drags deeply, coughs.*) Don't need the police to be frightened of them.

JOANNA (*putting a joint between her lips*). Can I have a light then?

PETER. What? Oh sorry. (*Half turns, tosses her the lighter without looking at her. It falls to one side.*) Sorry.

JOANNA *lights up, also drags deeply into her lungs. They sit smoking for a short while.* PETER *coughs once or twice.*

JOANNA. You've had a bad scene going recently, haven't you?

PETER *grunts.*

Look, if it helps, I'm just getting over one, too. (*Pause.*) But it's just a matter of time, that's all. I've got to the stage, you know, where I can tell myself it's over without even weeping. Dead. Terminado. Finito. Finished. Not that anything ever finishes, right? Christ, we were even going to get married!

PETER. That would have finished it.

JOANNA. His name was Josh.

PETER. Look, you really don't have to talk about it if you don't want to.

JOANNA. No, I want to.

PETER. Then I suppose it's irrelevant that you don't have to.

JOANNA. Right. (*After a pause.*) Witby.

PETER. Whatby?

JOANNA. Josh Witby . . . He directed the all black, all male *Way of the World* for the *Cellar in the Underground*, Islington. You know, the place where they guarantee your 30p. back if you don't like it and they have those posters up saying find out about experimental drama, it's only two hours of your life.

PETER. Can they guarantee those back?

JOANNA (*laughs. There is a pause*). My rival was Lady What's it, Wishfort, get it?

PETER. Got it. Witby's Lady Wishfort is all black and part male.

JOANNA. Josh's problem in a nutshell.

PETER. Sounds an excellent place for it.

JOANNA. I like sleeping with men, and so does he.

PETER. You have that much in common, at least. Most marriages start from far less.

JOANNA. Listen, I haven't got anything against homosexuals.

PETER. Nor have I. Even as bed-partners for heterosexuals.

JOANNA. And nothing against black boys either.

PETER. Nor have I. Even in parts written for white women in Restoration comedies.

JOANNA. Well, you sound as if you've got something against someone, is it me?

PETER. No, nothing against you either, and you're white, female and we've just shared a bed together. How tolerant do I have to be?

JOANNA. Bet you can't even bring yourself to look at me, can you?

PETER. Sorry. (*Turns, looks at her, looks away again.*) I am sorry. It must be that pre-coital depression I was worried about. It's struck.

JOANNA. But truly it doesn't matter. I don't mind.

PETER. Good. Unfortunately I do.

JOANNA (*comes over to him*). But you don't have to sit around like a sick dog, I mean the way you got out of bed and into your knickers—it was almost as bad as the way you got out of them—all doubled up and walking across the room in a crouch. You were ashamed before we even started, what of?

PETER. I think it must have been my paunch.

JOANNA. You know what you did while you were—I mean, you actually proposed to me.

PETER. Oh, you heard that, did you. I tried to make it sound like a love-cry. (*Pause.*) If you'd accepted on a *pro-tem* basis, things might have ended differently.

JOANNA. Perhaps, if you hadn't drunk so much, you might have done it.

PETER. Perhaps if I hadn't drunk so much, I wouldn't have tried.

JOANNA. Thank you. Thank you. (*Grinds out her cigarette.*) Oh Christ, this is all a lot of balls.

PETER. You don't need a lot, actually one will do. Bull-fighters manage on even less, so they say.

JOANNA. This hasn't happened to you before then, never?

PETER. No.

JOANNA. Never with your wife, even?

PETER. Not even. Except in Paris on our honeymoon, when I pretended for a fatal fraction of a thrust that we were on a dirty weekend.

JOANNA. Look, am I the only girl since you were married, apart from your wife?

PETER *says nothing.*

Well, am I? (*Little pause.*) I am, aren't I? Right?

PETER. Right, right. You're the only girl I've had apart from my wife. Right?

JOANNA. Wrong. You didn't have me. Right?

PETER. Right. Thank you. I'd forgotten your gift for instant recall. Perhaps because I try so hard to lack it myself.

JOANNA. What were you doing, practising! Christ! (*Goes to the rest of her clothes, begins to put them on.*) You know what you are, you're the type —

PETER. Don't bother. I *know* the type. (*Gets up, puts on shirt, etc.*) I gather all the other married men you've slept with have managed to come good.

JOANNA. But then they enjoyed it, too.

PETER. Even the guilt?

JOANNA. Even the sex. There was one I knew, he'd phone his wife from my bed and pretend he was at his desk. He even pretended to be the porter on the switchboard sometimes. (*Suddenly laughs.*) He used to say the best planned lays never gang agly.

PETER. And what happened to that little idyll?

JOANNA. His wife found out.

PETER. And put a stop to it pretty sharpish, right?

JOANNA. Wrong. As soon as he knew she knew he lost interest.

PETER. So he didn't want you, he just wanted the situation?

JOANNA. That was kind of you, to explain. What makes you think *I* wanted *you*, and not just the situation?

PETER. So that's why you limit yourself to a Josh on the one hand, or to married men on the other? But there's a large variety of males between homos and husbands, you know. When are you going to have a go at one of those?

JOANNA. I don't limit myself at all — except when I end up in the sack with somebody like you. Christ, there was a time today when I truly liked you — at the party, I thought you had something then, but it was just words, wasn't it, and then you had to be drunk to do it. I just hope you haven't given *me* anything catching, that's all.

PETER. What? Oh, you mean my inhibitions? But they don't get passed on by casual contact, only through an intimacy that digs deep into tissues you seem to have been born without. No, don't you worry, dear, you'll still be able to sleep around, smoke pot, promote your new jargons, bury our old language, and generally see our dying culture underground, right down to Josh's cellar —where my son—my son— (*Stands shaking.*)

JOANNA (*looks at him. Laughs*). And I was only talking about your dandruff. (*Goes out.*)

PETER (*after a moment*). So was I. (*Looks at shoulders, left and right, brushes futilely at them.*)

*Lights down.*

*Lights up.*

### Scene Two

*Muswell Hill. It is evening, about eight o'clock. Lights on.*

HILARY *enters left.*

JEREMY *off, left, calls out something.*

HILARY (*at the door*). No more cuddles tonight, you don't mean it anyway, sleep now. And no sneaking into my bed.

*Listens, sounds of JEREMY off, complaining. HILARY smiles, goes across to the desk, picks up her brief case, sits down at the desk, opens it. Takes out some papers, begins to look through them. Stops. Sits staring ahead.*

*There is a sudden rap on the window.*

HILARY *lets out a little scream. There is a crashing from the kitchen, and as* HILARY *rises in alarm,* CHARLES *enters.*

CHARLES. Hello, I thought I'd come this way so as not to disturb.

HILARY. Thank you.

CHARLES. In case Jeremy was asleep.

HILARY. Yes.

CHARLES. Actually it's the pot. Nindy's pot. We left it here that Sunday — and Nindy's suddenly taken against the old one, after using it for the last week. I don't know why, but she wants *hers* back. Alison's had to use the old sink ploy with the tap running — anyway I thought I'd just pop over and get it. You know? (*Little pause.*) I should have phoned.

HILARY. It's very nice to see you. I'll go and get it. (*Goes off, left.*)

CHARLES *goes to the drinks table.*

*Makes to squirt some soda water into a glass. The syphon farts emptily.* CHARLES *studies the bottom of the syphon, then raises the syphon, bending slightly at the knees, puts the tube into his mouth, and squirts and sucks.*

HILARY *re-entering with the pot, watches him from the door.*

CHARLES *not seeing, puts the syphon down.*

HILARY. Here you are. (*Hands him the pot.*)

CHARLES. Thanks.

HILARY (*after a pause*). Would you like a drink?

CHARLES. No, no thanks. Well, just some soda water, if there is any.

HILARY. I think it's empty.

CHARLES. There isn't another one in the cupboard — Pete — sometimes there's a spare in the cupboard.

HILARY (*goes to the cupboard, looks*). No.

CHARLES. Oh.

HILARY. Something else perhaps? There's some lime, or squash or ribena . . . ?

CHARLES. No, no thanks. I like soda water, you see. Its taste.

HILARY. But surely it doesn't have any taste.

CHARLES. Yes, that's what I like. And the way the bubbles shoot up against the roof of the mouth —

HILARY. Well, some coffee — or something to eat?

CHARLES. No, I had a nut and spinach cutlet before coming out. With boiled potatoes and blackberries. The blackberries were for pudding.

HILARY. Charlie — are we having this awkward conversation because you can't get into another awkward conversation you feel we should have. It occurred to me to check the waste-paper basket after you left. Have you come to report on your meeting?

CHARLES. He wasn't in, so I have nothing to report. (*Pause.*) Is everything all right though, Hilary?

HILARY. As long as you don't start re-interrogating me. I still don't want to talk about it.

CHARLES. All right. (*Sits down.*)

HILARY. It's very sweet of you to take it all so badly, but really I think it would be more helpful if you tried to take it well.

CHARLES (*nods*). But I think he's a little — (*Checks himself.*) Sorry Hilary. (*Sits in a sort of stupor.*)

HILARY. Is there something else the matter? Alison's all right — ?

CHARLES. Oh yes, yes. She's fine. (*Little pause.*) Perhaps a touch of pre-natal depression.

HILARY. Oh dear. But that's unusual, isn't it? She's generally so exuberant just before.

CHARLES. No, I meant me. I always get a bit low — but I don't let Alison see, of course. Or anyone. But this time it's worse than usual — what with you and Pete — a double touch really. Appropriate as we're going to have twins.

HILARY. Twins! Why, Charlie, that's marvellous, twins! How wonderful.

CHARLES. I thought you knew.

HILARY. Yes, Alison did tell me, as a matter of fact. But she said she wasn't going to tell you, she wanted it to be a surprise.

CHARLES. Well, she couldn't resist after all. She told me this evening. I think to cheer me up over Pete and everything. (*Sits.*)

HILARY. But Charlie, you don't mind, do you? Twins, just think —

CHARLIE. Oh, I'm sure once they're here. I wish she'd kept the surprise as a surprise though. Then I wouldn't have had time to prepare for it. Anyway I just used the pot as an excuse — I had to get away for a little, in case I couldn't cope. (*Little pause.*) It's monstrous of me to burden you with myself, isn't it?

HILARY. No, it isn't. I'm glad you came, it would be far more monstrous if Alison suspected — Charlie, you don't think a little whisky would help.

CHARLES. No, only a lot would. Sorry Hil. I suppose really it's an inevitable progression. We've been turning them out in singles for eight years, we were bound to advance. Recently in class I've taken to saying everything twice. Perhaps it was an early warning —

HILARY. Is it a matter of economics, your depression?

CHARLES. Well, I *have* got used to pacing them out in my mind and planning ahead. But if they're going to start coming in clusters — ? What can I do?

HILARY. Couldn't you count this as two goes' worth? Oh, of course, how silly of me, I'd forgotten Alison's Catholicism.

CHARLES. Her Catholicism's just a blind, Hilary. Lots of practising Catholics also practise contraception these days, while Alison scarcely bothers to practise Catholicism except in her attitude to contraceptives. When it comes down to it, the Pope's just her fertility symbol. She likes babies, lots and lots of babies. She likes cuddling them, burping them, changing them, feeding them, preferably while bearing them. (*Pause.*) Oh, I don't blame her, of course. I always knew she was a natural homemaker, it's one of the reasons I wanted to marry her. It's just that the house I'm paying the mortgage on isn't big enough for the home she's making. I haven't dared tell her yet — (*Stops.*)

HILARY. What?

CHARLES. Well, there was a chance of a house that belongs to the school — much larger than ours and the rent would be nominal. Bursar was sure it could be arranged, but Headmaster said no.

HILARY. Why?

CHARLES. Oh, he was very nice about it, of course. He wants to start a new school house for boarders — perfectly sensible, really. But it's always a bit of a shock being turned down — (*Little pause*) especially — (*Lets out a little laugh.*)

HILARY. Charlie?

CHARLES. Can I tell you something, in great confidence?

HILARY. If you're sure I ought to know.

CHARLES. It's something ridiculous. Something very ridiculous. On the other hand it's not. You must try not to laugh, but I shan't blame you if you do. You see — I asked Headmaster about the house at lunch, but at tea I suddenly thought I'd look in on him, just for a cup and — well, I often do you know, to talk about co-education or scholarships — but this time I also wanted him to see that I perfectly understood about not getting the house. Well, we had a very affable chat together, his wife was there and we always get along very well — it was very pleasant, I thought, very pleasant.

HILARY. Well, it sounds very pleasant.

CHARLES. Yes, it was. And when I left I decided to walk back to the car through their garden. I often go that way, especially if it's a fine evening. I wasn't at all depressed then, you know, of course I didn't know about the twins — well, perhaps I was a little depressed about Pete, thinking what a fool he was and why he couldn't count his blessings — and then I began to count my own, you know, the way one does — miscounting, as it turned out. But I began to feel rather happy. Rather happy, that's my point.

HILARY. And why shouldn't you be. You've got a great deal to be happy about.

CHARLES. Exactly, I know. And I wished I had Pete there, because I was sure I could persuade him — when suddenly I heard Headmaster's voice. He was talking to his wife. They didn't see me — in fact, they must have thought I was long gone. I was just about to squeeze through some shrubs, to let them know where I was, I didn't want them to think I was eavesdropping —

when I heard Headmaster say: 'But there must be some way of keeping the pest out of my house.'

HILARY (*after a pause*). Oh Charlie!

CHARLES. And his wife said: 'Oh, I know he's an appalling nuisance, but I can't help having a soft spot for him.'

HILARY. Oh Charles!

CHARLES. 'That's because he grovels whenever he sees you!' And then he said—

HILARY. Oh Charlie, don't go on. Please. I can't bear it.

CHARLES. Said 'The other day I saw him peeing over the roses. He's always squatting in the path and fouling it. He leaves fleas over the carpet, you've said so yourself.'

HILARY. They were talking about that stray—Alfonso! At least I hope they were.

CHARLES. So what it comes to is this. You don't think I have the physical habits of a dog, just the moral temperament of one.

HILARY. I think no such thing!

CHARLES. My God, I admired him though, for a moment.

HILARY. Headmaster?

CHARLES. Alfonso. I wished I could pee over his roses, drop turds on his path and shake fleas over his carpet. But I wouldn't grovel to his wife, I'd bite her ankles.

HILARY. I thought you liked them!

CHARLES. So did I. Until I thought I heard them talking about me like that.

HILARY. But they weren't talking about you. They were talking about Alfonso.

CHARLES. I know, I know. But you see, the fact that I *thought* they were talking about me must mean there's something in my idea of them that expects them to talk like that about me. And something in me that expects to be talked about like that. It's just the sort of thing I know Pete's always— (*Stops.*) Well anyway. But you know, almost the most shameful thing Hil— when I was in my car and well, trembling a little—a muddle of feelings, hate and anger for them, oh quite irrational, I realised it even at the time—but in the middle of all that I had this sudden very clear thought. Do you know what it was? Something *really* shameful?

HILARY (*after a moment*). I think so. That you'd better stop feeding Alfonso, now you know what Headmaster thinks of him.

CHARLES (*nods, despairingly*). And a second later I imagined myself making some casual reference to the effect—that perhaps we ought to have something done about him.

HILARY. Put down, you mean? Oh Charlie!

CHARLES. If you met me now, for the first time, you wouldn't dream of asking me back to your house for dinner, would you?

HILARY. Of course I would.

CHARLES. No you wouldn't. Alison's very attached to you, you know.

HILARY. Yes, I do know.

CHARLES. Still, she thinks you're a conceited little turnip.

HILARY. Turnip?

CHARLES. Sometimes parsnip. She hates the way you prattle boastfully on about your job. That's the sort of thing she says about you, although she loves you. So what sort of things do you say about her, although you love her if you do. About her constant pregnancies, for example, or her earth-mother laugh—or her unattractiveness.

HILARY. I think she's *very* attractive!

CHARLES. What's so attractive about her?

HILARY. She's got a lovely, open face, a marvellous complexion.

CHARLES. And a dreadful figure.

HILARY. She has not!

CHARLES. Yes, she has. What isn't dreadful about it?

HILARY. For one thing, she's got absolutely beautiful breasts. So full.

CHARLES. Yes, well they usually are, aren't they? (*Little pause.*) What about her bottom?

HILARY. Charlie, this has gone on quite long enough.

CHARLES. Actually, her bottom isn't as baggy as it looks when she's wearing those pregnancy trousers she usually wears. (*Little pause.*) You don't think I hate her, do you?

HILARY. No. I know you love her.

CHARLES. But you hate hearing me say things like this about her?

HILARY. Yes. But I'd rather you said them to me than to her.

CHARLES. I'll stop in a minute. Honestly. But do you know what would make it all right for me, absolutely? If I could just go to bed some evenings, and stretch, and turn on the reading light, and sigh luxuriously, and open a book. An Arthur Ransome. I long to re-read all the Arthur Ransomes.

HILARY. Surely you can manage that?

CHARLES. Alison always goes up before me. Then when I come in she stretches, turns off the reading light, and gives a luxurious sigh, and opens her legs. (*Little pause.*) No, that's not true. We have a long cuddle first, which I need. But that's how it ends. Every night. We have this joke, that she can't get to sleep without it. And recently since we've gone macrobiotic there's been a joke about not being able to get up without it, either.

HILARY. But not *every* night, Charlie, it's not possible.

CHARLES. But then there are bottles to warm up, or nappies to be changed, or mid-night wee-wees, or six week cholic — Otherwise every night. You see, she loves everything to do with babies, but especially the way they're made.

HILARY. But couldn't you, well, just hint — ?

CHARLES. Our marriage is constructed on our triumphant sex life, as you know. That, and our shared love of children.

HILARY. But you do *like* children. Don't you?

CHARLES. Nobody likes children these days. Why should I? They don't even like each other. But I love them, if that's what perpetually counting them and fretting for them and planning because of them amounts to. But I don't want to look at them, or hear them, let alone watch them eat, empty their pots and nappies —

HILARY. You sound just like Peter.

CHARLES. Oh God, I wish I *were* just like him, or even better be him! (*Little pause.*) Sorry Hilary, I wasn't referring to — to his current behaviour. But you see he's always been the younger one, the brighter one, the indulged one — the anarchic one. While I've just been the conventional one, the slow and loving and responsible one. The one-girl one. All those affairs he had before you —

HILARY. What? What affairs?

CHARLES. But surely he told you about them?

HILARY. No.

CHARLES. I shouldn't have spoken.

HILARY. No, I want to hear.

CHARLES. Are you sure?

HILARY. I want to hear.

CHARLES. But how could he have not confessed. The German ballerina, the Italian painter, Gide's daughter —

HILARY. *Gide's* daughter!

CHARLES. No, it wasn't Gide's, it was — I can't remember, a French writer. His daughter. The affair of his life until he met you. And he never said a word?

HILARY. I'd forgotten. It was all so long ago.

CHARLES. I suppose it was. But it still makes me angry to think of them. Because, you see, secretly, I wanted them, and if I couldn't have them, I wanted him to. Just as — just as — well, although I've always loved Alison, but was never actually in love with her, so I've — I've always been in love with you. Though now I love you too as my sister-in-law. From the first moment he showed you off to me. But you know that, don't you?

HILARY *nods.*

But you belonged to Pete, of course. Just as I did to Alison. All four of us were perfectly matched. You had lots of affairs too, didn't you, before you married Pete?

HILARY. Lots?

CHARLES. Well, quite a few.

HILARY. I suppose quite a few, yes.

CHARLES. How many?

HILARY (*after a pause*). Five, actually.

CHARLES (*whistles*). Five! Alison's always said — (*Pause.*) So you
see, you *were* perfectly matched. Almost mathematically. While I
was always the sort of chap to meet the sort of chap that Alison
is, without having anything before — and that was that. (*Little
pause.*) You've never been the slightest bit in love with me, have
you?

HILARY *shakes her head.*

And perhaps that's why I can't help being a little glad that you
and Pete have broken up. Oh, not only because of being in love
with you, but also — this is my very last confession, Hil.

HILARY. Thank God!

CHARLES. Because it's easier for me to bear being what I am, a
loving family man, an obsequious Assistant Headmaster in a minor
Public School, a bit of an old-fashioned Puritan, if *he's* behaving
despicably. I want him to live my destructive life for me, while I
go on living my decent life for myself. Oh God, how shameful!
I do want him to come back, I do, I do.

HILARY *puts her face to one side. She is in tears.*

Hil — Hil — Oh, I am sorry, I've been selfish. I'd no right — oh,
don't cry, please. (*Comes over, puts an arm around her.*) Did I
make you?

HILARY *shakes her head.*

CHARLES. Because of Pete and you?

HILARY. No, not especially, a little.

CHARLES. Because of Alison and me?

HILARY. A little, but not only.

CHARLES. Ah. *Lacrimae Rerum.* I felt them rising in me, when
Alison was laughing over the twins, and I was trying to laugh with
her. Pete will come back to you Hil. I know he loves you.

HILARY. So do I.

CHARLES. So you know he'll come back to you?

HILARY. Yes. I know it.

CHARLES. Then nothing's really too bad, is it?

*Lights down.*

*Lights up.*

*Muswell Hill. The sitting room is empty. There is the sound of the front door closing, left, then* PETER *enters. He has had a monstrous hair-cut, is neatly and newly suited. He is carrying flowers and chocolates. He stands staring, then hears noises in the kitchen. Moves towards it.* CHARLES *emerges. He is eating a carrot.*

*There is a long pause.*

PETER. Well Charlie, I'm back. Where's Hilary?

CHARLES. Gone to have a bath.

PETER. Ah! What are you doing here?

CHARLES. I came to collect the pot. I was just leaving.

*There is a pause.*

CHARLES. And how's your girl?

PETER. Did you mention her to Hilary?

CHARLES. No.

PETER. Thank you.

CHARLES. For Hilary's sake, not yours.

PETER. Naturally. (*Looks towards the door, then at* CHARLES.) Oh for God's sake don't look so censorious. My tail is back between my legs, where it belongs. Isn't that what you wanted?

CHARLES. But should you be smirking?

PETER. Am I? Well, it's a family trait in moments of embarrassment. As you should know.

CHARLES. Embarrassment? Is that what you call this mess? You walk out on your wife and son after weeks of the most repellent behaviour, all for the sake of some heartless little creature — and then you turn up with a hair cut and in a new suit and refer smirkingly to embarrassment. Well let me tell *you* —

PETER. No, please don't, Charlie. Please don't tell me anything. I know.

CHARLES (*biting angrily at the carrot*). *What* do you know?

PETER. Well, for one thing, I know that you couldn't just go off, could you, and have a casual affair with some heartless creature, just like that, after weeks of the most repellent behaviour. Could you?

CHARLES. No, I damn well could not!

PETER. Well nor could I. (*Sinks into the chair*.) I could manage the repellent behaviour, but not the heartless creature.

CHARLES. You mean nothing happened?

PETER. Nothing to speak of. Although I expect she'll speak of it, all right.

CHARLES. So you haven't betrayed Hilary after all?

PETER. Oh yes. I betrayed them both, given their different expectations. But incompetently. Neither a successful adulterer nor a faithful husband. Something between the two.

CHARLES. I did warn you that you couldn't go back.

PETER. To what?

CHARLES. To your old promiscuity. Your Gertas, your Friedas, your — (*Gestures*.)

PETER. My André Gide's daughters. (*Laughs*.)

CHARLES. Oh, I've remembered since. It was Cocteau's daughter.

PETER. You can't honestly believe Cocteau had a daughter either?

CHARLES. I don't honestly care whose daughter it was. Whose was it anyway?

PETER. Cocteau's.

CHARLES. You just said he didn't have a daughter.

PETER. Exactly.

CHARLES (*after a long pause, tensely*). What do you mean?

PETER. Isn't it perfectly obvious?

CHARLES. There isn't any famous French writer's daughter?

PETER. I'm sure there are lots. But I've never slept with them.

CHARLES. And the Gertas, the Friedas, the Italian painters, the ballet dancer who was old enough to be your mother.

PETER. I think it was the Italian painter who was old enough to be my mother. Unless it was a retired ballet dancer. Or Margot Fonteyn.

CHARLES. You made them all up?

PETER. *We* made them all up, really, Charlie. The two of us. Your indignation gave substance to my fantasies. Without your help they'd never have existed for me — and they seem to have gone on existing for you. They died for me years ago, isn't that funny.

CHARLES. So Hilary was the first girl you went all the way with.

PETER. The only anything I've ever been all the way with, except of course for that old sock.

CHARLES (*sits staring ahead*). You lied to me, all these years.

PETER. No. I lied to you years ago, and you've just gone on believing it all these years.

CHARLES. Why did you lie to me *then* then?

PETER. You seemed to expect that sort of thing from me. It seemed a shame to go on letting you down. Besides, you were so righteously convinced that I wasn't at all like you, it helped me to believe the same thing. I knew that we were both sheep, but my seeming a black one added a bit of colour to our joint self. (*Pause.*) But aren't you glad that underneath we're *both* such decent chaps. I've never done anything of which you'd *really* disapprove — at least not until after I left Hilary and even that — well, here I am after all.

CHARLES. We're not the same. We're not!

PETER. In what are we different then, except in Alison's fecundity. And I've frequently *longed* for more children. It's Hilary who's against that — since she started going back to work.

CHARLES. Well—well—you and Hilary, you made love long before you were married. Before you were engaged, even. Or was *that* a lie too?

PETER. Not quite. The first time we went to bed we didn't manage to get quite all the way. The second time we weren't engaged for most of the way, but we were by the time we'd gone all of it. It was a package deal. She insisted.

CHARLES. On your getting engaged?

PETER. On my going all the way. Getting engaged was my solution for getting there. Brothers Charlie, you see, under the skin. (*Gets up, shows his hands to* CHARLIE.) What do you see?

CHARLES. Your hands? (*Studies them.*) Nicotine stains, otherwise (*Shakes his head*) just your hands.

PETER. Not mine any longer. Daddy's. I never noticed them while he was alive but I recognise them now he's dead. Living heirlooms, without the liver spots. Doubtless they'll come.

CHARLES *looks at his own hands.*

You have Mummy's hands, to the very cuticle. As you don't smoke either. The rest of us is, of course, the usual hodge-podge of inherited characteristics, some too far back to be traceable. I wonder whose hands Jeremy will recognise when he gets to our age . . . (*Pause.*) Anyway, we're on our way, you and I.

CHARLES. On our way where?

PETER. Just on. And on. Through these early middle into the late middle, the late late middle or the early late—and so on and on, until pegging out. If not before. Somebody's father, somebody's husband, somebody's editor in my case, some Headmaster's Assistant in yours, somebody's brother in both our cases, eh Charlie? All relationships and no self. Not even our own hands.

CHARLES. So you attribute my—our—being faithful husbands to genetics, do you? What balderdash.

PETER. I'm not attributing it to anything, I'm merely saying that we are. It could be inherited. Daddy's mousiness, Mummy's prohibitiveness, it could be sweet-rationing.

CHARLES. Sweet-rationing?

PETER. Well, we did catch the last few years of it, remember, in our sweet-eating prime. Perhaps ration coupons for chocolates conditioned us to marriage licences for sex. I don't know.

CHARLES. And all those friends of yours that you cited — with their affairs and divorces.

PETER. I don't know. Perhaps their parents were on the black-market. Perhaps they were just unlucky. Or lucky. I don't know. But I'll tell you something, every breakup shocked me as much as it would have shocked you. (*Pause.*) Hilary knew I'd come back to her, Charlie, all the time. She knows me.

CHARLES. But why should she take you back?

PETER. Well, for one thing, if I'm to be a monogamous male, I'll need my only wife. (*Pause.*) But aren't you pleased that I'm a shining reflection of your own virtue: you don't seem to be. I don't expect much rejoicing in Heaven for the sheep back in the fold, as I've scarcely left it, but I thought you'd be — well, at the very least *satisfied*.

CHARLES (*after a pause*). But we're not the same in our attitudes to our work, are we?

PETER. I've been a most conscientious editor. Furthermore I like my job, on the whole.

CHARLES. But the way you've always sneered at my getting ahead. Virtually accused me of *ingratiating* myself —

PETER. Now there it's true I always thought there was a difference, I did despise some of your ploys. But not any more, Charlie. I've since found out that in a crisis we're identical there, too.

CHARLES. Identical in what?

PETER. At that party — the six simultaneous publications party — I made some remarks. At the top of my voice. Which I subsequently regretted. Actually, I regretted them a second before I made them.

CHARLES. Then why did you make them?

PETER. So as not to waste the regret. Anyway, my job hung in the balance, and I thought, as I set out to save it, that if you could do it with Headmaster and wife, I could do it with my lot.

CHARLES. Do what?

PETER. Grovel. With telegrams at first—I thought I might get a cheap deal with the post office. Apology cables on the lines of Greetings Cables. But I had to stop after the first two, I couldn't bear the operator's tone as he read them back to me. In the end I used taxis and grovelled direct. It was surprisingly easy.

CHARLES (*goes over to the drinks table*). You found it so, did you?

PETER. By drawing on your example. I pretended I was you and whomever I was grovelling to was either Headmaster, if a woman, or Headmaster's wife, if a man. In no time at all I was doing it *in propria persona*. And all these years I've sneered at you for practising what I was ashamed to realise in myself. So you see, Charlie, there's a good chance that we'll make it to the top together, just as Mummy would have wished, on all fours so to speak, and side by side. As you consult with Eton's Provost over your next raise or domicile, you'll be able to think of my fawning figure closing in on a Directorship in publishing.

CHARLES. Did you know you were out of soda water?

PETER. Then I shall order some more. Nuzek was so taken with my performance that he actually asked me to repeat it tomorrow, over lunch. At which I'll gobble down humble-pie with relish. (*Pause.*) Now I'd better go up and do some grovelling to my wife, eh? (*Looks at* CHARLES.) Charlie, what *is* it? You don't look yourself, and I've given you such a chance to be, only more so. You've skimped dreadfully on the I-told-you-sos. Haven't I earned them? (*Pause.*) Is everything all right at home? (*Pause.*) Alison all right? The kids?

CHARLES. Fine. Fine.

PETER (*hesitates, then brightly*). By the way, something occurred to me about that dog.

CHARLES. Dog?

PETER. Dog. Your adopted dog. Alfonso wasn't it—Hadn't you better make sure that Headmaster really doesn't mind him hanging about the garden before feeding him? Some people hate strays—

CHARLES *leaps across the room, seizes* PETER *by the lapels, shakes him vigorously.*

Hey—Hey—

CHARLES *lets him go.*

Christ, what was *that* for? Haven't I grovelled enough, even for you?

CHARLES (*hits him on the upper arm, sharply and spitefully*). You little—

PETER. Ow, you sod!

CHARLES. Bastard! (*Turns, walks off, stage left. Sound of front door slamming.*)

PETER. Christ! (*Rubs his arm, after a minute gets up, goes to the drinks table, picks up the scotch bottle, after a short struggle with himself puts it down. Hesitates, then goes across to the flowers and chocolates. Picks them up. Turns to the door, left.*)

HILARY *enters in a bathrobe. Looks at* PETER.

PETER (*turns. After a moment*) Good evening.

HILARY. Charlie left then?

PETER. Well, first he shook me half senseless, clouted me on the arm, and called me little bastard. Then he left. What was interesting is that he chose the place where he used to get me, day in and day out, up to fifteen years ago. It's soft and painful, doesn't do permanent damage, and leaves no bruise for a parental eye.

HILARY. Were you baiting him?

PETER. On the contrary. I was simply pointing out that we were brothers under the skin, and offering him some practical advice. Perhaps that's it—now I've shown him how my life has run, I've released all his sibling rivalry. (*Laughs nervously. There is a pause.*) Anyway I've come—(*Hesitates*) home. Groomed for the occasion. What do you think of my hair-cut, by the way? Executed by a great traditionalist in Holborn. He was so delighted to get back to old-fashioned hair-shearing that he tried to do it for nothing. I had to insist. (*Pause.*) But I didn't charge him much. (*Laughs.*) Well, the last time we spoke, you seemed to be hankering for what I'd once been. No other part of me is so immediately susceptible to backwards change. And look— (*Holds out chocolates and flowers.*) More *memorabilia* from our wooing past.

HILARY *makes no move.*

Am I smirking?

HILARY. Not noticeably.

PETER. Oh, well I ought to be. I'm very embarrassed. Not to say frightened even. (*Little pause.*) Surely you *knew* I'd come back.

HILARY. Yes.

PETER. And that I'd apologise for—well, you know.

HILARY. Yes.

PETER. Well— (*Puts the flowers and chocolates on the table.*) How's Jeremy?

HILARY. He's asleep.

PETER. Oh good. And how's school? His, I mean?

HILARY. All right.

PETER. Still not reading, I suppose?

HILARY. Since the weekend he's moved on to the second *Janet and John.*

PETER. Let's hope the narrative is beginning to gather pace. And how are you?

HILARY. Perfectly well, thank you.

PETER. Look Hil, I've missed you and him and everything— perhaps it was worth my going to find *that* out—not that I didn't know it. But now the fact of it makes me happy, as it did when we first lived together. (*Pause.*) I know the fault was mine, *entirely* mine. I was taking my frustrations out on you and was being altogether childish. I had no right to do it, no right to walk out— (*This very quickly.*)

HILARY. But I asked you to.

PETER. Well, I made it impossible for you not to, didn't I? A fairly familiar marital ploy, I expect, so that when one gets tired of playing the role of culprit one can have a go at being the victim. Well, I shan't do *that* anyway. I abjectly admit that it was all *my* doing.

HILARY. No it wasn't.

PETER. Oh yes it was Hil, I drove you past the point of tolerance, I know that. But now what I desperately want is to put it behind us, with the understanding of course that you can put it in front of me during any healthy little marital spat of the future. (*Smiles.*) I've brought you something else, by the way. (*Takes a sheet of paper out of his pocket, hands it to* HILARY.) The first items I've already made a start of putting into effect — the hair-cut is, I admit, a little excessive, but at least it takes care of the dandruff, for which there's no longer any room. I've also gargled my throat raw, my present huskiness isn't all emotion, you know, and as for items two and three, I haven't smoked since three this afternoon, and the scotch I needed before facing you I didn't actually swallow. Now you'll see that I've been able to give a firm commitment on Sainsbury's for Saturday mornings but that any evening treks would, of course, be subject to various career responsibilities. (*Little pause.*) Both our careers, that is. I admit that the way I've shared the business of taking Jeremy to school seems a trifle inequitable on a quick glance, but then I had to take into account that you drive and I don't. Three mornings for you and two for me therefore seems reasonable, but I am, you'll note, prepared to renegotiate as particular weeks make particular demands. (*Pause.*) The clause on sex at the end was, of course, the trickiest and required several draftings but you'll see that the only emphatic stipulation is a shared bed. The declaration with which I precede my signature is true. Where it says I love you and always will. (*Pause.*) I've kept a second copy for myself as a *memento mori* — I mean, *aide-mémoire* — but I thought of doing a third and circulating it to the registry office. They may feel it's worth incorporating into the current exchange of vows. Thus bridegrooms could make an immediate start on inflating into husbands. Of eight years' standing.

HILARY *finishes reading the paper.*

You don't seem very interested. Have I left something out?

HILARY. Nothing really.

PETER. But don't you want me to make a fresh start?

HILARY. But we're not very fresh any more, Pete. Either or us.

PETER. Well, what about an advance then, from where we used to be at our best? (*Pause.*) Hil—I'm not asking you for anything except the most precious thing in the world for me. To say that it's all right really.

HILARY. But it isn't.

PETER. But surely you *can* say—well, you know. That you love me, and always will, whatever.

HILARY. That's for children, not grown-ups.

PETER (*after a pause*). That's Jeremy taken care of. At least for your life-time, as he'll go on being your child, to the day he— (*Stops.*) And mine too. Ours. (*Pause, takes a step forward.*) Oh Hil— (*Steps towards her.*)

HILARY. Don't! (*Crying out.*)

PETER (*stops*). Because—just because—Charlie has been talking, has he?

HILARY. Almost non-stop. But not about you.

PETER. But then what is it? I mean, all right, all right, I've conceded that I deserve punishing—

HILARY. That's for children too.

PETER. Surely not these days. I thought that was why adults had to settle for punishing each other. (*Pause.*) All right, let me put it another way. I'm back in my own maisonette, what are you going to do about it?

HILARY. Ask you to leave.

PETER. Are you going to explain, or just go on being ruthlessly gnomic?

HILARY. I'm trying to avoid an ugly scene.

PETER. This is your idea of a pretty one, is it?

HILARY. Would you please leave, Peter. I'll tell you everything in a letter.

PETER. In a letter! (*Incredulously.*) A letter! Well darling, I promise you I shall receive it at my own front door. Because I'm bloody not going. I've discovered I'm too young to leave home. I'm sticking, upstairs, downstairs, in the kitchen, in your way. I'm your husband, Jeremy's father. And what are you going to do about that? Call in the lawyers and the policemen?

HILARY. If I have to. (*Pause.*) Anyway, now you know I really want you to go, and that I shall go on wanting you to go. And until you do—you stay down here. I'm going to bed.

PETER. No, you're not. (*Takes her arm.*) Do you really think you can get out of it after eight years of my love *and* devotion because I've given you a few bad times recently? Well, what about my bad times, the ones I can't escape from though I've just tried—and I'm not talking about your neglect of me for your work, your increasing frigidity and those calculated little aloofnesses that *you* started practising even before I started practising going to seed.

HILARY. Is that why you did it? So that I'd take a little notice of you?

PETER. I'm talking about the real bad times, the ones that have come every day of my life since I first began to love you. When the telephone rings in my office and before I answer it I think of you in a car crash or of Jeremy ill or maimed in some idiotic accident at school—or the sudden hopeless questions, such as 'But what should I do if anything happened to either of you?' as I know it's bound to, to both of you in the end, and that all I can really pray for is that it happens to me first, after a decent interval, and then that there are further decent intervals between your going and his. Except that life doesn't work according to decent intervals, which are anyway formulated by types like you and me out here in Muswell Hill.

HILARY. Shut up, shut up, this isn't fair.

PETER. Precisely my point. But it's true.

HILARY. Of course it's true. Do you think I haven't thought the same about Jeremy.

PETER. But not about me?

HILARY. Yes. But it doesn't matter.

PETER. Doesn't matter!

HILARY. Because I'm still going to live my own life. (*Pause.*) Oh God, Peter, it's not the beginning, when we were in love with each other. Or the end, when we could have cried over each

other, and probably still will, both those parts are easy, anyone
can do those. It's the stretch in between, that's our married life,
that I can't stand.

PETER. Because for a short time, a matter of months, what, three
months —

HILARY. Oh longer. Much longer.

PETER. Four then, at the most. Before that, I was a model
husband, father, the lot! Second only to Charlie.

HILARY. I wouldn't want to be married to Charlie either. But he's
found himself an Alison, why couldn't you?

PETER. What!

HILARY. Did you sleep with anyone, while you were away?

PETER. Is that what you think?

HILARY. Well, did you?

PETER. I certainly did not!

HILARY. Why not?

PETER. Because I couldn't — it's not in my nature — perhaps I tried,
I won't deny it — we went to bed together, yes, all right — but we
didn't make love! *You* know I couldn't!

HILARY. Why not?

PETER. You wouldn't let me! When it came to it I didn't want a
foreign body next to mine in bed, and that's the truth. I felt
clumsy and awkward and dirty, and that's the truth too. So you
can't make anything out of that Hilary. I may not be so in law,
but *you* know I'm a faithful husband.

HILARY. Yes, I know. And that's what I can't stand.

PETER. What?

HILARY. Pete — you're married to a faithless wife.

PETER. What?

HILARY. Oh why didn't you come back as you left — drunken and
sneering. You look so — so *clean!*

PETER. You mean there's somebody else?

HILARY *nods*.

In ten days you found a replacement—well, send him back. (*Goes and sits down.*)

HILARY. Not in ten days. A long time ago! I *wanted* you to go, I *wanted* you to go, I wanted you to *go*. I couldn't bear your wretched innocence, your oppressive faithfulness. It's been like deceiving a child.

PETER. It's not—(*Blankly, after a second*) fair. At that bloody school of yours, is he?

HILARY. Yes.

PETER. Well what is he—some damned—foreigner? What? A Turk, an Arab, a Spanish monk, a Frenchman—how low *have* you sunk?

HILARY. He's a teacher.

PETER. To the very bottom then! What's his name?

HILARY. What does it matter?

PETER. *What's his name!*

HILARY. Please, you'll wake Jeremy. George Green.

PETER. George Green. You've never mentioned any George Green. Nothing. Nothing. No passing references to any George Green, no murmurings in your sleep of George Green, no smiling by-the-ways-have-I-told-you-about-George-Green. Nothing. I don't believe it.

HILARY. It's true, Peter. I love him.

PETER. Love George Green! Well, come on, come on, what is he? Married, widowed, divorced, one of these fashionably converting homosexuals, he can't be single unless he's a mere boy, is he a mere boy, George Green?

HILARY. No. He's older than us, actually.

PETER. How much older?

HILARY. By ten years.

PETER. Divorced, eh? How many times?

HILARY. Twice.

PETER. A bit of a specialist then, but not versatile. Or has he just been practising until the right married woman, my wife, came along? How many children?

HILARY. Two by his first wife, one by his second.

PETER. But is he trained in children over five? Or does he pass them on at an early age? I'm speaking for Jeremy now.

HILARY. He sees a great deal of them.

PETER. And he sees a great deal of mine?

HILARY. Not yet. (*Pause.*) Peter, I —

PETER. Shut up!

HILARY (*after a pause*). I didn't set out to look for another man. I really didn't. It happened because, well, I didn't believe you'd go on being faithful.

PETER *laughs*.

HILARY. Well, nobody else has! You and Charlie are quite extraordinary, you see. After I'd gone back to work I suddenly realised that when I'm menopausal you'll be in your sexy forties, and in our fifties you'd be all right if you watched your eating and drinking, but I'd be a woman in my fifties, you see. And in our sixties you could be having it off with girls in their twenties even. I may feel a woman in my sixties, but to most men, including you, I'd be just a woman in my sixties, with almost certainly a hysterectomy — when God knows, I'd be struggling for the pride not to check your pockets or your underwear drawer before doing both, probably. (*Pause.*) So that when George showed he was interested in me at least I knew I was still desirable. I never meant it to turn serious.

PETER. It had no other way to turn, from such a beginning. And does he want to marry you?

HILARY. Yes.

PETER. And you him?

HILARY. I think so, yes. Anyway, I want you to move out straight away.

PETER. Oh, but just a minute darling, isn't it slightly unconventional to see me from our bedroom to the drawing-room sofa to the side-walk, back again and out again, all within ten

days. Most marriages conclude at a slightly more leisurely pace —
we're skimping on the niceties — we've been complacent witnesses
to a lot of break-ups in our time, we must owe returns to newly
re-weds and divorcees all over London. For God's sake let's stick
to form, by your own admission we haven't even begun to make
Jeremy miserable — what about the heart-searchings followed by
the heart-rendings, yours and mine — (*Stops, gestures futilely.*)

HILARY. But why did you think, why, that our marriage was
going to survive? Nobody else's has, that we know. Except for Jeff
and Davina Wainwright's, and isn't it better to end up apart than
together like them? (*Pause.*) If only you'd been unfaithful I
might have managed it — but you've always assumed I was to be
your full-time wife, even when you began to resent me, as
recently. When I became your full-time resentment. Your
dependence fills me with a guilt I can't bear, life's too short . . .
Don't you see . . . (*Coming over, puts her hand on his head.*)

PETER. Don't do that! (*Sharply, then.*) They still stock period
Brylcream in Holborn, my period anyway. (*Pause.*) Go to bed,
Hilary, leave me alone.

HILARY *hesitates, then turns, goes to the door, left.*

After all you'll have another of your hard days tomorrow won't
you, with all its explanations, caresses, half-plans, avowals and
pronunciation classes not to speak of collecting Jeremy from
school, then buying me a Chinese throw-away *and* facing me over
it —

HILARY *goes out.*

PETER *reaches for a cigarette, takes out the package, studies it,
then turns it on its side, studies the Government Warning, reads
it carefully, then takes out a cigarette, lights it. Sits staring ahead.
There is a crashing noise from the kitchen.* PETER *looks towards
the kitchen.*

CHARLES (*enters. He is carrying a syphon of soda water*). I got
you some. (*Holds up the syphon.*)

PETER. Thanks.

CHARLES. Well, I do drink so much of it — (*Carries it across to
the table, puts it down.*) Um, may I —?

PETER. Help yourself.

CHARLES (*squirts some into a glass*). I'm sorry about before. Drink?

PETER. Please.

CHARLES (*pours him a very small scotch, brings it over*). That's the first time in twenty years I've hit you.

PETER (*looking at the scotch in dismay*). At least it was evocative.

CHARLES. No hard feelings.

PETER. No. But I don't know why you did it.

CHARLES. Nor do I really. (*Pause.*) By the way, I don't know if Hilary told you, we're going to have twins.

PETER. You and Hilary?

CHARLES (*laughs*). Alison is, I should say.

PETER. Twins, Charlie. Congratulations.

CHARLES. Thanks. (*Little pause.*) Is everything all right between you two?

PETER. Oh yes.

CHARLES. Well, you said it would be. You told her everything, did you?

PETER. I think we're much clearer about each other, Charlie, thanks.

CHARLES. Even about that girl eh, and going to bed with her, even though—

PETER. She knows everything, even about Cocteau's daughter.

CHARLES. But I realised afterwards that she'd never known about her. Them. I mean, how could you tell her about affairs you never had?

PETER. I didn't have to tell her, she always knew I didn't have them. After all, she virtually had to give me directions on our engagement night.

CHARLES. She's very understanding. (*Little pause.*) You know, I'm sorry they didn't exist.

PETER. So am I. So, probably, is she. But then I'd have been a different sort of person and—

CHARLES. And she wouldn't have wanted to marry you.

PETER. Yes. A bit of a conundrum, that.

CHARLES. And she does love you. That's one thing Alison and I
have never doubted, through all this. Now that you've confessed
your self, which is real, after all, isn't it? Rather than your sins,
which weren't — That's too metaphysical for me. Still, Alison's
always said I'm more Catholic than she is by nature, so probably
you are too. (*Long pause, laughs.*) Remember how I confessed to
Mummy that I'd almost stolen some of those Laura Secord
Chocolates Aunt Mabel sent from Canada during the war.

PETER. But only to draw attention to the fact that I'd actually
stolen them. Didn't Mummy give you three of them as a reward?
Not really confessing, Charlie, more a sordid combination of
sneaking and scrounging.

CHARLES. That's a lie! I didn't know you had! (*Pause.*) Oh
Heavens, yes I did. You're quite right. I admit it. (*Laughs.*)

PETER *smiles.*

Anyway, I'm glad you're back, Pete. I missed you. I mean, the
great thing is, isn't it, to love one another in spite.

PETER. In spite? Yes, I'll drink to that. (*Raises his glass.*)

CHARLES (*raises his*). In spite. (*Then very emotionally.*) Welcome
home, Pete.

PETER. Thank you.

PETER *and* CHARLES *drink.*

CHARLES. Well. (*Gets up.*) I'd better be going, Alison will worry.
(*Turns to the door, right.*) Old Pete.

PETER. Old Charlie. (*Also emotionally. Gets up.*)

CHARLES (*exits, holding his glass*). Ooops! (*Crashing sound.*)

PETER *holding his glass, smiles. Picks up flowers and chocolates,
follows* CHARLES *into the kitchen.*

PETER (*from the kitchen*). For Alison. And the twins.

CHARLES (*from the kitchen*). Are you sure, but what about
Hilary?

PETER (*from the kitchen*). She's very fond — she'll be pleased.

CHARLES (*from the kitchen*). So will Alison. She's very fond too.

*The room, as they speak, fills with sunlight.*

JOANNA *after a moment enters. She is carrying a mug.*

PETER (*from kitchen*). Don't think of it as coffee, but as a quite other drink. Then try to like the other drink, and you're home.

JOANNA (*sips*). It's great. ( *Looks vaguely at the photograph.*)

PETER *enters. Hair slightly longer.*

I'm glad you like my covers, that really means a lot to me.

PETER. I hope you're going to do lots for me.

*There is a pause. PETER comes over, takes the mug from her. Puts it down.*

This can wait.

JOANNA. What for?

PETER *goes over to the sofa, begins to slip off the sofa mattress.*

I thought you said you had to see somebody at your office this afternoon.

PETER. Oh, he can wait, too.

JOANNA. I hope it's not a poet. I couldn't bear to keep a poet waiting.

PETER. I'm first, you can get around to him later.

JOANNA. What if that landlady of yours comes back?

PETER. On a Wednesday? (*Goes over to* JOANNA, *kisses her.*) It's her Sainsbury evening.

JOANNA. She's not your landlady, she's your wife, isn't she? You're married, aren't you?

PETER (*after a pause*). Am I?

*Lights.*

*Curtain.*

A selection of books published by Penguin is listed on the following pages.

For a complete list of books available from Penguin in the United States, write to Dept. DG, Penguin Books, 299 Murray Hill Parkway, East Rutherford, New Jersey 07073.

*Simon Gray*

## BUTLEY

One of the most successful plays of the recent British and American theater, *Butley* explores the complex relationship between a university lecturer, Ben Butley, and his former star pupil (now fellow lecturer), Joey. Within a background of petty academic politics, Butley makes some painful discoveries—about himself and those he loves or purports to love—when, in the course of a single day, he is obliged to face the fact that not only has his wife left him for another man but so has Joey, the friend with whom he has been sharing both office and apartment. Hard-bitten and cynical on the surface, brilliant and devious in his thought and language, Butley emerges as a moving and touching character.

## OTHERWISE ENGAGED AND OTHER PLAYS

*Otherwise Engaged* opens as Simon Hench, publisher and Wagnerite, prepares to listen to his new recording of *Parsifal*. The music begins but is interrupted—first by a visit from Hench's lodger, preoccupied with sexual problems, then by the arrival of Hench's brother, anxious about a job interview. Soon a string of intrusions has drawn Hench into a whirlpool of accusations, confusions, and recriminations. As Harold Hobson remarked in the *Sunday Times* (London), "*Otherwise Engaged* is not the kindest play in London, but it is the most entertaining and the most brilliant." This volume also includes the television plays *Two Sundays* and *Plaintiffs and Defendants*. Thematically related, the three plays show Simon Gray's dazzling ability to meet the different requirements of stage and screen.

*Arthur Miller*

## DEATH OF A SALESMAN

"By common consent, this is one of the finest dramas in the whole range of the American theater" is the way Brooks Atkinson described *Death of a Salesman*—now one of the most popular classics in our written literature. The name of Willy Loman, the central character, is as familiar as Babbitt. Willy's story is poignant, sometimes humorous, ultimately tragic—the story of a man steeped in the go-getter gospel who never got beyond his own daydream world. The absorbing drama of his downhill struggle is the heart-wrenching drama of wishful dreamers everywhere.

## A VIEW FROM THE BRIDGE

A play, as Arthur Miller points out in the Introduction to this edition of *A View from the Bridge*, is rarely given a second chance. This play is an outstanding exception. It did not find a large audience with its original Broadway production, but later it had great success in London and also in Paris, where it ran for two years, in the revised version printed here. Initially, in America, the play was in one act, with a set shorn of adornment. The British version, in two acts, had a background of fire escapes, passageways, and suggested apartments, so that Eddie Carbone lived out his horror in the midst of a recognizably familiar milieu. There was also additional material in the role of Eddie's wife. Altogether, the play became more human, warmer, and less remote, without in any way bowing to the sentimentality that Mr. Miller wanted to avoid. Both for the pleasure of reading the play itself and for the behind-the-scenes story of its presentation, this is a book that anyone interested in today's theater will find immensely rewarding.

*Edited by Eric Bentley*

## THE THEORY OF THE MODERN STAGE
An Introduction to Modern Theater and Drama

In this anthology, newly revised and edited by one of America's leading dramatic critics, Antonin Artaud, Bertolt Brecht, Gordon Craig, Konstantin Stanislavski, William Butler Yeats, and many other great theatrical theorists reveal the ideas underlying their productions and point to the possibilities of the modern theater.


*Sonia Moore*

## TRAINING AN ACTOR
The Stanislavski System in Class
(Revised Edition)

This extensively revised handbook demonstrates the *process* of learning the Stanislavski System—the key to spontaneous behavior on stage. Based upon tape-recordings made during Sonia Moore's famous classes, it poses—and solves—the various problems that actors face in creating believable characters. Twenty-four chapters progress from Mrs. Moore's opening comments on Konstantin Stanislavski's revolutionary discoveries to a final summary of her students' achievements. Demolishing the popular notion that Stanislavski's methods depend on private, self-centered expression, Mrs. Moore shows us that he taught a deliberate, controlled, conscious technique—internal and external at the same time—a technique that makes tremendous demands on actors but that rewards them with the priceless gift of creative life. With an additional chapter on directing, *Training an Actor* also includes data from Mrs. Moore's own recent research as well as from new Russian research on Stanislavski's last deductions.